Researching Online Foreign Language Interaction and Exchange

TELECOLLABORATION IN EDUCATION

Vol. 3

Edited by
Melinda Dooly & Robert O'Dowd

PETER LANG
Bern · Berlin · Bruxelles · Frankfurt am Main · New York · Oxford · Wien

Melinda Dooly & Robert O'Dowd (eds)

Researching Online Foreign Language Interaction and Exchange

Theories, Methods and Challenges

PETER LANG
Bern · Berlin · Bruxelles · Frankfurt am Main · New York · Oxford · Wien

Bibliographic information published by die Deutsche Nationalbibliothek
Die Deutsche Nationalbibliothek lists this publication in the Deutsche Nationalbibliografie; detailed bibliographic data is available on the Internet at ‹http://dnb.d-nb.de›.

British Library Cataloguing-in-Publication Data: A catalogue record for this book is available from The British Library, Great Britain

Library of Congress Cataloging-in-Publication Data

Owenby, Melinda Ann Dooly,

Researching online foreign language interaction and exchange : theories, methods and challenges / Melinda Ann Dooly Owenby & Robert O'Dowd.
p. cm. – (Telecollaboration in education; . 3)
Includes bibliographical references and index.
ISBN 978-3-03-431155-7 (alk. paper)
1. Language and languages–Study and teaching–Computer network resources.
2. Language and languages–Computer network resources. 3. Second language acquisition. 4. Human-computer interaction. I. O'Dowd, Robert II. Title.
P53.285.O94 2012
418.00285–dc23

2012018714

ISBN (pb.) 978-3-0343-1155-7 ISBN (eBook) 978-3-0351-0414-1

Hochfeldstrasse 32, CH-3012 Bern, Switzerland
info@peterlang.com, www.peterlang.com

Contents

Series Editors' Preface

This volume is the third in this series dedicated to promoting a wider understanding of the activity of telecollaboration to educational settings. For the purposes of this series, we understand telecollaboration to refer essentially to the application of global computer networks to student collaboration and interaction in both informal and institutionalized educational contexts (for more details see introduction).

The general focus of the series is on the pedagogical processes and outcomes of engaging learners in different geographical locations in virtual contact together, mediated through the application of online communication tools such as e-mail, synchronous chat and threaded discussion as well as the tools of Web 2.0 such as wikis, blogs, social networking and 3D virtual worlds. The application of such activity may include different subject areas (e.g. Foreign Language Education, History, Science) as well as different educational contexts, including but not limited to primary, secondary, university and adult education.

This volume aims to provide an accessible introduction to many of the methods and theoretical approaches currently being used to investigate online foreign language interaction and exchange in online environments as well as to present an overview of the key research issues which are emerging in the context of both Web 2.0 learning environments and the Web 2.0 educational mindset with its emphasis on the co-construction of knowledge, multimodality, intercultural relationship building and the constant blending of online and offline communicative activity. While it is impossible to be comprehensive of all research approaches emerging in this exciting field of language teaching and learning, we feel that the selection of work in this volume allows for a more indepth look at both better-known methods and innovative approaches to interactions in formal and informal language learning in an online mode.

The authors in this book have been carefully selected, based on their wide experience and professional practice in Foreign Language teaching and learning interaction in online environments. The sum of their expertise brings insight into the particular challenges and situations which this area of language learning implies and will be useful for newcomers and experienced practitioners and researchers alike.

Melinda Dooly, Universitat Autònoma de Barcelona, Spain
Robert O'Dowd, Universidad de León, Spain

17 March 2012

Acknowledgements

Our sincerest gratitude to all the authors who have made such timely and inspirational contributions to the current research in this fast-developing area of teaching and learning languages and intercultural competences. We would also like to thank all the reviewers who took the time to read and provide helpful comments on each of these chapters.

Researching Online Interaction and Exchange in Foreign Language Education: Introduction to the Volume

MELINDA DOOLY & ROBERT O'DOWD

The Rise of Online Interaction and Exchange in Foreign Language Education

In the first volume of this series on telecollaboration in education, Guth and Helm presented a collection of chapters which outlined how contemporary online communication technologies are currently being used in Foreign Language (FL) education to connect learners around the world in order to develop FL competency, intercultural awareness and e-literacies. Describing their field of activity as 'telecollaboration 2.0', the contributors to the volume demonstrated how the emergence of the Web 2.0 mindset and its technologies are shaping how FL education is being understood and is being practised at the turn of the 21st century.

Following on from the work of Guth and Helm, this volume continues with the themes of computer mediated communication (CMC) and telecollaborative exchange in FL education. However, instead of focussing exclusively on current 2.0 FL practice, this volume aims to provide an accessible introduction to some of the many methods and theoretical approaches being used to investigate the different configurations of FL interaction and exchange in online environments. We also aim to present an overview of the key issues which are very often unique to FL research contexts in the sense of being virtual, intercultural and multimodal. While the chapters in this volume do deal with how to investigate telecollaborative 2.0 activity, the authors also try to cater for a wider range of configurations of online FL interaction which includes in-class interaction, class-to-class interaction as well as learner interaction with the outside world. We have, therefore, deliberately avoided both the terms 'telecollaboration' and '2.0' in our title and have chosen to use the more generic term 'online interaction and exchange' in an attempt to attend to the many different ways in which online communication technologies are being used to engage FL learners in interaction around the world today. Another reason for doing this is that we are aware of the tendency of technologies and online communicative practises to date and to change quickly. We would hope that the methodologies and issues presented in this volume will still be relevant when '2.0' has been replaced by 'Web 3.0' or indeed 'Web 4.0' technologies.

At this stage, we believe that a publication on research methodology in this area is both relevant and necessary as there are many researchers who are coming from other areas of FL education or who are beginning their careers as researchers in the area of online interaction and exchange and we hope that this volume will provide them with insight into the particular challenges and situations which this area of language learning implies. Moreover, as more and more educators are beginning to engage their learners in this type of interaction the need for circumspection and reflection in their own practices indicates a growing need for practitioner research for improving and building on these innovative approaches (Dooly, 2009).

Since its emergence as a relatively new area of research within the field of Computer Assisted Language Learning in the late 1990's, online interaction and exchange has been the subject of a great deal of high quality published research in the literature. Various indexed journals have dedicated large amounts of space to research in this area (e.g. Language Learning and Technology, ReCALL, Computer Assisted Language Learning to mention but a few) and there is a growing number of monographs (Lamy & Hampel, 2007; Levy & Stockwell, 2006; O'Dowd, 2006) and edited collections (Belz & Thorne, 2006; Guth & Helm, 2010; Muyskens, 1998; O'Dowd, 2007;

Warschauer & Kern, 2000) on the area. But it is perhaps fair to ask at this stage why online interaction and exchange –and research in this area– have become such an important area of FL education. We would argue that this has come about due to a combination of various developments which are outlined briefly here.

The first of these is related to the significant increase in the availability of user-friendly online technologies in educational contexts around Europe and elsewhere, in a large part brought about by cheaper computer hardware and widespread access to high-quality internet connections. In many western countries at least, FL educators at primary, secondary and university level are now able to provide their learners with computers, laptops, tablets and other mobile devices at relatively low cost. A recent European Commission report on the use of ICT to support innovation and lifelong learning reported that already in 2006 67% of schools reported having broadband connections in their schools (Commission of the European Communities, 2008: 23–34). Increased internet access in educational institutions has coincided with the emergence of Web 2.0 tools such as blogs, wikis and podcasts as easy-to-use tools for FL education. The intuitive and user-friendly nature of many of these Web 2.0 tools has meant that FL educators can now engage their learners in online networking and publishing without possessing a great deal of technical knowledge or programming ability. This combination of cheap internet access and easy-to-use Web 2.0 technologies has meant that online interaction and exchange has become much easier to integrate into FL learning classrooms and, consequently, is also much easier to research.

However, we would argue that, apart from these 'technical' developments, there are three other principle reasons for the increased attention being paid to online FL interaction and exchange by both educators and researchers. The first of this has been the widespread acceptance in the FL education community of the importance of culture in FL learning and, furthermore, the recognition of the propensity for structured online intercultural interaction to support the development of learners' cultural awareness and skills of intercultural communicative competence. The importance of the role of culture for FL learners had already been highlighted regularly in FL circles during the 1990s (Byram, 1997, Kramsch, 1993), but it was the advent of the new millennium which heralded the entry of intercultural competence into state curricula and evaluation schemes. For example, tools for the evaluation of intercultural competence can be found in the Council of Europe's *European Language Portfolio* (2003) and the *Autobiography of Intercultural Encounters* (2007). Online interaction between learners in different cultures has been shown to be a potentially powerful tool for engaging learners in intercultural contact and for raising awareness of the role of culture in interaction and relationship building (O'Dowd, 2003, Belz, 2003, Ware, 2005; Möllering & Levy, this volume) and this has meant that many educators have turned to online interaction in order to facilitate the integration of intercultural objectives into their curricula. Thorne has gone so far as to suggest that the increased contact to 'real' members of other cultures facilitated by online exchanges has played an important role in the integration of the intercultural turn in FL education (Thorne, 2006).

A further reason for the rise of online FL interaction and exchange lies in the increasingly accepted paradigm of language learning as a sociocultural process facilitated through carefully constructed purposeful, plausible, communicative events. (We do not delve into the question of 'authenticity' of language use here, but for a concise overview problematising in/authenticity in computer-mediated language learning tasks, see Lamy & Goodfellow, 2010). Largely stemming from Dell Hymes' (1964) work on language use, the idea of communicative competence has been gradually adopted into approaches for language teaching; in the eighties the term 'communicative language teaching', (first coined by Savignon, 1983, 1991), gained ground and has come to represent a general paradigm that encompasses several different teaching models (Richards, 2005).

What these models have in common is an interactive approach to the teaching of multiply-integrated language competences, wherein learning is understood as an organic process, fostered through cognitively challenging, meaningful use of language. Inevitably, engaging learners in online networking and publishing implies greater opportunities for communicatively-based language learning, thus facilitating learner-mediated dialogical use of the target language (Dooly, 2008a; Müller-Hartmann & Schocker-v. Ditfurth, 2008; Meskill & Anthony, 2010; Müller-Hartmann, this volume).

A final reason for the growth of importance attributed to online FL interaction in classrooms has been the manner in which the areas of FL competence and e-literacies have merged inextricably as integral components of the new skills required in emerging labour markets. The growing importance of online technologies for the ways in which we work and learn in global networks has meant that today, instead of using technologies simply to learn FLs, learners need to learn how to combine both FL skills and 'e-skills' or 'new literacies' to be able to work and collaborate in new contexts where the borders between the virtual and the real and between the distant and the proximate are increasingly blurred (Fitzpatrick & O'Dowd, 2012; Dooly, 2008b; Dooly & Hauck, this volume). As online interaction has become such a pervasive way of learning and working, it is inevitable that there is considerable interest among policy makers and the research community as to how virtual tools and online collaboration and interaction should be structured and how learners can use online environments to learn, work and live together.

This tendency is clearly reflected in the policy documents currently emerging from the European Commission, the Council of Europe and elsewhere which highlight the need for European citizens to be engaged in learning scenarios where they can use both their intercultural communicative competence and their e-skills. In the European Commission's document *"Key competences for lifelong learning: European framework document"* (2010), three of eight key competences mentioned are FL competence, digital competence, cultural awareness and expression. These are seen to entail integral, interrelated skills which are essential prerequisites to achieving employability in a knowledge society. Furthermore, educators are being challenged to create learning scenarios which integrate the tools and communicative practices which learners will later face in their working lives.

The combination of these technical, pedagogical and professional developments has meant an important rise in online FL interaction taking place in educational contexts. But what form does this interaction take and how is it structured? In the following section we outline three main types of online FL interaction and exchange which can be found in the modern-day classroom.

Differing forms of Online Interaction and Exchange in FL Education

What form has online interaction and exchange taken in FL education? The many synchronous and asynchronous tools which have come into use since the emergence of the internet in the early 1990's have been employed in a myriad of ways by FL educators, but three general categories of online interaction and exchange can be identified to date, depending on the type of interaction involved (although it is acknowledged that overlapping can and often occurs between these categories). These can be described as 1) in-class interaction (described previously as Computer-Assisted Classroom Discussion or CACD by Ortega (1997)), 2) class-to-class interaction (also referred to as Online Intercultural Exchange or Telecollaborative exchange) and 3) class-to-world interaction (which coincides in many aspects with Telecollaboration 2.0). Although there is a certain historical evolution from categories 1 to 2 to 3, examples of category 3 can be found in early reports of online FL activity (see Warschauer, 1995), while categories 1 and 2 are still very much in use in classrooms and in online FL education courses around the world today. Each of these categories will now be presented briefly. Following that, the most common areas of research associated with each area will be looked at.

The first of these categories, in-class online interaction, refers to the activity of students within one particular class using online networks to interact together for the purpose of FL learning. This was particularly common when the internet was first beginning to emerge in the mid-1990's and educators did not yet have easy access to partner classes in distant locations and students did not have access to the internet outside of the classroom. In this context, learners in one class commonly used synchronous text-based communication, such as chats, MOO's and Local Area Networks (LAN) to interact together in the target language. The text-based nature of the communication was seen at the time as being a manner of allowing FL learners to create a "conversation in slow motion" (Beauvois, 1998: 93) which allowed students time to reflect on and plan their utterances in the FL before committing them to the online interaction with their classmates. Today, in-class online interaction is of course still quite common in FL education. However, this type of activity now generally tends to focus on asynchronous tools such as discussion forums and blogging etc. which are used for reflective discussion in distance education courses or by teachers wishing to promote greater interaction among students outside of their normal classroom contact hours.

In the late 1990's, improved online connections as well as the emergence of class-matching sites, such as the Intercultural E-mail Classroom Connections (IECC), iEARN, NickNack's Telecollaborative Projects, Global SchoolNet Foundation and the Tandem Network, led to a move away from in-class interaction and a dramatic increase in class-to-class interactions which involved virtual intercultural interaction and exchange between classes of FL learners in geographically distant locations. Originally, interaction was mainly text-based and asynchronous (see, for example, Eck, Legenhausen and Wolff, 1995). However, recent advances in online connections and communication tools have meant that synchronous oral communication (e.g. videoconferencing) as well as multimodal exchanges (involving combinations of different media such as blogs, Wikis etc.) are becoming increasingly popular.

As mentioned earlier, this second category of class to class exchange, or telecollaboration as it is commonly referred to, has come to be seen as one of the main pillars of the intercultural and communicative turn in FL education as it allows educators to engage their learners in regular, (semi-)authentic communication with members of other cultures in distant locations and also gives learners the opportunity to reflect on and learn from the outcomes of this intercultural exchange within the supportive and informed context of their FL classroom. Telecollaboration has traditionally taken one of two forms or models – each one reflecting the main learning aims prevalent in FL education at the time. The first well known model was e-tandem, which focussed on fostering learner autonomy and learners' ability to continue their language learning outside of the language classroom (O'Rourke, 2007). The second model is usually referred to as the 'telecollaborative model' and reflected the emphasis in the late 1990s and early 2000s on intercultural and sociocultural aspects of FL education (Belz, 2003, O'Dowd, 2010).

The use of telecollaboration in FL learning (particularly in primary education) still plays a rather minor role, perhaps due to assumed lack of communicative competences of the learners or because FL classes are introduced at around the age of twelve in many countries. Still, telecollaboration in many different disciplines does appear to be on the rise. In the secondary school sector in particular, it appears that the activity is gradually gaining in importance in classrooms in many countries –in Europe and the United States at least. To a great extent, this is due to the online structure and support offered by organisations such as Etwinning and ePals. The first of these is an online network of schools in Europe sponsored by the European Union's Lifelong Learning Programme[1]. In this network, schools from at least two different European countries create a project and use information and communication technologies (ICT) to carry out their work together. As schools communicate and collaborate via the Internet, there are no grants or administrative conditions connected to the scheme and face-to-face meetings are not required.

Etwinning provides collaborating teachers with online tools for their projects, a tool for finding partners in different countries as well

1 <http://www.etwinning.net>.

as 'kits' for developing projects appropriate to students' age and subject area. The network also offers training workshops, annual conferences and 'quality awards' for successful projects. The ePals network[2] also provides collaborative tools and virtual space for schools to connect and learn in a protected, project-based learning environment. However, ePals is based in the United States and members come from primary and secondary schools in over 200 countries and territories. According to the administrators of the platform, there are over 130,000 classes of primary and secondary pupils registered in ePals and several thousand new classrooms join each month.[3]

Although telecollaboration in Higher Education has received a considerable amount of attention in the research literature (see a brief overview in the next section), our own research in this area (O'Dowd, 2011) suggests that this activity has yet to achieve the same degree of integration or 'normalisation' in university FL education around Europe as it has in secondary education. Similarly, despite a growing interest in telecollaboration for FL learning in primary education, there is a paucity of research on situated, online interaction with young language learners (Dooly, 2011).

A third form of online interaction which has only begun to gain popularity in recent years is class-to-world interaction. This involves FL learners using their target language to enter into contact with individuals or groups in the 'real world' without this contact being previously organised by the teacher. While many educators have been drawn to class to class exchange due to its potential to bring learners into contact with 'authentic' texts written by native speakers and to give them the experience of 'real' intercultural communication, the authors Hanna and de Nooy have pointed out that in class-to-class telecollaboration

> [I]nteraction is restricted to communication with other learners, a situation that is safe and reassuring for beginners and younger learners, but somewhat limiting for more advanced and adult learners, who need practice in venturing beyond the classroom. (2009: 88)

2 <http://www.epals.com>.

3 <http://www.epals.com/content/ePalsSupport.aspx#s03>.

The authors propose that it is more authentic and more advantageous to engage learners in interaction in real L2 discussion forums such as those related to L2 newspaper and magazine publications. Their criticism of class-to-class telecollaboration reflects a more general preoccupation in FL pedagogy about the definitions of authenticity and authentic task (cf. Lamy and Goodfellow, 2010) and the question here is essentially whether structured class-to-class interaction is something which brings the classroom to genuinely intersect with the *real* world or whether it simply engages learners in tasks which 'approximate' or 'replicate' real world activity.

With this in mind, a wide variety of class to world interaction setups are beginning to emerge in order to complement traditional class-to-class exchanges. Described by Guth & Helm (2010) as Telecollaboration 2.0, this model is based on the Social Web which has emerged with the rise of Web 2.0 tools such as blogging, wikis and social networking sites and is characterised by a less text-based and more multimodal form of communication (see Guth & Helm, 2010; Lankshear & Knobel 2006). Examples of this model involve a type of intercultural exchange which is more classroom independent and which allows for a much greater spectrum of possible partners, language setups and forms of interaction. For example, instead of linking up with other classes, learners may collaborate in specialised interest communities or environments which focus on specific hobbies or interests. Thorne, Black and Sykes (2009), for example, describe the potential for intercultural contact and learning in online fan communities where learners can establish relationships will like-minded fans of music groups or authors and can even use Web 2.0 technologies to remix and create new artistic creations based on pre-existing books, movies and music. Learners also have increasing opportunities to use their FL skills and hone their intercultural communicative competence through participating in online multicultural communities such as multiplayer online games and public discussion forums, such as in the example by Hanna and de Nooy (2009) mentioned previously.

This emerging model requires learners to assume greater responsibility for how their intercultural learning progresses online as they are given greater freedom in their choice of potential intercultural learning partners and learning environments –many of which may be completely independent of organised classroom activity. Thorne describes this form of telecollaborative learning as 'intercultural communication in the wild' and speculates that this learning may be:

> [...]situated in arenas of social activity that are less controllable than classroom or organised online intercultural exchanges might be, but which present interesting, and perhaps even compelling, opportunities for intercultural exchange, agentive action and meaning making. (2010: 144)

The fact that online language learning can be categorized into different types of interaction holds two significant implications; firstly there is a noticeable increment of such practices, so much so that heuristic categories of interaction can now be discussed. Secondly, the link between the opportunities provided by social networking technology and the way in which these tools are used to mediate language learning means that the physical and mental boundaries of the traditional classroom are breaking down (Dooly, 2010), whether by the teacher who designs dynamic, CMC-oriented learning processes (Meskill & Anthony, 2010) or the learner that participates in incidental learning while taking part in online gaming or virtual worlds. This blurring of boundaries carries the implication that definitions of what constitute formal and informal learning need to be interrogated more closely. This is beyond the scope of this introduction and, indeed, the majority of the chapters in this book consider educational research from the perspective of different 'class-based' situations. However, it is felt that the research methods and approaches discussed here are adaptable and applicable to all domains of learning that involve online interaction and exchange in FL learning.

Researching Online Interaction and Exchange in FL Education: Changing Foci and Approaches

Inevitably, online interaction and exchange has a relatively short history and collections of classroom practice and anecdotal research (see, for example, Muyskens, 1998; Warschauer, 1995) were not replaced by in-depth studies of online interaction and exchange until the late 1990's. Indeed, at the turn of the millennium, Warschauer and Kern were still lamenting that:

> [...]the corpus of NBLT [Network-based Language Teaching] research includes few published studies that examine in depth the development of discourse and discourse communities in on-line environments. (2000: 14)

When research did begin to emerge, the focus of studies on in-class interaction (category 1) was mainly on comparing online synchronous interaction with face-to-face student interaction in the target language in an attempt to explore how online interaction could replace or supplement face-to-face student interaction. Reports suggested that, compared to face-to-face interaction, online in-class interaction reduced student anxiety, increased student participation, enhanced student motivation to participate in discussions in the FL and provided more time for students to develop and refine their comments in the target language (see Warschauer, 1996 for an overview of research in the area). The methodology used was mainly quantitative and experimental in nature and involved control groups of students engaged in face-to-face interaction. The emphasis in general was on quantitatively analysing –counting and categorising– the linguistic features, language functions and learning resources used in online communication.

Many research studies focussing on the contribution of in-class interaction to FL education continue to appear in the literature. Much of these come from the interactionist perspective to FL education and pyscholinguistic theories of SLA such as Long and Robinson's (1998) Interaction Hypothesis. This theory proposes that when language learners have to negotiate meaning in interaction, they are exposed to input which is both linguistically and interactionally modified. Such input draws learners' attention towards grammatical form, pushes them to modify their own output, and consequently helps them to develop their interlanguage. In an interactionist approach, negotiation of meaning and peer correction are seen as processes which occur relatively naturally as interlocutors seek to understand and clarify each others' utterances. For researchers coming from this background, the aim of online interaction is therefore to maximize the need for negotiation of meaning and to then explore the development of complexity, accuracy and fluency in online task performance (Blake, 2000; Pellettieri, 2000). Some of these studies have been based on interactions between learners with teacher supervision in task-based instructional settings (Sotillo, 2000), while others have looked at how in-class online interaction can make up for the lack of face-to-face contact in distance based FL courses (Tudini, 2003).

Investigations into the learning outcomes of the second category, class to class or telecollaborative exchange, have been dominated by a sociocultural perspective which are critical of the interactionist approach for its overly cognitive orientation and for depicting learning as taking place solely through the negotiation of linguistic meaning and for reducing the function of communication to the exchange of information. Research coming from a sociocultural approach puts much greater emphasis on the social aspects of language and contextualization of the language learning process (situated learning). Within this perspective, the role of language as a mediating tool for learning is crucial, and the fact that the target language is itself an object of learning implies that the entire language learning process hinges on being a dialogic process. Furthermore, proponents of this approach point out that, apart from the exchange of information, communication also has socio-psychological and sociological functions such as face saving and the expression of ethnolinguisitic identity (Block, 2002).

This nexus of sociocultural learning and online exchange has been fruitful for research in intercultural communicative competence. Kramsch reminds us that communication is also used for "establishing and maintaining relationships" and as "an opportunity to understand oneself and one's own culture better" (Kramsch, 1993: 183). With this in mind, researchers of class-to-class interaction have examined its contribution to the development of learner autonomy (Schwienhorst, 2000), linguistic competence (Belz & Kinginger, 2002) and intercultural communicative competence (Müller-Hartmann, 2000; O'Dowd, 2003; Ware, 2005). Studies have also focused on the pedagogical structure and design of on-line exchange projects and their tasks (Müller-Hartmann, 2000; Meskill & Ranglova, 2000, O'Dowd & Ware, 2009, Dooly, 2011) as well as on the institutional barriers to integrating online exchange (Belz & Müller-Hartmann, 2003) and on the reasons for intercultural misunderstanding and conflict in online interaction (O'Dowd & Ritter, 2006; Ware & Kramsch, 2005).

The methodology used in socioculturally-oriented studies has been essentially qualitative in nature, with researchers using combinations of a wide variety of methods such as interactional micro-analysis to study language learning in process (Dooly, 2011), ethnographic interviewing (O'Dowd, 2006), participant surveys, think-aloud protocols and case studies (Thorne, 2006; Bauer, de Benedette, Furstenburg Levet & Waryn, 2006). However, there are also examples of linguistic analysis (Belz, 2003) and microgenetic corpus analysis (Belz & Vyatkina, 2008) of students' online intercultural interaction.

Research into the third category –student to world interaction– is still in its relative infancy, but an important body of research is already emerging which explores how aspects of FL learning –linguistic competence, intercultural awareness, learner independence etc– are being developed in and outside the classroom through learners' use of wireless devices and Web 2.0 tools and communities. Some studies, such as that by Hanna and de Nooy (2009) or Sadler and Eröz (2008), are still relatively 'class-based' in that classes of learners are engaged in an organised fashion by their teachers in web-based public discussion forums. This is perhaps not surprising, given that much research is propelled by the triangulation (and tension) between institutions such as teacher education, schools and policy-makers, as is evidenced by the aforementioned European policies on FL teaching and learning.

Other studies have gone a step further to explore how learner interaction outside of the FL classroom context can influence learners' FL development. Thorne, for example, used activity theory to analyse the relationship between academic and social-personal use of blogs by FL learners (2004) while Pasfield-Neofitou (2011) analysed a corpus of blogs, e-mails, SNS interactions, chat conversations, game profiles, and mobile phone communications between 12 Australian learners of Japanese with Japanese partners they had contacted outside of their formal learning environment in order to explore issues of language choice, identity construction and feelings of national identity and 'foreignness' online.

Inevitably, as novel developments in online communication technologies and innovative opportunities for online exchange appear, new foci and approaches for research in this domain will emerge. However, these approaches are best grounded in sound theoretical principles. The chapters in this book aim to provide that foundation to guide and promote further research in this exciting field of learning.

The Challenges of Researching Online Interaction and Exchange

Any researcher approaching the area of online interaction and exchange in FL education is faced with a wide array of decisions to make as regards choosing the appropriate research framework, using and combining quantitative and qualitative methods, dealing with ethical issues as well as questions related to intercultural competences, multimodality, task design etc. While the individual chapters of this volume will look at all these issues in some detail, it is worthwhile to briefly review some of the principal arguments and concepts which are currently being discussed in this field of research.

Just as the paradigms, or conceptual frameworks of the participants will influence the way in which online interaction and exchange is employed by the teacher and pupil for language learning, the researcher's paradigm will shape his or her methodological approach to understanding these exchanges. Croker (2009) argues that "positivist" research "strive(s) to find a singular, universal truth" (p. 6), while constructivists and socioconstructivists do not believe in a universal truth since individuals construct meaning through interaction with their world (Merriam, 2002).

As the focus of research dealing with online interaction and exchange shifts towards an attainment of a deeper understanding of how learners experience their learning progression, many researchers have reallocated the foci from looking only at 'end-products' to considering processes and meanings. These processes and meanings are not necessarily rigorously or experimentally examined or measured "in terms of quantity, amount, intensity, or frequency" (Denzin & Lincoln, 2003: 13), allowing for a interpretative, naturalistic approach (Denzin & Lincoln, 2003), including multimethodological research.

We have alluded to the 'paradigmatic differences' between 'cognitivist' and 'socioculturalist' in SLA (cf. Zuengler & Miller, 2006; Reinhardt, this volume) earlier in this introduction. It is not our intention to wade into the arguments between the two positions, instead we call attention to the fact that this debate underscores a significant challenge for researchers of language acquisition –what exactly entails learning and how can you determine if competences have been assimilated? More and more, researchers and theorists working in language acquisition foreground the complexity involved in cognitive processes –as is evidenced by growing interest in the application of research frameworks like Cultural-Historical Activity Theory (Thorne, 2004; Wolff-Michael & Yew-Jin, 2007; Blin, this volume), Complexity (or Chaos) Theory (Larsen-Freeman, 2007, 2008) and Dynamic Systems Theory (De Bot, Lowie, & Verspoor, 2007; Verspoor, de Bot, & Lowie, 2011).

Added to this, the complications of additional dimensions to the 'traditional' classroom entailed in the use of online interaction and exchange implies that research grounded in rationalism –and subsequent 'isolatable' variables– falls short when trying to determine whether and how language learning takes place (Basharina, 2007; Dooly, 2011). What these frameworks have in common is the emphasis on the dynamic interaction of various (and varying) elements of one or more systems over time, along with a growing recognition that results of these interactions are not entirely predictable. They also highlight recursive loops and bifurcation of learning (e.g. noticing, recalling, applying, incorporating, etc.) as opposed to a linear process of these language learning features.

At the same, the inherent problems of attempting to transform theories such as Complexity Theory, originally conceived for mathematics or physics, into a 'metaphorical' framework for understanding human behavior are patent (Swan, 2004). The boundaries for defining activities, members and systems tend to be 'fuzzy' and there is inevitable overlapping in systems and membership (which are often multiple). Furthermore, the rules in mechanical physics are related to a series of physical or chemical reactions, whereas 'rules' in human behaviour might be metaphorically linked to "mental models" (Plsek & Greenhalgh, 2001), but these models cannot be seen and even need not be logical. This is directly related to the agency of humans and implies constantly evolving (unpredictable) behaviour

Still, despite these challenges associated with applying dynamic theoretical frameworks, researchers working in Computer-Mediated Communication in potential learning situations increasingly recognize the need to acknowledge the multiple dimensions and complexity involved in online interaction and exchange. For instance, in considering the question of how the internet and other communication technologies alter the nature of literacy, Coiro, Knobel, Lankshear and Leu state that "[…] we currently lack the adequate theories, constructs, and methods to match the complexity of the question" (2008: 1). These authors argue for a multidisciplinary approach with different theoretical frameworks and epistemological approaches to understand the development of new literacies and their role in education: "The richness of these multiple perspectives provides us with the best opportunity to understand fully the many issues associated with the changing nature of literacy (p.2)".

In our particular field of online FL interaction and exchange, many authors have called for greater use of qualitative methodology. Lamy & Hampel suggest that qualitative research is more suited to CMC research in FL education since the interaction involved is "liable to be affected by an unmanageably high number of variables" (2007: 17), while Bax (2003) claims that "we need more careful qualitative –I would argue for ethnographic– analyses, in order to understand CALL" (p. 2). Similarly, Levy and Stockwell (2006) argue in favour of the need to use rich qualitative data – such as that collected in ethnographic and case studies and justify this in the following way:

> The strength of this kind of research also derives from the researchers' rich description and understanding of the context, and their ability to convey this to the readers, who need to be convinced of its authenticity and potential value. (Levy & Stockwell, 2006: 168)

Other researchers suggest mixed methods (cf. Livingstone, Van Couvering, & Thumim, 2008), arguing that all research methods have limitations and weaknesses and the use of triangulation of different methods compensates for these weaknesses. Tashakkori and Teddlie (2003) have described mixed methods as a method in its own right because it combines quantitative and qualitative approaches while transcending them by responding to issues which could not be otherwise comprehended.

Nonetheless, Bazeley (2004) foregrounds some of the problems of mixed methods research, beginning with the issue that exactly what constitutes this method is often ill-defined.

> After a period in the paradigmatic wilderness, mixed methods research has regained not just acceptability, but popularity, with a significant number of studies arguing its virtues in terms of greater understanding and/or validation of results. But all is not "plain sailing" – working with mixed methods raises a range of issues above and beyond those encountered within a particular

> methodology. Not the least of these is that there is no one mixed methods methodology, and the term can be applied to widely divergent approaches to research. (p. 141)

Also, mixed methods approaches to data collection remains a source of contention as many researchers argue that there is an inherent lack of rigorousness. Similarly, Kendall (2008) warns of the common practice of using qualitative interview data to illustrate or 'liven up' statistical information gained from surveys. This approach stops analytical categories from emerging from the interview data.

Counter-arguments to this criticism is that through critically examining the quantitative/qualitative dichotomy, mixed methods can provide an innovative approach to empirical investigation (Teddlie & Tashakkori, 2003). This is supported by researchers in language acquisition, for instance Dörnyei (2007) argues that that these methods are not mutually exclusive, and that combining them is a viable possibility. And according to Croker (2009), sound research requires two features: unassailable data collection skills and an appropriate methodological approach that provides a framework for the research process. Mixed method approach also corresponds with virtual, intercultural and multimodal FL research contexts, each unique to its own situation and type of interaction (see Reinhardt; Ware & Rivas, this volume).

CMC settings also provide potentially rich opportunities for multiple, multimodal data (see Dooly & Hauck; O'Rourke this volume) and, ostensibly, data compilation for online interaction can be a relatively straightforward task, including the possibility of large corpora of metadata (Vyatkina, this volume). However, as Kitade (2008) points out, examining only the online interactions risks leaving out a significant portion of how the learner engages with the task at hand, especially in the case of 'classroom-based' activities. Along these lines, Warschauer & Kern argue that:

> [t]o understand the full impact of new forms of interacting in the language classroom, we must look beyond the texts of interaction to the broader contextual dynamics that shape and are shaped by those texts. (2000: 15)

Warschauer (2003) describes the complex relationship between online interaction and the context in which it takes place as the 'social embeddedness of technology' and explains the concept in the following way:

> [...]technology does not exist outside a social structure, exerting an independent force on it, but rather the technological and social realms are highly intertwined and continuously co-constitute each other in myriad ways. (Warschauer, 2003: 26)

Just as technology is socially embedded, research into the use of technology is equally embedded into the lives of the participants of the study and this gives rise to certain ethical issues. For example, as interest in how language learning can take place through online interaction grows, more studies involving young learners will take place. Not only must parental or guardian consent be given, it is recommendable to offer pre-study meetings with parents and teachers to discuss possible concerns that they may have and all subjects should be anonymised. However, making the participants' identities anonymous in data that has been captured online is not always easy (e.g. screenshots of video conferences) but there are programmes that can be used to blur facial features, erase meta-data of document programmes and blanking out of onscreen data that may give clues to participant identity.

Even for study participants of legal age, the question of individual privacy when it comes to recording (text, voice or video) in online 'public' spaces is important. Forums, open chats (or membership chats that the researcher has joined), or Virtual Worlds can easily be recorded without online participants even being aware that they are recorded (Panichi & Deutschmann, this volume). For researchers interested in capturing natural data, this may be an ideal means of doing so, however, the ethical issues of hidden recorders are patent. It is best to revise carefully the norms and regulations of the institution that is supporting the research as well as the rules that govern each online environment. In all cases, the researcher should act with prudence and consider possible repercussions carefully.

Kern (2006: 202) states that it is vital to get participants' acceptance before using their data in studies. Of course, the question of how to get consent from online participants distributed across the world, all of whom use online identities is another issue for researchers working in the domain of the third category of 'student to world interaction'. Added to this is the question of what constitutes consent – permission provided by participants with their 'online' identities or 'real-world' identities?

In many cases, the issues described above are questions faced by all social and educational researchers. In other cases, the issues are more pertinent to the specific circumstances of research in this area. As the use of contemporary online communication technologies becomes more commonplace in FL education in order to develop FL competency, intercultural awareness and e-literacies, the need for sound research in these contexts is apparent.

Individual Contributions to the Volume

The first section of this volume looks at different approaches which can be used for investigating and understanding CMC research such as sociocognitive and interactionist approaches, mixed methods approach and Cultural Historical Activity Theory. In the first chapter of this section, Reinhardt explores the related and sometimes contentious histories of interactionist and sociocognitive paradigms in SLA, arguing for an integrative, pragmatic approach that allows for an ecological perspective on telecollaborative interaction that views technological constraints, communication breakdown, and learner history as dynamic affordances of the context and language learning process. Next, Blin explores ways of using Cultural Historical Activity Theory (CHAT) and Engeström's theory of expansive learning to design and analyse language learning activities taking place in a variety of CMC environments. In the third chapter of this section, Ware and Rivas consider particular issues which may arise from ethnographic and mixed methods studies applied to CMC language learning contexts. Examples from an international online language learning project in secondary schools in the US and Spain exemplify possible resolutions to these issues.

Following that, in the second section, the authors suggest how different tools for data-collection techniques, diverse online contexts and varying approaches can contribute to our understanding of online FL interaction. First, Dooly and Hauck discuss the interdependence of multimodal communicative competence and the language learning process and the significance this has for research aimed at interrogating multi-faceted, multi-modal interactions. In the second chapter of Section Two, Müller-Hartmann examines the role of the teacher in CMC environments. The author outlines how to research the micro processes on the classroom level and online interaction through classroom-based action research. Following this, Panichi and Deutschmann discuss issues related to research in virtual world environments for language learning, including the use of educational communities, the nature of communication and human interaction in educational processes in these environments and the methods and tools currently at disposal for investigation. In the last chapter of this section, Möllering and Levy provide a review of research methods used in analysing the development of Intercultural Communicative Competence in Computer-mediated interactions.

Finally, the third section provides an overview of the emerging issues and challenges which are confronting FL CMC researchers and provides concrete suggestions as to how they can be dealt with. Vyatkina shows the use of learner corpus analysis applied to telecollaborative discourse, exemplified by email and internet chat exchanges between German and American college-level language learners. In the last chapter, O'Rourke discusses the importance of gaze data, collected with eye-tracker technology, for rich data compiled in synchronous computer-mediated communication, illustrated with analyses of gaze data from tandem MOO sessions.

The intended audience of the volume includes current researchers in the area, but in particular we intend to address the needs and interests of young researchers (for example, students at Master or PhD level) or new-comers to the area who are hoping to learn about the current state of the field before embarking on their own research studies. With this in mind, all of the chapters provide a comprehensive overview of their theme including an extensive literature review, before going on to provide extracts of real data to illustrate the theories, methods or issues in question. The aim of this book is to provide everyone with interest is this exciting field of study with a feel for different research designs and to offer an introduction that allows the reader to view different facets and perspectives of diverse research processes.

References

Basharina, O. (2007). An activity theory perspective on student-reported contractions in international telecollaboration. *Language Learning & Technology*, *11*(2), 82–103.
Downloaded 1 September 2011 from <http://llt.msu.edu/vol11num2/pdf/basharina.pdf>.

Bauer, B., de Benedette, L., Furstenberg, G., Levet, S., & Waryn, S. (2006). Computer-mediated intercultural foreign language education: The Cultura Project. In J.A. Belz & S.L. Thorne (Eds.), *Internet-mediated intercultural foreign language education* (pp.31–62). Boston, MA: Heinle & Heinle.

Bax, S. (2003). CALL – past, present and future. *System*, 31,1, 13–28.

Bazeley, P. (2004). Issues in mixed qualitative and quantitative approaches to research. In R. Buber, J. Gadner, & L. Richards (Eds.), *Applying qualitative methods to marketing management research* (pp. 141–156). UK: Palgrave Macmillan.

Belz, J. (2003). Linguistic perspectives on the development of intercultural competence in telecollaboration. *Language Learning & Technology, 7,* 2, 68–99. Downloaded 1 September 2011 from <http://llt.msu.edu/vol7num2/BELZ/default.html>.

Belz, J.A., & Kinginger, C. (2002). The cross-linguistic development of address form use in telecollaborative language learning: Two case studies. *Canadian Modern Language Review/Revue canadienne des langues vivantes, 59*(2), 189–214.

Belz, J.A.,& Müller-Hartmann, A. (2003). Teachers as intercultural learners: Negotiating German-American telecollaboration along the institutional fault line. *The Modern Language Journal, 87*(1), 71–89.

Belz, J., & Thorne, S. (2006). *Internet-mediated intercultural foreign language education.* Boston, MA: Heinle & Heinle.

Belz, J.A., & Vyatkina, N. (2008). The pedagogical mediation of a developmental learner corpus for classroom-based language instruction. *Language Learning & Technology, 12*(3), 33–52.

Beauvois, M. (1998). Conversations in slow motion: Computer-mediated communication in the foreign language classroom. *The Canadian Modern Language Review, 54*(2), 198–217.

Blake, R. (2000). Computer mediated communication: A window on L2 Spanish interlanguage. *Language Learning & Technology, 4*, 120–136. Downloaded 1 September 2011 from <http://llt.msu.edu/vol4num1/blake/default.html>.

Block, D. (2002). 'McCommunication': A problem in the frame for SLA. In D. Block & D. Cameron (Eds.), *Globalization and language teaching* (pp. 117–133). London: Routledge.

Byram, M. (1997). *Teaching and assessing intercultural communicative competence.* Clevedon: Multilingual Matters.

Commission of the European Communities (2008). *The use of ICT to support innovation and lifelong learning for all- A report on progress.* Brussels: European Commission.

Council of Europe (2003). *European Language Portfolio.* Strasbourg: Council of Europe.

Council of Europe (2007). *Autobiography of Intercultural Encounters.* Strasbourg: Council of Europe.

Croker, R. A. (2009). An introduction to qualitative research. In J. Heigham & R. A. Croker (Eds.), *Qualitative research in applied linguistics: A practical introduction* (pp. 3–24). Basingstoke: Palgrave Macmillan.

De Bot, K., Lowie, W., & Verspoor, M. (2007). A dynamic systems theory approach to second language acquisition. *Bilingualism: Language and Cognition, 10* (1), 7–21.

Denzin, N. K., & Lincoln, Y. S. (2003). Introduction: The discipline and practice of qualitative research. In N. K. Denzin & Y. S. Lincoln (Eds.), *The landscape of qualitative research: Theories and issues* (pp. 1–47). Thousand Oaks, CA: Sage Publications.

Dooly, M. (2008a). Understanding the many steps for effective collaborative language learning. *Language Learning Journal, 36*(1), 95–78.

Dooly, M. (2008b). Technology integrated into language learning: Introduction. In M. Dooly & D. Eastment (Eds.), *How we're going about it: Teachers' voices on innovative approaches to teaching and learning languages* (pp. 159–164). Newcastle: Cambridge Scholars Publishing.

Dooly, M. (2009). New competencies in a new era? Examining the impact of a teacher training project. *ReCALL 21*(3), 352–369.

Dooly, M. (2010). Teacher 2.0. In S. Guth & F. Helm (Eds.), *Telecollaboration 2.0: Language, literacies and intercultural learning in the 21st century* (pp. 277–303). Bern: Peter Lang.

Dooly, M. (2011). Divergent perceptions of telecollaborative language learning tasks: Task-as-workplan vs. task-as-process. *Language Learning & Technology, 15*(2), 69–91. Downloaded 1 September 2011 from <http://llt.msu.edu/issues/ june2011/dooly.pdf>.

Dörnyei, Z. (2007). *Research methods in applied linguistics.* Oxford: Oxford University Press.

Eck, A., Legenhausen, L. & Wolff, D. (1995). *Telekommunikation und Fremdsprachenunterricht: Informationen, Projekte, Ergebnisse.* Bochum: AKS-Verlag.

European Commission (2010). *Key competences for lifelong learning: European framework document.* Strasbourg: Council of Europe.

Fitzpatrick, T., & O'Dowd, R. (Eds.) (2011). *E-Vollution.* Strasbourg: Council of Europe.

Guth, S., & F. Helm (eds) (2010). *Telecollaboration 2.0: Language, literacies and intercultural learning in the 21st Century.* Bern: Peter Lang.

Hanna, B., & de Nooy, J. (2009). *Learning language and culture via public internet discussion forums.* New York: Palgrave Macmillan.

Hymes, D. (with J. Gumperz, eds.) (1964). The ethnography of communication. *American Anthropologist, 66*(6), Part 2.

Kendall, L. (2008). The conduct of qualitative interview: Research questions, methodological issues, and researching online. In J. Coiro, M. Knobel, C. Lankshear & D. Leu (Eds.), *Handbook of research on new literacies* (pp. 133–149). New York: Lawrence Erlbaum Associates.

Kern, R. (2006). Perspectives on Technology in Learning and Teaching Language. *TESOL Quarterly, 40* (1), 183–210.

Coiro, J., Knobel, M., Lankshear, C., & Leu, D. (Eds.) (2008). *The handbook of research on new literacies.* Mahwah, NJ: Erlbaum.

Kramsch, C. (1993). *Context and culture in language teaching.* Oxford: Oxford University Press.

Lamy, M-N., & Goodfellow, R. (2010). Telecollaboration and learning 2.0. In S. Guth & F. Helm (Eds.), *Telecollaboration 2.0: Language, literacies and intercultural learning in the 21st century.* (pp. 107–138). Bern: Peter Lang.

Lamy, M-N., & Hampel, R. (2007). *Online communication in language learning and teaching.* London: Palgrave Macmillan.

Lankshear, C., & Knobel, M. (2006). *New literacies: Everyday practices and classroom learning (2nd edition).* Maidenhead & New York: Open University Press.

Larsen-Freeman, D. (2007). On the complementarily of chaos/complexity theory and dynamic systems theory in understanding the second language acquisition process. *Bilingualism: Language and Cognition, 10*, 35–37.

Larsen-Freeman, D., & Cameron, L. (2008). *Complex systems and applied linguistics.* Oxford: Oxford University Press.

Levy, M., & Stockwell, G. (2006). *CALL dimensions: Options and issues in computer-assisted language learning.* Mahwah, NJ: Lawrence Erlbaum.

Livingstone, S., Van Couvering, E., & Thumim, N. (2008). Converging traditions of research on media and information literacies: Disciplinary, critical, and methodological issues. In J. Coiro, M. Knobel, C. Lankshear & D.J. Leu (Eds.), *Handbook of research on new literacies* (pp. 103–132). New York: Lawrence Erlbaum Associates.

Long, M., & Robinson, P. (1998). *Focus on form theory, research, and practice.* Stuttgart: Ernst Klett Sprachen.

Merriam, S. B. (2002). Introduction to qualitative research. In S. B. Merriam (Ed.), *Qualitative research in practice: Examples for discussion and analysis* (pp.3–33). San Franscisco: Jossey-Bass.

Meskill, C., & Ranglova, K. (2000). Sociocollaborative language learning in Bulgaria. In M. Warschauer & R. Kern (Eds.), *Network-based language teaching: Concepts and practice* (pp. 20–40). Cambridge: Cambridge University Press.

Meskill, C., & Anthony, N. (2010). *Teaching languages online.* Bristol: Multilingual Matters.

Müller-Hartmann, A. (2000). The role of tasks in promoting intercultural learning in electronic learning networks. *Language Learning and Technology 4* (2), 129–147. Downloaded 1 September 2011 from<http://llt.msu.edu/vol4num2/muller/default.html>.

Müller-Hartmann, A., & Schocker-v. Ditfurth, M. (Eds.) (2008). Research on the use of technology in task-based language teaching. In A. Müller-Hartmann & M. Schocker-v. Ditfurth (Eds.), *Aufgabenorientiertes Lernen und Lehren mit Medien: Ansätze, Erfahrungen, Perspektiven in der Fremdsprachendidaktik* (pp. 12–64). Frankfurt: Peter Lang.

Muyskens, J. (Ed.) (1998). *New ways of learning and teaching: focus on technology and foreign language education.* Boston, MA: Heinle & Heinle Publishers.

O'Dowd, R. (2003). Understanding 'the other side': intercultural learning in a Spanish-English email exchange. *Language Learning and Technology 7*, 2, 118–144. Downloaded 1 September 2011 from <http://llt.msu.edu/vol7num2/odowd/default.html>.

O'Dowd, R. (2006). *Telecollaboration and the development of intercultural communicative competence.* Berlin: Langenscheidt.

O'Dowd, R. (Ed.) (2007). *Online intercultural exchange: An introduction for foreign language teachers.* Clevedon: Multilingual Matters.

O'Dowd, R. (2010). Issues in the assessment of online interaction and exchange. In S. Guth & F. Helm (Eds.), *Telecollaboration 2.0: Language, literacies and intercultural learning in the 21st century* (pp. 337–358). Bern: Peter Lang.

O'Dowd, R. (2011). Online foreign language interaction: Moving from the periphery to the core of foreign language education? *Language Teaching, 44*, 368–380.

O'Dowd, R., & Ritter, M. (2006). Understanding and working with 'failed communication' in telecollaborative exchanges. *CALICO Journal, 23*, 623–642.

O'Dowd, R., & Ware, P. (2009). Critical issues in telecollaborative task design. *Computer Assisted Language Learning, 22*(2), 173–188.

O'Rourke, B. (2007). Models of telecollaboration (1): eTandem. In R. O'Dowd (Ed.), *Online intercultural exchange* (pp. 41–61). Clevedon, UK: Multilingual Matters.

Ortega, L. (1997). Processes and outcomes in networked classroom interaction: Defining the research agenda for L2 computer-assisted classroom discussion. *Language Learning and Technology, 1* (1), 82–93. Downloaded 1 September 2011 from <http://llt.msu.edu/vol1num1/ortega/default.html>.

Pasfield-Neofitou, S. (2011). Online domains of language use: second language learners'experiences of virtual community and foreignness. *Language Learning and Technology 15* (2), 92–108. Downloaded 1 September 2011 from <http://llt.msu.edu/issues/june2011/pasfieldneofitou.pdf>.

Pelletieri, J. (2000). Negotiation in cyberspace: The role of chatting in the development of grammatical competence. In M. Warschauer & R. Kern (Eds.), *Network-based language teaching: Concepts and practice* (pp. 59–86). Cambridge: Cambridge University Press.

Plsek, P.E, & Greenhalgh, T. (2001). The challenge of complexity in health care. *British Medical Journal, 323* (7313), 625–628.

Richards, J.C. (2005). Communicative language teaching today. *International Journal of Applied Linguistics, 8* (2), 233–250.

Sadler, R., & Eröz, B. (2008). Getting the message: Training language teachers in the theoretical and practical application of forums. In M. Dooly & D. Eastment (Eds.) *How we're going about it: Teachers' voices on innovative approaches to teaching and learning languages* (pp. 187–197). Newcastle: Cambridge Scholars Publishing.

Savignon, S.J. (1983). *Communicative competence: Theory and classroom practice.* Reading, MA: Addison-Wesley.

Savignon, S.J. (1991). Communicative language teaching: State of the art. *TESOL Quarterly, 25*(2): 261–277.

Schwienhorst, K. (2000). *Virtual reality and learner autonomy in second language acquisition.* Unpublished Ph.D. thesis, Trinity College Dublin.

Sotillo, S. M. (2000). Discourse functions and syntactic complexity in synchronous and asynchronous communication. *Language Learning & Technology, 4*(1), 82–119. Downloaded 1 September 2011 from <http://llt.msu.edu/vol4num1/sotillo/>.

Swan, M. (2004). Complex quantum chaos and the present perfect. *ELT Journal, 58*(1), 68–70.

Tashakkori, A., & Teddlie, C. (Eds.) (2003). *Handbook of mixed methods in social and behavioral research.* Thousand Oaks, CA: Sage.

Thorne, S. L. (2004). Cultural Historical Activity Theory and the object of innovation. In O. St. John, K. van Esch & E. Schalkwijk (Eds.), *New Insights into FL learning and teaching* (pp. 51–70). Frankfurt: Peter Lang Verlag.

Thorne, S.L (2006). Pedagogical and praxiological lessons from Internet-mediated intercultural foreign language education research. In J. Belz & S. Thorne (Eds.), *Internet-mediated intercultural foreign language education* (pp. 2–30). Boston: Heinle & Heinle.

Thorne, S.L (2010). The "intercultural turn" and language learning in the crucible of new media. In S. Guth & F. Helm (Eds.), *Telecollaboration 2.0: Language, literacies and intercultural learning in the 21st century* (pp. 139–164). Bern: Peter Lang.

Thorne, S. L., Black, R. W., & Sykes, J. (2009). Second language use, socialization, and learning in internet interest communities and online games. *Modern Language Journal, 93*, 802–841.

Tudini, V. (2003). Using native speakers in chat. *Language Learning & Technology, 7*(3), 141–159. Downloaded 1 September 2011 from <http://llt.msu.edu/vol7num3/pdf/tudini.pdf>.

Verspoor, M. H., de Bot, K., & Lowie, W. (Eds.) (2011). *A dynamic approach to second language development. Methods and techniques.* Amsterdam, Netherlands: John Benjamins.

Ware, P. (2005). "Missed" communication in online communication: Tensions in fostering successful online interactions. *Language Learning & Technology, 9*(2), 64–89. Downloaded 1 September 2011 from <http://llt.msu.edu/vol9num2/default.html>.

Ware, P., & Kramsch, C. (2005). Toward an intercultural stance: Teaching German and English through telecollaboration. *Modern Language Journal, 89* (2), 190–205.

Warschauer, M. (Ed.) (1995). *Virtual connections: Online activities and projects for networking language learners.* Honolulu, HI: University of Hawai'i Second Language Teaching and Curriculum Center.

Warschauer, M. (1996). Comparing face-to-face and electronic communication in the second language classroom. *CALICO Journal, 13*(2), 7–26.

Warschauer, M. (2003). *Technology and equity: A comparative study.* Paper presented at the Annual Meeting of the American Educational Research Association, April 24, 2003, Chicago, Illinois.

Warschauer, M., & Kern, R. (Eds.) (2000). *Network-based language teaching: Concepts and practice.* Cambridge: Cambridge University Press.

Wolff-Michael, R., & Yew-Jin, L. (2007). "Vygotsky's neglected legacy": Cultural-historical activity theory. *Review of Educational Research, 77*(2), 186–232.

Zuengler, J., & Miller, E.R. (2006). Cognitive and sociocultural perspectives: Two parallel SLA worlds? *TESOL Quarterly*, *40*, 35–58.

Section I: Theoretical Approaches to Researching Online Exchange

Accommodating Divergent Frameworks in Analysis of Technology-Mediated L2 Interaction

JONATHON REINHARDT

Researchers have used a variety of methodological frameworks to analyze technology-mediated interaction between second/foreign (L2) learners and expert/native speakers, both inter- and intra-class. For example, researchers of telecollaborative interaction grounded in an input-interactionist paradigm have found negotiation for meaning to occur in online inter-class chat (e.g. Pellettieri, 2000; Smith, 2003; Jepson, 2005; Lai & Zhao, 2006), while those using socio-cognitive paradigms (Kern & Warschauer, 2000; Atkinson, 2002) have found evidence for the development of intercultural and pragmatic competence in intra-class telecollaboration (e.g. Ware, 2005; Jin & Erben, 2007; Abrams, 2009). Each approach offers heuristic value for the researcher of L2 learning.

While the interactionist (Long, 1983; Varonis & Gass, 1985) and socio-cognitive (Atkinson, 2002) frameworks these methods entail are often seen as ontologically incommensurable (Firth & Wagner, 1997; Block, 2003; Zuengler & Miller, 2006), some research has attempted synthesis or balance of the two, while others have made conciliatory nods and acknowledged the heuristic strength of multiple perspectives. This chapter examines research from both paradigms, focusing on methodological approaches and the areas they share: interaction and negotiation for meaning. It concludes with consideration of a recently emerging paradigm, broadly labelled ecological (e.g. Leather & van Dam, 2003; van Lier, 2004; van Geert 2008; Larsen-Freeman & Cameron, 2008a) that has been claimed to potentially transcend the debate and resolve incommensurabilities (e.g. Lafford, 2007; Chapelle, 2009).

There has long been discussion in applied linguistics and second/foreign language acquisition/development[1] (SLA) about the appropriate object and method of investigation, between those concerned with the psychological aspects of acquisition and those oriented more towards the social aspects of learning. This 'cognitive-social' divide, in some ways, is the fundamental debate of the field, with parallels among rationalist-positivists and social relativists in many fields across the academy. While its origins lie in ontological debates in education, the social sciences, philosophy, and linguistics, the debate in SLA coalesced around theoretical camps in the 1990s (Long, 1990; Lantolf, 1996; Gregg, 1996; Firth & Wagner, 1997), and is ongoing (e.g. Seidlhofer, 2003; Block, 2003; Jordan, 2004; Watson-Gegeo, 2004; Zuengler & Miller, 2006; Hill, 2006; Lafford, 2007; Larsen-Freeman, 2007). On the cognitive side, theorists (e.g. Jordan, 2004) use rationalist arguments to claim that language acquisition is an internal cognitive phenomenon. In this line of thought, input-interactionists (e.g. Long & Robinson, 1998; Gass & Mackey, 2006) explore the psychological mechanisms of language acquisition using input processing metaphors (Block, 2003). In contrast, researchers from traditions like sociocultural theory and language socialization (e.g. Lantolf & Thorne, 2006; Atkinson, 2002; Watson-Gegeo, 2004), what might be called "social-informed" theories, criticize interactionist tenets (Block, 2003) and claim that language learning is socio-cognitive in nature, that is, cognition cannot be considered separately from social interaction. In this view, language learning is inseparable from language use, and participation is the dominant metaphor (Lave & Wenger, 1991; Sfard, 1998).

For the researcher of L2 interaction, these debates can be confusing and sometimes daunting, because of their implications for research design and implementation. Any empirical study of L2 interaction uses a theoretical framework that also implicates the use of

1 The inclusion of both "acquisition" and "development" in this acronym intentionally reflects a crucial difference in how cognitive and social-informed research conceptualizes L2 learning (Firth & Wagner, 1997; Block, 2003). For the purpose of clarity, however, SLA is used throughout the chapter.

particular methods. For example, input-interactionists privilege experimental, psychometric methods, which align with the theoretical underpinnings of a cognitive framework. Socio-cognitive frameworks, in contrast, implicate the use of qualitative and ethnographic methods. In practice, however, many researchers stretch, adapt, and combine frameworks and methods, which on one hand may lead to new insight, but on the other, may lead to commensurability issues.

When technology-mediated L2 interaction contexts are added to the equation, the choice of method becomes even more complex, as researchers are faced with a variety of technologies and class configurations. Early SCMC (synchronous computer-mediated communication, or chat) research tended towards comparison with face-to-face communication, discussion of the speech-writing hybrid nature of the medium, and general description of CMC benefits (e.g. Beauvois, 1992; Chun, 1994; Kern, 1995; see Blyth, 2008, for discussion). Research found evidence that in intra-class SCMC, learners would produce more language; that they would produce a wider range of discourse types; that their participation would be re-distributed; and that their fluency would benefit, although possibly at the expense of accuracy. Building on these findings, cognitive researchers using input-interactionist frameworks (e.g. Pellettieri, 2000; Smith, 2003) claim to find in SCMC an environment conducive to negotiation of meaning (c.f. Ortega, 2009). Most have found traditional frameworks need adaptation to account for the disjunct turn structures and textual persistence of chat, which, some hypothesize, seems to promote noticing (Schmidt, 1990), the *sine qua non* of SLA.

In contrast to interactionist research, socio-cognitive research (Kern & Warschauer, 2000; Atkinson, 2002; Watson-Gegeo, 2004) can be seen broadly to encompass several social-informed approaches, including sociocultural theory, language socialization, situated learning, and dialogic perspectives (Zuengler & Miller, 2006). Because socio-cognitive frameworks emphasize the role of cultural context, they are often used in the study of telecollaboration (Belz & Kinginger, 2002; Warschauer, 1997), or internet-mediated intercultural language education (Belz & Thorne, 2006). These studies find evidence for the development of linguistic, pragmatic, and intercultural competence in the internet-mediated social interactions at the center of telecollaborative partnerships.

As both interactionist and socio-cognitive approaches have heuristic value to the researcher of technology-mediated interaction, the primary purpose of this chapter is to explore their potential complementarities. The chapter will first examine the theoretical backgrounds, methodologies, and criticisms of each framework, focusing on recent research that employs them. Several studies that combine the two frameworks in varying degrees will then be presented, followed by a discussion of their shared key concepts of "interaction" and "negotiation for meaning". An ecological approach (van Lier 2000, 2004; Larsen-Freeman & Cameron, 2008b; Lafford, 2009) is then introduced, as a framework that has been touted to offer new insights into SLA and potentially transcend much of the cognitive-social debate.

The Interactionist Approach

The interactionist approach to SLA research (Long, 1983; 1996; Gass, 1997; Long & Robinson, 1998), also known as input-interactionism, hypothesizes that interaction between a learner and other language users is central to language learning, since this interaction provides opportunity for the negotiation for meaning (NfM). Besides NfM, the concepts of input, feedback, noticing, and output are the main constructs of the approach, as each plays an important role in the acquisition process. A learner is subject to input and produces output based on comprehension of that input, which effects feedback from an interlocutor. This may subsequently lead to the learner noticing particular formal qualities of her production (Swain, 1985) that led to that particular feedback. This noticing may then lead to acquisition.

Interactionist approaches are coherent with a rationalist-positivist understanding that language acquisition is primarily a cognitive phenomenon, that is, it occurs in an individual's brain. Linguistic knowledge is primarily informational in nature, negotiated in interaction, and quantifiable. Methodologically, controlled experiments using highly structured tasks lead to implications about what factors may co-occur, or even have a causative relationship, with particular outcomes. For example, if task type is hypothesized to influence the quantity and quality of negotiation, a researcher might design a classroom experiment where two groups complete different kinds of tasks, with every other variable kept the same. The transcripts of the interactions would then be coded and analyzed for negotiation for meaning, using a taxonomy that is commensurable with the theoretical framework. If one group had more negotiations than the other, it would be evidence that the task they did was more conducive to negotiation.

The approach has been criticized for several reasons, primarily because it seems to marginalize the role of social context by considering it a matter of individual difference, rather than an integral part of the hypothesis. Moreover, the constructs central to the approach appropriate ontological metaphors that originate in computer science and reduce conceptualization of communication to simple transmission. If learning is facilitated during negotiation of meaning, the implication is that negotiation-free interaction is less conducive to acquisition than communication breakdown. The model privileges grammatical over pragmatic knowledge, and reduces the learner, so the criticism goes (e.g. Firth & Wagner, 1997), into a theoretically knowable collection of variables.

These criticisms have been answered with claims that the approach is not in fact intended to be comprehensive, and that researchers do not deny the role of context, but rather do not focus on it. Gass (1998) notes that interactionists "have never meant to understand language use *per se*" (p. 84), and that while context is important, researchers have focused on language rather than the communicative act itself. While particular tasks may promote negotiation, it is not claimed that this is the only way that noticing leads to uptake. The approach is conceptualized using isolatable, measurable constructs to allow for experimental, psychometric research and to claim internal and external validity, so that causation may be implied and findings may be generalized to other individuals and contexts[2].

Interactionist Treatments of Technology-Mediated L2 Interactions

Interactionist frameworks have been used widely in analyses of L2 learner interactions in SCMC. Pellettieri's (2000) work was one of the first to show that meaning could be negotiated in chat. She used Varonis and Gass' (1985) "Trigger-Indicator-Response-Reaction to Response" (TIRR) taxonomy to code learner interactions, and found that with goal-oriented, language focused tasks, students would negotiate meaning. She noted a preponderance of reaction to responses (93% of all interactions), and attributed this to the lack of visual cues in the chat medium. In another early study using the TIRR model, Blake (2000) also found negotiation to occur in jigsaw tasks in chat, noting that breakdown wasn't necessary "in the classical sense, since there is no incidental communicative misunderstanding" (p. 132). Smith (2003) also used Varonis and Gass' framework, and found that learners negotiated task-targeted items mostly in decision-making tasks, but incidental items in jigsaw tasks, confirming Blake's findings. Smith also found, like Pellettieri, an excess of reaction moves, and speculated this was due to the fact that when acknowledging understanding in CMC, an interlocutor must use a text-based cue, while in face-to-face, some reaction moves can be non-verbal, like a nod of understanding.

To accommodate their findings, researchers have found that extended interactionist taxonomies are useful for analysis of chat. Smith

2 It is important to note, however, that many of the concepts adopted by the approach, like negotiation of meaning, noticing, and uptake, have their own body of research, some of which may not claim affiliation with input-interactionist theory.

expanded the NfM model by incorporating the notion of "task-appropriate response" (2003), and later (2009) noted that self-initiated self-repair, including of grammatical forms, was evident in SCMC if appropriate data collection techniques were used. Lee (2001) expanded Long's CCC (Confirmation, Comprehension, and Clarification check) model to account for invented words, use of English, and symbolized discourse markers (emoticons). Toyoda and Harrison (2002) expanded Varonis and Gass' trigger specification, by looking at lexical, sentential, and discourse trigger types. Similarly, O'Rourke (2005) examined the signal or indicator of negotiations to determine which were most prominent in telecollaborative interactions.

With regards to method, the resources available to the researcher, as well as the purpose of an NfM analysis, influence the choice of study features, especially relative speaker status (NS or NNS) and learner proficiency, and pedagogical factors such as task type or institutional configuration. Many interactionist-informed studies have been of NNS-NNS L2 learners in intra-class chat (Pellettieri, 2000; Blake, 2000; Smith, 2003, 2004), but have also been of Heritage-NNS (Blake & Zyzik, 2003), NS-NNS in telecollaboration (Tudini, 2003) or tandem learning partnerships (Kötter, 2003; O'Rourke, 2005). Most use experimental set-ups, although some utilize open-ended or classroom configurations. Focus is on identifying which factors, such as speaker status, proficiency level, task medium, or task design, effect which outcomes.

More recent interactionist-informed research has delved further into these factors. For example, Sotillo (2005) compared NS-NNS and advanced NNS-NNS pairings, finding that learners negotiated less with NS than with other learners. Jepson (2005) found more repair in voice chat than in text chat. Satar and Ozdener (2009) found results similar to Jepson (2005), but added there was less anxiety in text chat, which might make it more appropriate for lower proficiency levels. Kitade (2006) used the TIRR model to analyze asynchronous (e-mail) exchanges, and found a lack of reaction moves, an understandable finding, considering their spoken discourse function as confirmation or acknowledgement devices. Lai and Zhao (2006) found that learners generally noticed more in text chat than in face-to-face interaction, which they speculate may be due to the explicit nature of chat-based negotiation and persistent quality of the text. Recasts, however, were noticed less, which Lai later, with Fei and Roots (2008), speculated were due to contingency, or how close they were to their triggers. In SCMC, discontinuous or split turn sequences may mean that recasts are noticed less. Smith (2009) notes the need for new research techniques that record how some SCMC users compose, then delete, utterances before contributing them, in order to better account for noticing and uptake, since such moves are not apparent in a final chat transcript.

Socio-cognitive Perspectives

In her review of interactionist research in SCMC, Ortega (2009) notes that the evidence on the benefits of SCMC for L2 learning is inconclusive, as the amount of NfM found in SCMC has varied quite widely. She observes that the wide variety of findings may point towards the role of contextual variables, for example, task type, age, gender, and the familiarity and proficiency differences between interlocutors. Researchers using socio-cognitive frameworks would certainly agree with Ortega, but they might also argue that a positivist, experimental framework could not truly get at many of the reasons for the variation. From a socio-cognitive perspective, the reduction of language, language learning, and language learners into theoretically measurable collections of variables misses the mark. Getting at these issues, they would argue, demands more social-informed definitions of language and learning, along with commensurate research techniques.

Socio-cognitive perspectives on L2 learning and development include those social-informed approaches that, even if they do not articulate it explicitly[3], imply that social and cognitive activity are interdependent and inseparable. Primary among these approaches are sociocultural theory (Lantolf & Thorne, 2006), language socialization (Schieffelin & Ochs, 1986; Ochs, 1988; Watson-Gegeo, 2004), and situated learning (Lave & Wenger, 1991). According to socio-cognitive perspectives, language is a social accomplishment, a tool which people use "to act in and on their social worlds" (Atkinson, 2002, p. 526), existing first externally and then acted or "participated" into being. According to Atkinson's (2002) interpretation of a socio-cognitive approach, grammar is a shared resource fundamental to social interaction that emerges as an epiphenomenon (see also Hopper, 1998), and is thus neither *a priori* nor analyzable separately from cognition. Cognitive development is interdependent with social activity, and all learning is concomitant with socialization (Gee, 1996; Watson-Gegeo, 2004). L2 development is not acquisition or internalization, but "engagement and participation in a dynamic and changing mind–body–world continuum" (Atkinson, Churchill, Nishino, & Okada, 2007, p. 170). Insofar as such a continuum rejects, or transcends, dualistic thought, including subjective-objective dichotomies (Lakoff & Johnson, 1980), socio-cognitive approaches can be considered monistic and relativistic.

Methodologically, socio-cognitive researchers place primary importance on ecological validity, where research conditions are as close to the actual conditions of learning as possible. Analysts strive to capture the 'emic' view, or the participant's perspective, on the phenomenon under study. Because 'socio-cognitive' is not a single

3 The term 'socio-cognitive' has been used in several different ways, sometimes as an umbrella term for the social side of the cognitive-social debate (e.g. Kern & Warschauer, 2000), sometimes as a particular social-informed approach distinct from other approaches (e.g. Atkinson, et al., 2007), and sometimes as a means of transcending the debate itself (e.g. Larsen-Freeman, 2007). This chapter (see also Reinhardt, 2008) adopts the first definition, considering that some major social-informed approaches, e.g. sociocultural theory (Lantolf & Thorne, 2006) and language socialization (Watson-Gegeo, 2004), theorize that cognition is real, and may have inter-psychological qualities, but is inseparable from social activity.

cohesive approach, but rather a family of approaches with common perspectives on L2 development, they do not share a single framework like NfM studies using the TIRR taxonomy. Instead, various combinations of qualitative and ethnographic methods are used in conjunction with discourse analysis, although quantitative methods, for example the use of surveys and corpus analysis, are not necessarily eschewed. Studies tend to be descriptive and longitudinal rather than experimental and synchronic. For example, a study might examine how participation structures change over the course of a telecollaborative partnership, analyzing learner interactions for the use of particular forms and corroborating these observations with learner interviews.

Criticisms of socio-cognitive methods are that they seem inexact and not particularly rigorous, and that findings sometimes seem overly interpretive and phenomenological. In response, socio-cognitive researchers argue that their methods involve inclusive consideration, rather than exclusion, of factors like learner histories, socio-institutional influences, and pragmatic and interpersonal meanings. Socio-cognitive techniques can therefore be very "messy", involving sometimes very large amounts of data like interviews, videos, and student work, and cycles of grounded interpretation and re-interpretation, often longitudinally. Without an understanding of this methodology, readers may find that the presented results, which are most likely only a small portion of all the data, seem anecdotal and less solidly empirical. Another criticism is that the research may not seem scientific in the positivistic sense, and that it lacks validity and generalizability to other contexts. For socio-cognitive research, however, it is understood that context is fundamental, not ancillary, to any application. Since each context is different, ecological validity is of utmost importance, and should not be sacrificed for generalizability. Socio-cognitive research is usually post-positivist, in that the researcher does not claim total objectivity, and is "aware that unobservable cognitive processes alter our understanding of science, rather than allowing science to dictate whether cognition is observable or not" (Hill, 2006, p. 821).

Socio-cognitive Treatments of Technology-Mediated L2 Interaction

A number of studies of telecollaborative interaction have used socio-cognitive theoretical and methodological frameworks. Some studies use a socio-cognitive lens more broadly to examine the development of intercultural competence (Furstenberg, Levet, English, & Maillet, 2001; O'Dowd, 2003; Ware & Kramsch, 2005; Jin & Erben, 2007) and participation in communities of practice (Kramsch & Thorne, 2002; Hanna & de Nooy, 2003; 2009; Darhower, 2007; Black, 2007; Abrams, 2009). Others make specific use of social-informed frameworks like sociocultural theory (Belz, 2002; Thorne, 2003; Belz, 2004; Belz & Kinginger, 2003; Oskoz, 2009), dialogic approaches (Ware, 2005), and language socialization (Lam, 2004). Using these frameworks, researchers have found, for example, that telecollaborative environments in particular offer expanded discourse options and the opportunities for development of sociopragmatic competence (Abrams, 2009). Several of the more recent studies are worth examining closer for theoretical and methodological trends[4], as they also address areas particularly well-suited to socio-cognitive research (Atkinson, 2002), for example self-presentation and identity development (Lam, 2004), the use of contextualization cues (Ware, 2005), the development of intercultural competence (Jin & Erben, 2007), community participation structures (Darhower, 2007), and interaction structures (Oskoz, 2009).

Although her work is not on formal instructed environments, Eva Lam's work (2004; 2009) on immigrant teen use of internet technologies to develop new identities and literacy practices illustrates how L2 learning through new media has been researched using a socio-cognitive approach. Using a language socialization framework, Lam (2004) examined how, through participation in online Cantonese chat rooms, two Chinese immigrant teenagers assumed new plurilingual identities by mixing and demonstrating expertise in multiple languages.

4 For comprehensive reviews of earlier research, see Reinhardt, 2008, and Thorne, 2008.

Methodologically, Lam uses case studies, following the teens for months, developing relationships with them, and conducting interviews and participant observation. Her research shows that the transnational realities of contemporary culture and identities that influence language practice are often plurilingual and "glocal" (i.e., both global and local), so that older conceptualizations of culture no longer hold, an important implication for telecollaboration.

Ware (2005) provides an example of longitudinal, qualitative research for the study of telecollaboration. In her analysis of "missed communication" in a German-American partnership, she uses a socio-cognitive framework based on Bakhtin's concept of dialogic interaction and the use of affordances and contextualization cues for meaning creation. As a participant observer and instructor of the courses she analyzed, she was able to adopt an emic view, that is, the perspective of the course participants. She uses a variety of qualitative methods, including simple corpus techniques, interviews, and discourse analysis of discussion board posts and coursework, to determine common themes that might explain the tensions that emerged, including different academic expectations, socio-institutional factors, and individual differences among participants. For each of her categories she provides data examples from interviews and coursework to support her assertions.

Building on the earlier work of Furstenberg, et al. (2001), O'Dowd (2003), and Belz & Thorne (2006), Jin & Erben (2007) provide an example of how a methodological approach should be commensurate with a theoretical framework. Using Byram's Intercultural Communicative Competence model (1997, in Jin & Erben, 2007), where learners develop competence over time through reflective interaction with others, they examined intercultural learning in telecollaborative partnerships between Americans and Chinese students using instant messenger over several months. A variety of qualitative and ethnographic techniques were employed, including surveys, student coursework, interviews, and participant observation, in conjunction with a grounded analysis of instant messenger transcripts. They found a variety of development trajectories among individual students, and supported observations of changes in quantitative survey results with interview data.

Socio-cognitive researchers often compliment existing theoretical frameworks with grounded and content analyses of interaction data to establish ecologically valid constructs, which are illustrated with individual examples of learner data. For example, Darhower (2007) used the community of practice concept (Lave & Wenger, 1991; Wenger, 1998), as well as the ecological concept of affordances (van Lier, 2004, see below), to explore the development of online community among Spanish learners in the US and English learners in Puerto Rico who engaged in weekly chats. Of the huge number of transcripts generated, Darhower chose data from groups whose interactions demonstrated best his overall finding that community-building differed dramatically among groups. He read through transcripts using Brown's (2001, in Darhower, 2007) framework of community to categorize the data broadly, used grounded techniques to identify emergent trends, and then found discourse samples to illustrate his findings.

Oskoz (2009) provides an example of how socio-cognitive researchers combine methods, often first presenting quantitative data and then discourse examples from individuals. Adopting a sociocultural framework for analysis of scaffolded assistance in interaction, she examined whether learners in SCMC engage in peer assistance to the same extent as in face-to-face, and whether that assistance leads to learning, or, in sociocultural terms, microgenetic development. She finds that in general, learners created their own learning agendas, and that considerable variation existed among groups. Oskoz first uses content analysis to identify when and to what degree of explicitness a learner noticed an error, as well as the kinds of intervention offered by peers, and then determines the frequency of each type. She presents the findings quantitatively, and from those observations, then offers discourse examples to illustrate the different feedback types found. Oskoz' study is also a good example of a socio-cognitive treatment of an area, peer feedback, traditionally treated with interactionist frameworks.

Combining Frameworks

Some have claimed that the differences in interactionist and socio-cognitive frameworks are so great that they are incommensurable (Zuengler & Miller, 2006), and that the cognitive-social debate may never be resolved because it is based in competing metaphors (Watson-Gegeo & Nielsen, 2003; Larsen-Freeman, 2007). Chapelle (2009), however, notes that while a single L2 learning theory is limited, "CALL activities can span a broad range of learning opportunities" (p. 747), and so require balanced consideration. As both socio-cognitive and interactionist frameworks have become more widespread and recognized, more researchers are drawing elements from both perspectives in an attempt to gain new insights, a pragmatic view increasingly legitimized by the growing acceptability of mixing methods. These studies are worth examining for what they perceive as common ground.

Many studies find it pragmatically useful to acknowledge both interactionist and socio-cognitive approaches in outlining their theoretical frameworks, although they don't necessarily synthesize the approaches methodologically. Jepson (2005), for example, examined repair moves in text- and voice-based chat rooms among L2 English speakers, by using a combined conceptualization of interaction as a theoretical framework. However, his application of Long's (1983) CCC framework to categorize data makes little reference to socio-cognitive concepts, and he leaves socio-cognitive insights to the future by concluding that "further research based on sociocultural theory would likely unearth a plethora of data from conversational chat rooms with NNS participants" (p. 91).

In his study of Irish-German tandem learning in a MOO, O'Rourke (2005) makes explicit the hybrid nature of his theoretical framework, thus justifying his methodological choices. O'Rourke acknowledges the socio-cognitive position that the function of CMC tools is not technologically determined but rather dynamic and socially co-constructed (e.g. Thorne, 2003), but also that pedagogical environments "must have distinctive, if indirect, effects on interaction since they have distinctive properties" (p. 435). O'Rourke then adapts an NfM TIRR framework to analyze telecollaborative interactions, with a caveat that he does not adopt the position that NfM leads directly to L2 acquisition, but rather metalinguistic awareness. Like others, he finds that the TIRR framework needs significant modification because of the unique text-only qualities of the MOO environment.

Lee (2008) employed a hybrid approach to examine learner-expert interactions in Spanish, in that her set-up was experimental as in interactionist research, while her interpretive framework was sociocultural theory. Working with learner-expert pairs, she examined various kinds of classroom tasks to determine which result in more self-repair and scaffolding episodes, finding that open-ended question tasks produced more self-repair than jigsaw or spot-the-differences tasks. She used a grounded approach to categorize episodes, finding qualitative differences in the use of expert scaffolding, the use of L1, and self-correction. Learner interviews found that some learners appreciated the expert assistance, while others found it distracted from communication. It is interesting to compare Lee's research design to that of Oskoz (2009), who also investigated scaffolding and feedback, but used a less structured task design, which is more consistent with socio-cognitive methods.

Others make use of methodological constructs that are more commensurate with both frameworks, for example, Language Related Episodes (LREs), Swain's conceptualization of collaborative dialogue (2000; also Swain & Lapkin, 1998), a unit broader than TIRR exchanges and more consistent with a socio-cognitive perspective on interaction. In an analysis of noticing in intra-class chat, Shekary and Tahririan (2006) claim using LREs reflects "an integrated approach to interaction theory" (p. 560), drawing on interactionist as well as socio-cognitive concepts. They found that learners recalled items they negotiated in SCMC-mediated LREs better than incidentally discussed items. Ware and O'Dowd (2008) also use LREs to examine differences in feedback styles between Spanish-

American telecollaboration partners. They note that input-interactionist frameworks are useful for examining real-time interaction, but not for looking at the other ways interactants may provide each other feedback on form.

Although it didn't involve CMC, Foster and Ohta's (2005) study shows the heuristic strength of combining interactionist and sociocultural frameworks in a principled manner to analyze learner face-to-face interaction. They question the notion that NfM is key to language learning for several reasons: 1) it may be face threatening, 2) it is more often lexical than morphosyntactic, 3) it is difficult to identify, and 4) opportunities for learning may be outside NfM episodes. They examine two classroom tasks for NfM, classifying them according to broader conceptualizations of Long's CCC framework, and showing that many such checks can be understood as continuation markers rather than communication breakdowns. From a sociocultural perspective, these are evidence of mutual collaborative assistance. In their data, they showed that fewer than half of the CCC exchanges actually involved NfM, and could instead be interpreted as collaborative episodes involving co-construction, other-correction, self-correction, or continuers. In other words, NfM defined in the strictest sense may not capture all the learning going on, and thus may not be the ultimate standard by which to measure the pedagogical value of classroom tasks.

In a similar way, Reinhardt (2008) showed that the same German-American telecollaborative data could be interpreted from both interactionist and socio-cognitive perspectives, each enhancing the other. An interactionist analysis showed more self-corrections and reaction to responses than in face-to-face interactions, a phenomenon attributable to the technological medium. There were also very few true NfM episodes, which Reinhardt attributed to the advanced proficiency of the learners, the mixed NS-NNS nature of the pairings (see also Ortega, 2009), and the open-ended nature of the task. Using a socio-cognitive perspective, Reinhardt then drew on the social identities of the learners to show how, in the same episodes, learners were negotiating face and identity, in other words interpersonal meaning, besides ideational or transactional meaning. The turn delay and textual trace afforded by the technology gave learners the ability to self-repair and thus save face.

Towards Middle Ground

Many researchers have adapted interactionist and socio-cognitive frameworks to examine computer-mediated and telecollaborative L2 learning, and while some have attempted synthesis or balance of the two, many more have only made conciliatory nods and acknowledged the heuristic strength of multiple perspectives. The debate remains entrenched, and it may be an "agree to disagree" situation as Larsen-Freeman (2007) notes, where each side pursues "its own research agenda, each accounting for a different dimension and each providing the necessary checks and balances in preventing hegemony in either direction" (p. 781).

As some of the studies combining approaches demonstrate, however, middle ground might be found by exploring the regions where theories and methods overlap. The field of SLA agrees on a fair amount, for example, the role of noticing or attention, the importance of context, and the centrality of interaction. The analysis of interaction is not always interactionist, and has been at the heart of research on language learning since the emergence of applied linguistics (Sacks, Schegloff, & Jefferson, 1974), and a variety of frameworks have been applied to its analysis. Conversation analysis, for example, broadly conceived to address SLA, has been proposed as a framework for socially-informed analysis of interaction (Hellermann & Cole, 2008; Mori & Markee, 2009). Interactional analysis, theoretically based on the notions of interactional competence and discursive practice (Young, 2009) has also grown in popularity as a research method (e.g. Abrams, 2009).

Moreover, when informed by the notion of interaction understood broadly, negotiation for meaning (NfM) is not necessarily bound to an input-interactionist framework. It is interesting to note that because of the preposition "for", the phrase "negotiation for meaning", can be read to imply that meaning emerges during negotiation. The use of "of" in "negotiation of meaning", in contrast, might imply that meaning is already there and must simply be re-established. The meaning of "meaning" is really at the heart of the difference between the two perspectives, whether it's defined primarily as transactional or ideational in nature, primarily interactional or interpersonal, or both. Methodologically, this translates to whether and to what degree a researcher values etic or emic perspectives and the research techniques those values implicate.

Transcending the Debate: Ecological Approaches

A new perspective on interaction and negotiation, and a refreshing response to the cognitive-social debate, may be found in ecological approaches. Ecological frameworks have been explicated with increasing detail over the last decade or so, as 1) a new, loosely cohesive perspective on language learning informed by ecological metaphors (e.g. Leather & van Dam, 2003), 2) a broadened, sociocultural theory and semiotics-informed perspective on language learning and use (van Lier, 2000; 2004), and 3) an overarching term for more specified accounts of complexity theory (Larsen-Freeman 1997; 2007; Larsen-Freeman & Cameron, 2008a, 2008b) and dynamic systems theory (e.g. de Bot, Lowie, & Verspoor, 2007; van Geert, 2008) interpreted for language learning. Lafford (2007) notes that these frameworks may offer a means towards synthesized understanding of the polar opposites (Ellis & Larsen-Freeman, 2006, in Lafford, 2007: 751) of the cognitive and social, or a means towards "superposition" of opposites, a concept in complex systems theory where a phenomenon (such as a research framework) exhibits features of otherwise incompatible properties simultaneously. Chapelle (2009) notes that complex systems theory may offer a "metatheory that would put the theory pieces together to create a fuller picture" (p. 748), by allowing consideration of multiple factors working together simultaneously[5].

Analogies have always been drawn between technology and learning, and ecological metaphors for understanding learning have parallels in our most recent conceptualizations of technology as ecological. Lam and Kramsch (2003; see also Kern & Warschauer, 2000) note historical parallels in how we metaphorically conceptualize computers and learning, with a shift from 1) mainframes and central processing units in the 1960s and 1970s, corresponding to the information processing metaphors of input-interactionism for learning, to 2) individual use of personal computers as tools in the 1980s and 1990s, corresponding to cognitive and constructionist metaphors for learning, and finally to 3) today's distributed, networked use of ubiquitous gadgets, involving cloud applications and crowd-sourcing, which correspond to new learning metaphors of dynamic, chaotic, and complex ecologies. Larsen-Freeman & Cameron (2008a), however, note that "ecological" is not just a metaphor, but a group of increasingly explicated heuristics for understanding and researching language learning and teaching, especially in the case of dynamic and complex systems theories.

With their origins in biological and natural sciences, ecological approaches view language, user communities and practices, language learning, and language learners as inextricable elements of an ecology, the relationships among which are the focus of analysis, although never in isolation from one another (Lafford, 2009). Ecological approaches investigate emergence and co-adaptation, "a kind of mutual causality, in which change in one system leads to change in another

5 Interestingly, before this observation, in her overview of SLA in CALL, Chapelle (2009, p. 744) categorized Complexity Theory under "Approaches to Language in Social Context", while she categorized Associative-Cognitive CREED theory under "General Human Learning", separate from "Cognitive Linguistic" or "Psycholinguistic" approaches.

system connected to it" (Larsen-Freeman & Cameron, 2008b, p. 202). In this way, co-adaptation is a feature of alignment, accommodation, and establishment of intersubjectivity, and might be seen as another way to conceptualize negotiation. Learning is dynamic, contingent, non-linear, and self-organizing in nature, and systems of language use/learning emerge in nested patterns. These patterns are not predicted but "retrodicted" or described *post priori*, since interrelationships are so complex that causation in the traditional sense is untenable.

Methodologically, because interrelationships are so intertwined, ecological approaches take a comprehensive approach towards research, without isolating particular variables in an attempt to imply causation. Qualitative and descriptive techniques are thus often used to describe a system or set of systems. As in socio-cognitive approaches, conditions of observation should be as genuine as possible, since ecological validity is paramount. As in input-interactionist approaches, however, quantitative techniques are also used, since it is important to identify complex, recurrent patterns of usage and activity.

Ecological Treatments of Technology-Mediated L2 Interaction

Several recent studies of technology-mediated L2 interaction, some in telecollaborative environments, make use of ecological constructs to varying degrees. They use a combination of quantitative and qualitative techniques, but perhaps because the approach is still relatively new, their methods are not as standardized as those used in interactionist or socio-cognitive studies.

Some studies conceptualize interaction using the notion of "affordance" (Gibson, 1979), or "possibilities for action that yield opportunites for engagement and participation, that can stimulate intersubjectivity, joint attention, and various kinds of linguistic commentary" (van Lier, 2004, p. 81). For example, Darhower (2007; 2008) utilizes the concept in his analyses of learner-expert Spanish-English interactions in telecollaborative chat rooms. He notes parallels between feedback and affordances, which he operationalizes as discourse moves in interaction that "intend or appear to activate a learner's awareness of specific language structures and/or lexical meaning" (Darhower, 2008, p. 50). Darhower uses a grounded method with learner surveys to categorize affordance-related episodes, finding many more potential affordances than were actually acted upon. In this way, affordances are not much different from LREs or NfM episodes, except that the episodes not acted on are also noted in an attempt to identify complex patterns.

In her analyses of learner interactions on a video-enhanced online discussion board, Berglund (2009) uses the concept of affordance to show that different multimodal technologies afford participation rates and qualities in different ways, depending on tool, task design, and user. She describes the learning context as an ecology, and similar to Darhower, she uses quantitative techniques to categorize episodes. She also uses qualitative methods, in conjunction with conversation analysis, to further identify interactional patterns afforded by the technologies.

Zheng, Young, Wagner, and Brewer (2009) also use the notion of affordance to examine how L2 learners at a distance complete joint activities in the game-based virtual world Quest Atlantis. They consider how negotiation involves a dynamic, emergent cycle of action and perception, embedded and embodied in the virtual world. Like Darhower and Berglund, they analyze chat transcripts for affordances, but they go further and focus on the ecological notions of scaffolding, information pickup, and agent attunement. They use a grounded approach to identify perception-action cycles as units of analysis, and find that different game quest activity designs afford different sorts of "negotiation for action".

While the above studies recognized the parallels between affordances and negotiation episodes, they might be critiqued from an ecological perspective because they did not identify change in patterns over time. One such attempt was by Johnson (2008), although his participants were graduate students in online discussions, rather than L2 learners in telecollaboration. Using longitudinal quantitative and qualitative techniques, he identifies non-linear trajectories of learner participation in terms of "turbulence" and "resistance", and shows how sets of interaction patterns do not occur in isolation from one another, but can be understood as elements of a larger system, the classroom ecology. Johnson's approach is exemplary in its principled application of an ecological, complex systems approach, and illustrates what might be done with L2 learner telecollaboration data[6].

Conclusion

Studies on technology-mediated inter- and intra-class L2 interaction have employed a variety of approaches, including input-interactionist, socio-cognitive, and ecological frameworks, beneath which lie various theoretical and methodological implications, some more or less commensurable with others. Any perspective on SLA entails particular views of the object of, means to, and reasons for investigation, although these entailments are not always obvious. In other words, a theory of language learning will imply what should be investigated, how it should be done, and for what reasons. A researcher's understanding of language learning, whether or not she realizes its epistemological implications, influences what she sees in her data and chooses to note. Her implicit beliefs about what language is, what learning is, and what counts as valid evidence for the truth of something underlie her investigation. In more philosophical terms, while a rationalist accepts reason as a source for knowledge, and a true empiricist accepts only experience as evidence, modern positivistic inquiry involves both rational reasoning and empirical evidence. In contrast to positivism, however, relativists add that all knowledge is

6 While they consider their framework socio-cognitive, Kinginger & Belz (2005) use a combination of qualitative and quantitative techniques to show dynamic, recurrent patterns of development, so their approach could be considered ecological.

relative to the experiencer, and that culture and language influence how we interpret truth, which is socially constructed. Most likely, a researcher is influenced by both positivist and constructivist thought, although she may run into commensurability issues if she combines theories and methods from different philosophies.

Broadly speaking, interactionist frameworks are theoretically commensurate with experimental, quantitative methods, and socio-cognitive frameworks are coherent with naturalistic, qualitative methods. In practice, however, researchers often stretch heuristics to meet their needs and accommodate their findings, thereby redefining and strengthening the framework. Researchers employing input-interactionist frameworks have found it necessary to adapt analytic taxonomies and research techniques in order to deal with new technologies and uses, and are challenged to account for the role of context (Ortega, 2009). At the same time, socio-cognitive research has adopted new discourse analytic and qualitative research techniques, without being aligned to a formal description of language (Hill, 2006). This continuous re-evaluation and adaptation in the face of new challenges is healthy for the field. Besides interaction and negotiation, other constructs central to input-interactionism, including input, output, noticing, and uptake, can only be strengthened through re-conceptualization within other frameworks, just as the methodological rigor of socio-cognitive approaches might benefit from the addition of quantitative heuristics, for example corpus analytic methods (see Belz & Vyatkina, 2005), without sacrificing ecological validity.

Ecological approaches are promising in their potential to transcend the cognitive-social debate, although it remains to be seen whether they will be accepted as something new, or judged as just the latest iteration of a socio-cognitive paradigm. In any case, researchers will continue to be faced with new problems and questions about learning and teaching in technology-mediated L2 learning environments, as technology continues to evolve. Ecological frameworks may be ideally suited for examination of these new problems, but they too will eventually be adapted, challenged, and re-conceptualized. As is the nature of scientific change, new theories, methods, and paradigms eventually supersede older paradigms (Kuhn, 1962). These new paradigms often emerge when we are driven to innovate and adapt to new research and teaching situations, forcing upon us new perspectives.

References

Abrams, Z. (2009). Sociopragmatic features of learner-to-learner computer-mediated communication. *CALICO Journal, 26*(1), 1–27.

Atkinson, D. (2002). Toward a sociocognitive approach to second language acquisition. *Modern Language Journal, 86*(4), 525–545.

Atkinson, D., Churchill, E., Nishino, T., & Okada, H. (2007). Alignment and interaction in a sociocognitive approach to second language acquisition. *Modern Language Journal, 91*(2), 169–188.

Beauvois, M. (1992). Computer-assisted classroom discussion in the foreign language classroom: Conversation in slow motion. *Foreign Language Annals, 25*(5), 455–463.

Belz, J., & Kinginger, C. (2002). The cross-linguistic development of address form use in telecollaborative language learning: Two case studies. *The Canadian Modern Language Revue/La revue canadienne des langues vivantes*, 59, 189–214.

Belz, J., & Kinginger, C. (2003). Discourse options and the development of pragmatic competence by classroom learners of German: The case of address forms. *Language Learning*, 53, 591–647.

Belz, J., & Thorne, S. (2006). *Internet-mediated intercultural foreign language education.* Boston, MA: Heinle & Heinle.

Belz, J., & Vyatkina, N. (2005). Learner corpus research and the development of L2 pragmatic competence in networked intercultural language study: The case of German modal particles. *Canadian Modern Language Review/Revue canadienne des langues vivantes*, 62, 17–48.

Belz, J. (2002). Social dimensions of telecollaborative foreign language study. *Language Learning & Technology*, *6*, 60–81.

Belz, J. (2004). Learner corpus analysis and the development of foreign language proficiency. *System*, *32*, 577–591.

Berglund, T. (2009). Multimodal student interaction online: An ecological perspective. *ReCALL*, *2*, 186–205.

Black, R. (2007). Digital design: English language learners and reader reviews in online fiction. In M. Knobel & C. Lankshear (Eds.), *A new literacies sampler* (pp. 95–114). New York: Peter Lang.

Blake, R., & Zyzik, E. (2003). Who's helping whom? Learner/heritage-speakers' networked discussions in Spanish. *Applied Linguistics*, 24, 519–544.

Blake, R. (2000). Computer mediated communication: A window on L2 Spanish interlanguage. *Language Learning & Technology*, *4*, 120–136.

Block, D. (2003). *The social turn in second language acquisition*. Washington, DC: Georgetown University Press.

Blyth, C. (2008). Research perspectives on online discourse and foreign language learning. In S. Magnan (Ed.), *Mediating discourse online* (pp. 47–70). Amsterdam: Johns Benjamins.

Chapelle. C. (2009). The relationship between second language acquisition theory and computer-assisted language learning. *Modern Language Journal*, *93*, 741–753.

Chun, D. (1994). Using computer networking to facilitate the acquisition of interactive competence. *System, 22*, 17–31.

Darhower, M. (2007). A tale of two communities: Group dynamics and community building in a Spanish-English telecollaboration. *CALICO Journal, 24*(3), 561–589.

Darhower, M. (2008). The role of linguistic affordance in telecollaborative chat. *CALICO Journal, 26*(1), 48–69.

de Bot, K., Lowie, W., & Verspoor, M. (2007). A dynamic systems approach to second language acquisition. *Bilingualism: Language and Cognition*, *10*, 7–21.

Ellis, N., & Larsen-Freeman, D. (2006). Language emergence: Implications for applied linguistics—Introduction to the special issue. *Applied Linguistics*, 27, 558–589.
Ellis, N., & Larsen-Freeman, D. (Eds.) (2009). Language is a complex adaptive system. Special issue. *Language Learning, 59*, Supplement 1, 1–26.
Ellis, N. (2006). Cognitive perspectives on SLA: The associative cognitive CREED. *AILA Review, 19*, 100–121.
Ellis, N. (2008). The dynamics of second emerge: Cycles of language use, language change, and language acquisition. *Modern Language Journal, 92*, 232–249.
Ellis, N. (2009). The psycholinguistics of the interaction hypothesis. In A. Mackey & C. Polio (Eds.), *Multiple perspectives on interaction in SLA: Second language research in honor of Susan M. Gass* (pp. 11–40). New York: Routledge.
Firth, A., & Wagner, J. (1997). On discourse, communication, and (some) fundamental concepts in SLA research. *Modern Language Journal, 81*, 285–300.
Foster, P., & Ohta, A. S. (2005). Negotiation for meaning and peer assistance in second language classrooms. *Applied Linguistics 26*(3), 402–430.
Furstenberg, G., Levet, S., English, K., & Maillet, K. (2001). Giving a virtual voice to the silent language of culture: The Cultura project. *Language Learning & Technology, 5*, 55–102.
Gass, S. & Mackey, A. (2006). Input, interaction and output: An overview. *AILA Review, 19*, 3–17.
Gass, S. (1997). *Input, intearction, and the second language learner.* Mahwah, NJ: Lawrence Erlbaum Associates.
Gass, S. (1998). Apples and oranges: Or, why apples are not oranges and don't need to be. A response to Firth and Wagner. *Modern Language Journal, 82*, 83–90.
Gee, J. (1996). *Social linguistics and literacies: Ideology in discourses.* London: Falmer Press.
Gibson, J. (1979). *The ecological approach to visual perception.* Hillsdale, NJ: Erlbaum.

Gregg, K. (1996). The logical and developmental problems of second language acquisition. In W. Ritchie & T. Bhatia (Eds.), *Handbook of second language acquisition* (pp. 49–81). San Diego: Academic Press.

Hanna, B., & de Nooy, J. (2003). A funny thing happened on the way to the forum: Electronic discussion and foreign language learning. *Language Learning & Technology, 7*, 71–85.

Hanna, B. E., & de Nooy, J. (2009). *Learning language and culture via public Internet discussion forums.* New York: Palgrave Macmillan.

Hellermann, J., & Cole, E. (2008). Practices for social interaction in the language-learning classroom: Disengagements from dyadic task interaction. *Applied Linguistics 30*(2), 186–215.

Hill, K. (2006). Comments on J. Zuengler and E. R. Miller's "Cognitive and sociocultural perspectives: Two parallel SLA worlds?" A reader responds: A sociocognitive perspective: The best of both worlds. *TESOL Quarterly, 40*(4), 819–826.

Hopper, P. (1998). Emergent grammar. In M. Tomasello (Ed.), *The new psychology of language* (pp. 155–177). Mahwah, NJ: Erlbaum.

Jepson, K. (2005). Conversations—and negotiated interaction – in text and voice chat rooms. *Language Learning & Technology, 9*(3), 79–98.

Jin, L., & Erben, T. (2007). Intercultural learning via instant messenger interaction. *CALICO Journal, 24*(2), 291–311.

Johnson, N. (2008). Postcards from the (turbulent) edge (of chaos): Complexity theory and computer mediated communication. In S. Magnan (Ed.), *Mediating discourse online* (pp. 73–92). Amsterdam: Johns Benjamins.

Jordan, G. (2004). *Theory construction in second language acquisition.* Amsterdam: Johns Benjamins.

Kern, R., & Warschauer, M. (2000). Introduction: Theory and practice of network-based language teaching. In M. Warschauer & R. Kern (Eds.), *Network-based language teaching: Concepts and practice* (pp. 1–19). Cambridge: Cambridge University Press.

Kern, R. (1995). Restructuring classroom interaction with networked computers: Effects on quantity and characteristics of language production. *Modern Language Journal, 79*, 457–476.

Kinginger, C., & Belz, J. (2005). Socio-cultural perspectives on pragmatic development in foreign language learning: Microgenetic case studies from telecollaboration and residence abroad. *Intercultural Pragmatics, 2–4*, 369–421.

Kitade, K. (2006). The negotiation model in asynchronous computer-mediated communication (CMC): Negotiation in task-based email exchanges. *CALICO Journal, 23*(2), 319–348.

Kötter, M. (2003). Negotiation of meaning and codeswitching in online tandems. *Language Learning & Technology, 7*, 145–172.

Kramsch, C., & Thorne, S. (2002). Foreign language learning as global communicative practice. In D. Block & D. Cameron (Eds.), *Language learning and teaching in the age of globalization* (pp. 83–100). London: Routledge.

Kuhn, T. (1962). *The structure of scientific revolutions.* Chicago: University of Chicago Press.

Lafford, B. (2007). Second language acquisition reconceptualized? The impact of Firth and Wagner (1997). *Modern Language Journal, 91*, 735–756.

Lafford, B. (2009). Toward and ecological CALL: Update to Garrett (1991). *Modern Language Journal, 93*, 673–696.

Lai, C., & Zhao, Y. (2006). Noticing and text-based chat. *Language Learning & Technology, 10*(3), 102–120.

Lai, C., Fei, F., & Roots, R. (2008). The contingency of recasts and noticing. *CALICO Journal, 26*(1), 70–90.

Lakoff, G., & Johnson, M. (1980). *Metaphors we live by.* Chicago: University of Chicago.

Lam, W. S. E., & Kramsch, C. (2003). The ecology of an SLA community in computer-mediated environments. In J. Leather & J. van Dam (Eds.), *Ecology of language acquisition* (pp. 141–158). Dordrecht, The Netherlands: Kluwer Publishers.

Lam, W. S. E. (2004). Second language socialization in a bilingual chat room: Global and local considerations. *Language Learning & Technology, 8*(3), 44–65.

Lam, W. S. E. (2009). Multiliteracies on instant messaging in negotiating local, translocal, and transnational affiliations: A case of an adolescent immigrant. Reading Research Quarterly, *44*(4), 377–397.

Lantolf, J. P., & Thorne, S. L. (2006). *Sociocultural theory and the genesis of second language development.* Oxford: Oxford University Press.

Lantolf, J. (1996). SLA theory building: Letting all the flowers bloom. Language Learning, *46*(4), 713–749.

Larsen-Freeman, D., & Cameron, L. (2008a). *Complex systems and applied linguistics.* Oxford: Oxford University Press.

Larsen-Freeman, D., & Cameron, L. (2008b). Research methodology on language develpment from a complex systems perspective. *Modern Language Journal, 92*, 200–213.

Larsen-Freeman, D. (1997). Chaos/complexity science and second language acquisition. *Applied Linguistics, 26*, 141–165.

Larsen-Freeman, D. (2007). Reflecting on the cognitive–social debate in second language acquisition. *Modern Language Journal, 91*(5), 773–787.

Lave, J., & Wenger, E. (1991). *Situated learning: Legitimate peripheral participation.* Cambridge: Cambridge University Press.

Leather, J., & van Dam, J. (Eds.) (2003). *Ecology of language acquisition.* Dordrecht, The Netherlands: Kluwer Academic Publishers.

Lee, L. (2001). Online interaction: Negotiation of meaning and strategies used among learners of Spanish. *ReCALL, 13*, 232–244.

Lee, L. (2008). Focus-on-form through collaborative scaffolding in expert-to-novice online interaction. *Language Learning & Technology, 12*(3), 53–72.

Long, M. (1983). Linguistic and conversational adjustments to non-native speakers. *Studies in Second Language Acquisition*, 25, 37–63.

Long, M. (1990). The least a second language acquisition theory needs to explain. *TESOL Quarterly, 24*, 649–666.

Long, M. (1996). The role of linguistic environment in second language acquisition. In W. Richie & T. Bhatia (Eds.), *Handbook of second language acquisition* (pp. 413–478). San Diego: Academic Press.

Long, M., & Robinson, P. (1998). Focus on form: Theory, research and practice. In C. Doughty & J. Williams (Eds.), *Focus on form in second language acquisition* (pp. 15–41). Cambridge: Cambridge University Press.

Mori, J., & Markee, N. (2009). Language learning, cognition, and interactional practices: An introduction. *International Review of Applied Linguistics, 47*, 1–9.

O'Dowd, R. (2003). Understanding the "other side": Intercultural learning in a Spanish-English e-mail exchange. *Language Learning & Technology, 7*, 118–144.

O'Rourke, B. (2005). Form-focused interaction in online tandem learning. *CALICO Journal, 22*, 433–466.

Ochs, E. (1988). *Culture and language development: Language acquisition and language socialization in a Samoan village.* Cambridge: Cambridge University Press.

Ortega, L. (2009). Interaction and attention to form in L2 text-based computer-mediated communication. In A. Mackey & C. Polio (Eds.), *Multiple perspectives on interaction in SLA: Second language research in honor of Susan M. Gass* (pp. 226–253). New York: Routledge.

Oskoz, A. (2009). Learners' feedback in online chats: What does it reveal about students' learning? *CALICO Journal, 27*(1), 48–68.

Pellettieri, J. (2000). Negotiation in cyberspace: The role of chatting in the development of communicative competence. In M. Warschauer & R. Kern (Eds.), *Network-based language teaching: Concepts and practice* (pp. 59–86). Cambridge: Cambridge University Press.

Reinhardt, J. (2008). Negotiating meaningfulness: An enhanced perspective on interaction in computer-mediated foreign language learning environments. In S. Magnan (Ed.), *Mediating Discourse Online* (pp. 219–244). Amsterdam: Benjamins.

Sacks, H., Schegloff, E. A., & Jefferson, G. (1974). A simplest systematics for the organization of turn-taking for conversation. *Language*, *50*, 696–735.

Satar, H. M., & Ozdener, N. (2009). The effects of synchronous CMC on speaking proficiency and anxiety: Text versus voice chat. *Modern Language Journal, 92*(4), 595–613.

Schieffelin, B. & Ochs, E. (1986). *Language socialization across cultures.* Cambridge: Cambridge University Press.

Schmidt, R. (1990). The role of consciousness in second language learning. *Applied Linguistics, 11*, 129–158.

Seidlhofer, B. (2003). *Controversies in applied linguistics.* Oxford: Oxford University Press.

Sfard, A. (1998). On two metaphors for learning and the dangers of choosing just one. *Educational Researcher, 27*(2), 4–13.

Shekary, M., & Tahririan, M. (2006). Negotiation of meaning and noticing in text-based online chat. *Modern Language Journal, 90*(4), 557–573.

Smith, B. (2003). Computer-mediated negotiated interaction: An expanded model. *Modern Language Journal, 87*(1), 38–57.

Smith, B. (2004). Computer-mediated negotiated interaction and lexical acquisition. *Studies in Second Language Acquisition*, 26, 365–398.

Smith, B. (2009). The relationship between scrolling, negotiation, and self-initiated self-repair in an SCMC environment. *CALICO Journal, 26*(2), 231–245.

Sotillo, S. (2005). Corrective feedback via instant messenger learning activities in NS-NNS and NNS-NNS dyads. *CALICO Journal, 22*(3), 467–496.

Swain, M. K. (1985). Communicative competence: Some roles of comprehensible input and comprehensible output in its development. In S. M. Gass & C. G. Madden (Eds.), *Input in second language acquisition* (pp. 235–253). Rowley, MA: Newbury House.

Swain, M. (2000). The output hypothesis and beyond: Mediating acquisition through collaborative dialogue. In J. Lantolf (Ed.), *Sociocultural theory and second language learning* (pp. 97–114). Oxford, U.K.: Oxford University Press.

Swain, M., & Lapkin, S. (1998). Interaction and second language learning: Two adolescent French immersion students working together. *Modern Language Journal, 82*, 320–337.

Thorne, S. (2003). Artifacts and cultures-of-use in intercultural communication. *Language Learning & Technology, 7*(2), 38–67.

Thorne, S. (2008). Mediating technologies and second language learning. In D. Leu, J. Coiro, C. Lankshear & M. Knobel (Eds.), *Handbook of Research on New Literacies* (pp. 417–449). Mahwah, NJ: Lawrence Erlbaum.

Toyoda, E., & Harrison, R. (2002). Categorization of text chat communication between learners and native speakers of Japanese. *Language Learning and Technology, 6*, 82–99.

Tudini, V. (2003). Using native speakers in chat. *Language Learning & Technology*, 7, 141–159.

van Geert, P. (2008). The dynamic systems approach in the study of L1 and L2 acquisition: An introduction. *Modern Language Journal, 92*(2), 179–199.

van Lier, L. (2000). From input to affordance: Social-interactive learning from an ecological perspective. In J. Lantolf (Ed.), *Sociocultural theory and second language learning* (pp. 245–259). Oxford: Oxford University Press.

van Lier, L. (2004). *The ecology and semiotics of language learning: A sociocultural perspective.* Dordrecht: Kluwer.

Varonis, E., & Gass, S. (1985). Non-native/non-native conversations: A model for negotiation of meaning. *Applied Linguistics, 6*, 71–90.

Ware, P. (2005). "Missed" communication in online communication: Tensions in a German-American telecollaboration. *Language Learning & Technology, 9*(2), 64–89.

Warschauer, M. (1997). Computer-mediated collaborative learning. *Modern Language Journal*, 81, 470–481.

Ware, P., & Kramsch, C. (2005). Toward in intercultural stance: Teaching German and English through telecollaboration. *Modern Language Journal, 89*(2), 190–205.

Ware, P. & O'Dowd, R. (2008). Peer feedback on language form in telecollaboration. *Language Learning & Technology, 12*(1), 43–63.

Watson-Gegeo, K. A., & Nielsen, S. E. (2003). Language socialization in SLA. In C. Doughty & M. H. Long (Eds.), *The handbook of second language acquisition* (pp. 155–177). Malden, MA: Blackwell.

Watson-Gegeo, K. A. (2004). Mind, language, and epistemology: Toward a language socialization paradigm for SLA. *The Modern Language Journal, 88*, 331–350.

Wenger, E. (1998). *Communities of practice: Learning, meaning, and identity.* Cambridge: Cambridge University Press.

Young, R. (2009). *Discursive practice in language learning and teaching.* Malden, MA: Wiley-Blackwell.

Zheng, D., Young, M., Wagner, M., & Brewer, R. (2009). Negotiation for action: English language learning in game-based virtual worlds. *Modern Language Journal, 93*(4), 489–511.

Zuengler, J., & Miller, E. (2006). Cognitive and Sociocultural Perspectives: Two Parallel SLA Worlds? *TESOL Quarterly 40*(1), 34–58.

Introducing Cultural Historical Activity Theory for Researching CMC in Foreign Language Education

FRANÇOISE BLIN

In recent years, the rapid development of the Social Web has presented foreign language educators and researchers with many opportunities and challenges. Defined by O'Reilly (2005) as sites for collective activity, which "[grow] organically in response to user activity", Web 2.0 applications (e.g. blogs, wikis, social bookmarking), social networks (e.g. Facebook, MySpace, etc.), and virtual worlds (e.g. Second Life) offer new affordances, as well as constraints, for foreign language learning and the development of intercultural competence. Indeed, their collective orientation, embedded in their specific functionalities (e.g. commenting, linking, co-authoring, revising, remixing, sharing, 'liking', etc.), not only shape new forms of online interactions, often of a multimodal nature, but they also provide opportunities for new forms of collective language learning activities. While Web 1.0 undoubtedly enabled asynchronous and synchronous intercultural exchanges, via discussion forums, emails, and chat for example, Web 2.0 further "extends the opportunities for interaction with peers of the learner or target community" (Alm, 2006: 32) by providing a context for authentic language use and fostering the emergence of new communicative and literacy practices (see for example Thorne & Payne, 2005; Thorne & Black, 2007).

As new forms of online interactions and of communicative and literacy practices have been finding their way into education, learning paradigms focusing on mediated activity and shared knowledge creation are increasingly attractive to researchers and educational technologists working in the areas of CMC in general and Computer Supported Collaborative Learning (CSCL) in particular (see for example Paavola & Hakkarainen, 2005). Such paradigms, strongly influenced by Vygotsky's (1978, 1986) seminal work on mediation or Leontiev's (1978) concept of collective activity, often entails a shift from individual actions to joint activity, or from individual to collective cognition, as the primary unit of analysis (Lund & Smødal, 2006; Lund, 2008). They constitute analytical frameworks that allow for the in-depth systemic analysis of context-bound individual and collective actions. In particular, cultural historical activity theory (CHAT) and Engeström's (1987) theory of expansive learning increasingly provide the theoretical foundations underpinning the design and analysis of new CMC environments in a variety of professional and educational contexts (Lund, Rasmussen, & Smødal, 2010) as well as studies of the emergence and transformation of social practices in these environments (Nardi, 1996; Engeström & Miettinen, 1999).

Activity theory, "the best kept secret of academia" (Engeström, 1993: 64) until the mid-nineties (see also Engeström & Miettinen, 1999; Roth, 2004; Lantolf & Thorne, 2006; Roth & Lee, 2007), has been defined as "an approach in psychology and other social sciences that aims to understand individual human beings, as well as the social entities they compose, in their natural everyday life circumstances" (Kaptelinin & Nardi, 2006, p. 31). In the last decade, it has become particularly influential in the fields of Human Computer Interaction (Kaptelinin & Nardi, 2006), educational technology (Jonassen, 2000; Lim & Hang, 2003; Mwanza & Engeström, 2005; Raven, 2006; Amory, 2010) and educational research (Hardman, 2007; Roth & Lee, 2007). To a much lesser extent, it is also gaining popularity in applied linguistics and Second Language Acquisition (Lantolf & Pavlenko, 2001; Thorne, 2005; Lantolf & Thorne, 2006; Thorne & Tasker, 2011), CALL (Blin, 2004, 2005, 2010; Lund 2008; Lund & Rasmussen, 2008), and teacher education (Jahreie & Ottesen, 2010; Feldman & Weiss, 2010).

The complexity of its underpinning philosophical, epistemological and methodological assumptions, which at times translate into somewhat obscure terminology and arguments, may well act as a deterrent for researchers willing to use CHAT as an analytical and interpretive framework to investigate CMC in the context of foreign language education (hereafter CMCL). This chapter introduces the main tenets of CHAT as they may relate to CMCL research. Following a brief overview of the genesis of CHAT, it explicates the basic concepts and principles of contemporary cultural historical activity theory, also known as 'third generation activity theory' (Engeström, 1987). It then illustrates and discusses how CMCL researchers can begin to operationalize it in their own contexts.

The Genesis of Cultural Historical Activity Theory: An Overview

Drawing on the philosophy of Hegel and Marx, on the Russian cultural-historical psychology of Vygotsky and Luria, and most importantly on Leontiev's model of activity (Leontiev, 1978), "activity theorists seek to analyse the development of consciousness within practical social activity" (Daniels, 2008: 115). For them, following Marx' belief that "the activity of an individual and individual consciousness derive from collective activity" (Lektorsky, 2009: 76), consciousness is "located in and emergent of the practices of everyday life, including the cultural and material structuring of environments and the manner of our participation in them" (Lantolf & Thorne, 2006: 210–211).

Contemporary activity theory is however far from being a unified theory (Holzman, 2006). Daniels (2008) notes that "there are undoubted tensions between different contributions to the development of activity theory" (p. 117), and more particularly between Russian and Western approaches. Russian approaches to activity are mainly developed in the domain of psychology, and define activity "as an explanatory principle" (Hakkarainen, 2004: 10), which "determines the genesis, structure, and contents of the human mind" (Roth & Lee, 2007: 189). On the other hand, the Western approach, commonly referred to as cultural historical activity theory (CHAT), is multidisciplinary and defines activity "as an object of scientific study and management" (ibid.). For Daniels (2008) however, differences within and between Russian and Western variants of activity theory should not be "allowed to distract attention from the fundamental contribution to social science that is being made by the field" (p. 117). One of the most influential contributions to the development of activity theory in the West is to be found in the work of Yrjö Engeström (1987) and the Centre for Activity Theory and Developmental Work Research[1] at the University of Helsinki.

First generation activity theory

Tracing its evolution since its inception in the Soviet Union in the 1920s, Engeström (2001) identifies three generations of activity theory. The first generation has its origin in Vygotsky's revolutionary idea that human actions are mediated by cultural artefacts, thus overcoming "the split between the Cartesian individual and the untouchable societal structure" (Engeström, 2001: 134). Vygotsky was however criticised by some of his own students, and in particular by A. N. Leontiev, "for not taking into account the role of practical activity in the process of mediation" (Lektorsky, 2009: 77). Stressing the role of mediating tools and instruments, as well as of the collective nature of activity, Leontiev (1978) elaborated the first variant of activity theory as summarised by Lektorsky:

> [...] activity consists of actions, the latter of operations. Activity presupposes a corresponding motive, which coincides with an object of activity; actions are aimed at concrete goals; and operations are connected to certain tasks. These relations are flexible: an action can become an activity, a goal can transform into a motive, a task can become an operation, and so on. According to Leont'ev, it is important to understand actions as deriving from the whole proc-

1 Since 2008, known as the Center for Research on Activity, Development and Learning (CRADLE), <http://www.helsinki.fi/cradle/index.htm>.

> ess of activity, because a meaning of an action is dependent on its role in activity. (2009: 77)

Donato and McCormick (1994) illustrate Leontiev's hierarchical structure of an activity in the context of foreign language learning from the perspective of a student (a *subject*) engaged in the activity of learning a new language. The student's language learning activity may be motivated by individual or societal needs, which are crystallised into an *object* giving direction to the student's activity. Typical objects of language learning activities can "range from full participation in a new culture to receiving a passing grade required for graduation" (Donato & McCormick, 1994: 455). Language learning activities consist of a number of actions (e.g. reading the newspapers or writing an essay), which are aimed at concrete goals (e.g. improving his/her reading comprehension or writing proficiency), which in turn consist of operations, that are actions that have become routinised and automated through frequent repetitions. For example, "contextual guessing during reading becomes automatized once the learner becomes adept at this strategy" (Donato & McCormick, 1994: 455).

Second and Third Generation Activity Theory

Although Leontiev claimed that activities were collective formations, the focus of his work largely remained on "the activity of an individual and individual actions and operations" (Lektorsky, 2009: 77). Similarly, it can be argued that the focus of earlier activity theoretical contributions to SLA (see for example Donato & McCormick, 1994; McCafferty, Roebuck, & Wayland, 2001) has largely remained on the activity of individual language learners, and their individual (inter-) actions and operations.*Second generation activity theory* on the other hand understands activities as object-oriented collective systems. Engeström (1987) expanded Leontiev's activity model by introducing entire activity systems as the new unit of analysis, which explicitly include not only Leontiev's tool-mediated relationship between subject and object, but also social elements (i.e. rules, community, and division of labour).

Strongly influenced by the Russian philosopher Il'enkov (1977, 1982), Engeström (2001) developed "the idea of internal contradictions as the driving force of change and development in activity systems" (p. 135). Here, contradictions are to be understood in the context of Marxist philosophy, and more specifically in the context of Marx' labour theory of value: the *primary contradiction* in capitalist societies is between the use and exchange value of commodities and "pervades all elements of our activity systems" (Engeström, 2001: 137). For example, the primary contradiction in the object of the language learning activity briefly discussed earlier may be between full participation in the foreign culture and passing the examination.

Activity systems are not static but constitute instable and multi-voiced entities that interact with other activity systems and evolve over time in response to internal and external contradictions. *Third generation activity theory* thus seeks to "develop conceptual tools to understand dialogue, multiple perspectives, and networks of interacting activity systems" (Engeström, 2001: 135). It has been particularly enriched by Ritva Engeström's (1995) integration of conversational analysis with Bakhtin's (1982, 1987) ideas on dialogicality and utterance and with Leontiev's concept of activity, and by the elaboration of the concept of boundary crossing, which "occurs because human beings are involved in multiple activities and have to move between them" (Engeström, 2009: 313). The next section will further explicate the basics of contemporary CHAT.

Contemporary CHAT: The Basics

As briefly outlined in the previous section, Engeström's (1987) formulation of second generation activity theory is an expansion of Leontiev's triadic model (subject–tools–object) of collective activities.

Collective activities are oriented towards one or more *objects*, motivated by the need to transform these into desired outcomes. This motive gives sense and direction to the tool-mediated, goal-oriented actions, which are intentional and carried out by the *subjects* (individuals or teams) of the activity. Activities and actions differ not only because of their orientation (i.e. object/motive oriented vs. goal oriented) but also because of their respective time structure, which is qualitatively different (Engeström, 1999a). Action time is linear and finite "whereas activity time is recurrent and cyclic" (Engeström, 1999a: 33). Furthermore, the relationship between activity and action is dialectical: "actions constitute activities, but activities motivate particular action sequences" (Roth & Lee, 2007: 201). Similarly actions are realised through routinised operations, which "emerge in response to the relationship of goal and current state of the action and its material context" (Roth & Lee, 2007: 202).

Activity systems represent the structures of activities and constitute the primary unit of analysis. They now include the *community*, composed of participants sharing the same object or motive, as well as the *rules* and *division of labor* governing the community and mediating individual and group actions.

The Mediational Structure of Activity Systems

An activity system has thus a complex mediational structure, which is commonly represented by triangles (Engeström, 1987) depicting the mutual relationships that exist between all its constituents. Figure 1 below illustrates a fictitious wiki activity system, seen from the perspective of the participating students (*subjects*), and shaped by its *object* (e.g. the collective production of linked pages on a given topic). The activity is mediated firstly by tools and artefacts, and secondly by "social mediators" (Engeström, 2008: 27). *Tools and artefacts* may include the communicative and collaborative technologies available to students as part of the wiki platform, language and methods, as well as print and/or multimedia resources made available, online or offline, by the teacher, content creators, or native speakers of the target language.

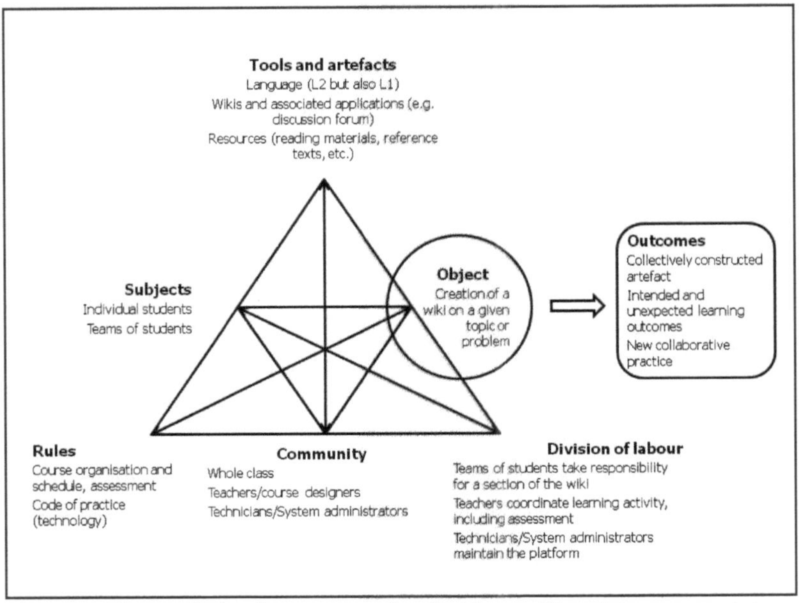

Figure 1. The mediational structure of a fictitious wiki activity system (adapted from Engeström, 1987)

Social mediators comprise the implicit or explicit *rules* governing the actions carried out by the subjects of the activity (e.g. course organisation and schedule, required assignments and marking scheme, expected mode of interaction between participants and online behaviour, etc.), the *community* involved in the construction of the wiki (e.g. members of the class or group, teachers, technicians/system administrators), and finally, the *division of labour* (e.g. the role, power, and responsibilities of various members of the community).

The bottom part of the figure represents what Engeström (2008) calls the "hidden curriculum" (p. 86), mediated by the "deep social structure of the activity" (p. 90). The top sub-triangle (subject – tools & artefacts – object) depicts the "visible curriculum", the "tip of the iceberg" (Engeström, 2008: 90). It represents "individual and group actions embedded in a collective activity system" (Engeström, 2001:

134). According to CHAT, individual and group actions can only be understood "when interpreted against the background of entire activity systems" (Engeström, 2001: 136), which constitute the primary unit of analysis.

Engeström's Five Principles of Third Generation CHAT

In third generation CHAT, "the basic model is expanded to include minimally two interacting activity systems" (Engeström, 2001: 136). Engeström (2001) formulates five principles summarizing the main tenets of third generation CHAT: (1) activity systems as the primary unit of analysis, (2) multi-voicedness, (3) historicity, (4) contradictions as source of development, and (5) possibility of expansive transformations.

According to the first principle, the primary unit of analysis consists of a "collective, artifact-mediated and object-oriented activity system, seen in its network relations to other activity systems" (Engeström, 2001: 136). Secondly, activity systems are multi-voiced. Different subjects in the community, whether individual or team, bring their own histories and construct the object in different ways, at times conflicting, through their position in the division of labour and their level of familiarity with the mediating tools available to them (Engeström, 2001: 136). Consequently, the object of the activity is "constantly in transition and under construction, and *it manifests itself in different forms for different participants and at different moments* of the activity" (Hasu & Engeström, 2000: 4). Thirdly, activity systems are not static but constantly evolve over a long period of time. Activity systems need to be analysed against the local history of their objects and against the global history of the tools, procedures and concepts that shape, and are shaped, by the local activity (Engeström, 2001: 136).

The fourth principle emphasizes the central role of contradictions as sources of change and development. Contradictions emerge within and between interacting activity systems as the activity unfolds. They "manifest themselves as problems, ruptures, breakdowns, clashes" (Kuutti, 1996: 34), or as disturbances, which "are essentially actions that deviate from the expected course of normal procedure" (Engeström, 2008: 27). They "offer a potentially powerful lens for understanding the interconnection between micro-level events and macro-level structures" (p. 26), or between individual actions and collective activity.

Activity systems move through cycles of transformations in response to emerging contradictions within and between interacting activity systems. Engeström's (2001) fifth principle "proclaims the possibility of expansive transformations in activity systems" (p. 137), which result in expansive learning:

> Activity systems move through relatively long cycles of qualitative transformations. As the contradictions of an activity system are aggravated, some individual participants begin to question and deviate from its established norms. In some cases, this escalates into collaborative envisioning and a deliberate collective change effort. An expansive transformation is accomplished when the object and motive of the activity are reconceptualized to embrace a radically wider horizon of possibilities than in the previous mode of the activity. A full cycle of expansive transformation may be understood as a collective journey through the *zone of proximal development*[2] of the activity. (Engeström, 2001: 137, italics in original)

Expansive transformations thus lead to new forms of activity, shaped by new objects and characterised, for example, by the adoption of new technologies and of a different organisation of the division of labour. Expansive learning "involves the creation of new knowledge and new practices for a newly emerging activity: that is, learning embedded in and constitutive of qualitative transformation of the entire activity system" (Daniels, 2008: 127). For Engeström (2009), "expan-

2 Engeström (2001) defines the zone of proximal development as "the distance between the present everyday actions of the individuals and the historically new form of the societal activity that can be collectively generated as a solution to the double bind potentially embedded in the everyday actions." (Engeström, 1987: 174)

sive learning is above all stepwise expansion of the object" (p. 327). Likewise, individual learning occurs "during the expansion of the subject's action possibilities in the pursuit of meaningful objects in activity" (Roth & Lee, 2007: 198).

The dialectical relationship between collective activity and individual actions as well as the systemic and dynamic properties of activities as embedded in the five principles briefly outlined above, make CHAT a powerful conceptual framework that can be used by researchers seeking to better understand "the collective activities underlying language production and the content such activities result in" (Lund, 2008: 40) and to analyse their relationship with language use and development in CMCL environments. Using CHAT as an analytical framework however entails that CMCL studies focus on collective language learning rather than be primarily concerned with individual or group actions oriented towards specific language learning goals and mediated by a CMC task or technology.

Operationalising CHAT: Developmental Work Research

CHAT is however much more than an interpretive framework. It is also a "developmental theory that seeks to explain and influence qualitative changes in human practices over time" (Engeström, 1999b: 378). The five principles of CHAT and the theory of expansive learning summarised above underpin the Developmental Work Research (DWR) method, also known as the Change Laboratory method, developed by Engeström and his colleagues to study work and organisations. In line with Vygotsky's (1978) method of double stimulation (Engeström, 2007), the Developmental Work Research method seeks to discover the potential for expansion through formative experiments and developmental interventions that "open up the zone of proximal development of the activity system" (Engeström, 2009: 327).

Engeström (2009) outlines three methodological rules that direct developmental interventions in complex settings (see also Engeström, Engeström, & Kerosuo, 2003). These are:

> (1) *follow the objects* of activity in their temporal and sociospatial trajectories; (2) *give the objects a voice* by involving the clients or users in dialogues where the object is made visible, articulated, and negotiated; (3) *expand the objects* by organizing intervention sessions and assignments where the producers and clients construct new shared models, concepts, and tools to master their objects. (Engeström, 2009: 327)

In practice, data are collected over a longitudinal period, using ethnographic materials, which are analysed and negotiated by researcher-interventionists and participants together. The intervention sessions are videotaped, analysed and then serve as a stimulus for further reflection. Participants collaboratively construct new models and tools, which they then implement. Throughout the research, the objects are followed (Engeström, 2009). According to Engeström,

> The procedure allows for the collection of rich longitudinal data on the micro-interactions and cognitive processes involved in expansive learning as the participants make their work visible, moving between actions and activity, between the past, the present, and the envisioned future. (2009: 328)

Exploring the full potential of formative experiments and developmental interventions to explain and influence changes in learners' practices in CMCL contexts is beyond the scope of this chapter. Nevertheless, the developmental work research methodology offers tools and instruments that can be used to analyse the qualitative transformations of CMCL activity systems.

Analysing CMCL Activity Systems

In the CHAT literature, the term *activity system* mostly relates to work practices and organisations (see for example Roth & Lee, 2007, p. 201). According to Engeström (2008), "entire organizations as well as their relatively autonomous departments, units, or teams may be analyzed as activity systems" (p. 27). Similarly, teaching and learning activities can be analysed at the institutional, departmental or classroom level (Lim & Hang, 2003; Engeström, 2008). Entire programmes (macro level), courses or modules (meso level), units of learning (micro level) can also be analysed as activity systems.

Third generation CHAT posits that activity systems are always "a part of a network of activity systems that in its totality constitutes human society" (Roth & Lee, 2007: 200). The fictitious wiki activity system represented in Figure 1 (above) interacts with a multitude of activity systems. The participating students are also the subjects of other learning, work or social activities, and so are other members of the community (e.g. teachers, course designers, administrators, technicians). Furthermore, "the outcomes of actions become part of the newly transformed system" (Roth & Lee, 2007: 199). For example, a first version of a wiki page produced by one member of a student team (outcome) soon becomes the object of conscious actions on the part of other team members who revise it. It also becomes a resource for other teams who decide to create a link to it from their own page.

Delineating the boundaries of the activity system that will constitute the unit of analysis, i.e. "the minimal meaningful context for an activity" (Hall, 2001: 208), can thus represent a challenge to CMCL researchers. This challenge is aggravated by the dialectical relationship between collective activity, individual or group actions, and routinised operations, as ignoring Leontiev's (1978) three levels of activity may lead to misinterpretations of the data (Roth & Lee, 2007: 202). Yet, the boundaries between activity, actions and operations are somewhat blurred and depend on the subject and object of real life activities and situations (Kuutti, 1996: 32): what constitutes an action as seen by a course designer or system administrator may be an activity for the teacher or student.

Single Activity Systems as the Unit of Analysis

Cole's (1999) garden-as-culture metaphor illustrates the above issues in the case of single activity systems. It also reiterates the need for researchers to move back and forth between the different levels of activity systems (e.g. macro, meso, and micro levels) that provide the overall context for the CMCL activity of interest to them:

> Broadly speaking, like gardeners, activity theorists must attend simultaneously to two classes of concerns: what transpires inside the activity system ("garden") they study (or design and study) and what transpires around it. These issues often seem to be addressable independently of each other, but in reality, they are as interdependent as tasks and context, thought of as the text and context of development. [...] Gardens do not, obviously, exist independently of the larger ecological system within which they are embedded. (Cole, 1999: 92)

Figure 2 below illustrates the ecology of the chosen unit of analysis in Blin's and Appel's (2011) study of the emergence and transformation of the collaborative structure of a Computer Supported Collaborative Writing in L2 (CSCWL2) activity, which was conducted at the Universitat Oberta de Catalunya (UOC). The selected activity system (meso level) is a constituent part of a larger activity system (macro level), i.e. a language module entirely delivered online, and corresponds to the realization of a task[3] involving the collaborative production of an essay on a medical ethics problem. The emerging collaborative writing practice of a team of four students was examined through a detailed analysis of the online moment-to-moment interactions (micro level) that constituted the activity, while being motivated by it.

3 From an activity theory point of view, the terms *activity* and *task* are not interchangeable. A *task* is what teachers (or researchers) want learners to do (Roebuck, 2000). Tasks act as a stimulus and provide an initial structure, a "behavorial blueprint" (Coughlan & Duff, 1994: 175, cited in Thorne, 2005: 399) for students' actions, whereas activity is what students actually do (Roebuck, 2000).

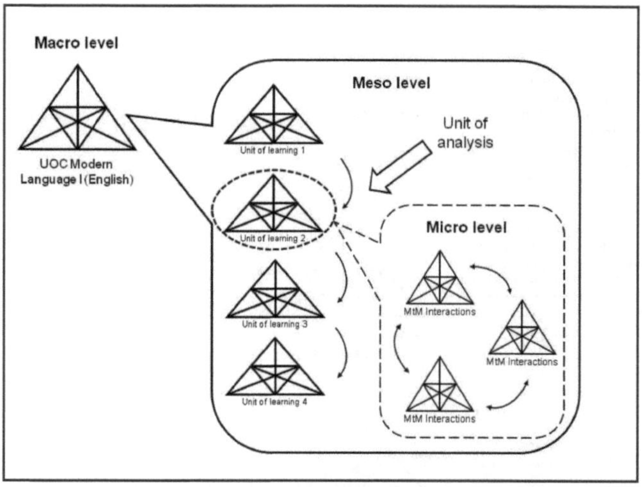

Figure 2. Single activity system as unit of analysis (adapted from Blin & Appel, 2011)

Upon completion of the chosen unit of learning, students were expected to demonstrate their ability to write formally, and collaboratively, opinions stated by others on a topic relating to medical ethics. More specifically, these *intended learning outcomes* included the acquisition of domain related vocabulary, the ability to produce grammatically correct sentences, as well as the ability to structure a text in order to convey opposing points of view. Students were also expected to demonstrate sustained participation and engagement with the task. To that effect, students carried out individual and group actions, which ultimately resulted in the production of a collective text dealing with Euthanasia.

The goal-oriented actions, triggered by the task guidelines and instructions, produced artefacts and other outcomes that became elements of the activity system itself as illustrated by Figure 3 below. Such actions, observable through the analysis of students' postings to the group forum and use of their shared area in the virtual language classroom, include studying pre-task materials and making initial team decisions (e.g. choice of topic), writing individual essays and sending it to the group, revising one's own essay as well as those produced by the other members of the team, and integrating the individual essays into a single text using Google Docs.

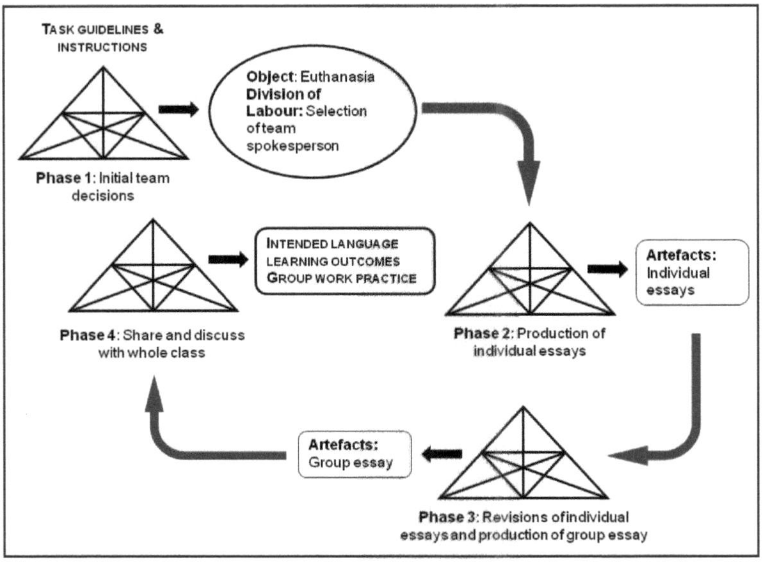

Figure 3. The ongoing transformation of the activity system (adapted from Blin & Appel, 2011)

Joint activity systems as the unit of analysis

Single activity systems, such as the aforementioned CSCWL2 activity system, constitute appropriate units of analysis to study 'intraclass' CMCL activities. Telecollaboration activities involving two or more partners from different institutions, often from different countries, are likely to require that joint activity systems, partially sharing not only their object (Engeström, 1987, 2001) but also elements of the division of labour (e.g. cross-institutional teams may be constituted from the outset) as well as some tools and artefacts (e.g. communicative technologies, language, etc.), be taken as the unit of analysis as illustrated in Figure 4 below. Initially, each activity system is characterised by a different mediational structure, which embodies the cultural-historical processes that has shaped, and has been shaped by, their particular context (Thorne, 2003: 40).

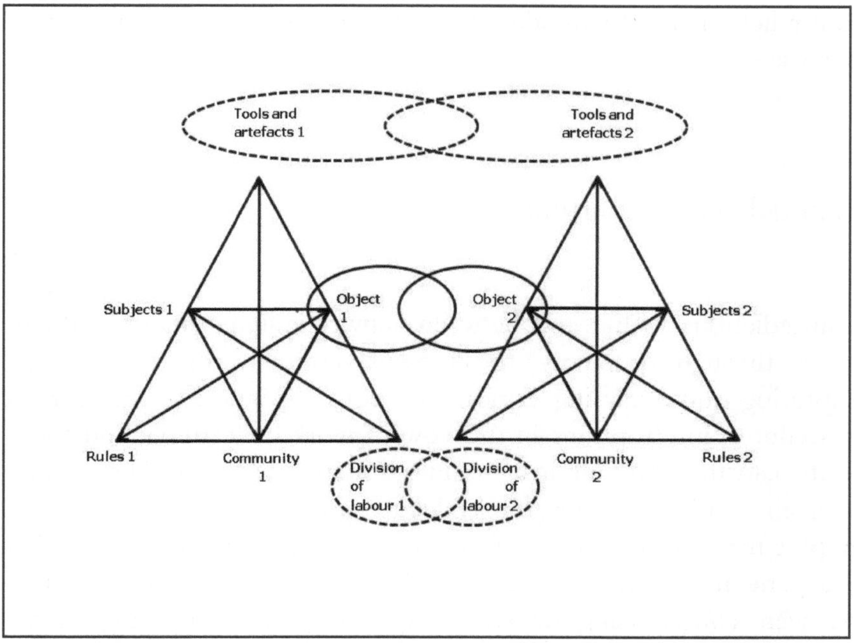

Figure 4. Telecollaboration joint activity system (adapted from Engeström, 2001)

Participants may also bring to the joint activity different cultures-of-use of "an ostensibly 'shared' or 'common' mediational artifact [that] may invoke divergent communicative expectations" (Thorne, 2003: 57). Intercultural telecollaboration activities showcase the multi-voicedness of activity systems, which, according to Engeström (2001), "is a source of trouble and a source of innovation, demanding actions of translation and negotiation" (p. 136) as evidenced by the "special attention in recent studies [...] paid to tensions and misunderstandings that might hinder intercultural learning" (Basharina, 2007: 82). In telecollaboration activities, interacting activity systems move towards the construction of a shared object and the mutual transformation of their mediational structure, thus creating a "third space", defined by Gutiérrez as "a transformative space where the potential for an expanded form of learning and the development of new knowledge are heightened" (2008: 152). The creation of the 'third space' implies however that emerging internal and external contradictions are firstly identified, and secondly resolved in expansive ways.

Material-semiotic artefacts

Contradictions within and between activity systems manifest themselves through problems, breakdowns, conflicts, or disturbances. Capturing and analysing critical incidents, deviations from normal procedures, interruptions in the flow of work or learning, and focus shifts, can thus provide insights into systemic tensions. The capture of such incidents entails the collection of a large body of ethnographic materials by means of physical or virtual observation (e.g. log files generated by the system, recordings of interactions taking place via web conferencing or within virtual worlds), and interviews. CMCL activity systems also produce, and are mediated by, a wide range of digital artefacts, which have been created by individual or groups, and which are normally available for analysis.

Transcripts of synchronous and asynchronous interactions, wiki pages and blog posts, images and podcasts are only but a few examples of *material-semiotic artefacts*, defined by Lemke (2001) as material objects "that [carry] significant information across time and space and that serves, through local interpretation, to create coherences between distal events" (2001: 21). Material-semiotic artefacts serve a variety of purposes in the overall activity on a much longer timescale than either the events of publishing or posting these particular artefacts, or the event of accessing, downloading or reading them. For example, they may appear first as the outcomes individual actions before becoming mediators of subsequent group actions. They "afford heterochrony" (Lemke, 2000: 281): they link longer-term processes and shorter-term events. In other words, they connect the longer-term object-oriented activity and shorter-term individual goal-oriented actions. As they make the interdependence between collective activity and individual actions visible, material-semiotic artefacts may uncover the transformations (or lack thereof) of the activity. They are also likely to reveal some of the emerging contradictions within and between interacting activity systems.

The (non-) expansion of a CMCL activity system

This section illustrates some of the concepts and principles presented thus far, using a sequence of short moment-to-moment interactions, which occurred during the early stages of the UOC CSCWL2 activity (Medical ethics) briefly described earlier (Blin & Appel, 2011). The aim is not to present a comprehensive activity theoretical analysis of the chosen activity system, but rather to provide a snapshot of a moment in time as it relates to the bigger activity.

The interactions presented below took place at the very beginning of the activity, when students' actions were directed towards the need to organize their division of labour, to select what would constitute the object of the next phase, and to familiarise themselves with the learning environment. The team of four (Laura, Isabel, Miguel and David) had just been formed and had chosen a name (*London*). Team interactions take place exclusively online and through the medium of the target language (English), normally in the UOC virtual classroom assigned to the course. At the time of the study, no synchronous tool had been made available to them within the institutional VLE, and students were expected to interact via their dedicated group forum. Identifying a need for synchronous communication, Isabel proposes to use Messenger. While Laura responds favourably to the idea, neither Miguel nor David reacts to the suggestion. Interaction within the team thus remained asynchronous for the duration of the task.

> Isabel: Tonight I can connect more time, now just wanted to greet and I'm at work, if you want to use the messenger that is parallel to a more synchronous conversation.... You ok?
> My messenger address is: [...]

Laura: For me that's ok. My messenger address is: [...]. But I can't connect today until ten o'clock.

Isabel's suggestion is an example of an attempt to deviate from normal procedures, which could have potentially led to the transformation of the communicative and collaborative practice through the introduction of new tools in the activity system. A few days later, Laura also tries to introduce a deviation from the planned procedures by proposing a new process to share individual essays, based on what she had learned in her ICT course. David and Isabel initially adopt Laura's proposal. Miguel, however, soon returns to the old practice while reminding the group of the teacher's instructions. In fact, throughout the realization of the activity, Miguel gently silenced any attempt to deviate from normal procedures. Any effort to expand the team's repertoire of tools and procedures, as well as the object of the learning activity, remained unsuccessful (see Blin & Appel, 2011 for a full discussion).

The above exchange between Isabel and Laura also points to emerging tensions between the different activity systems to which students belong. As can be expected in the context of part-time distance learning, work and family commitments introduce disruptions in the flow of the learning activity, making it difficult at times for students to coordinate their online presence and interaction, whether technologies facilitating synchronous communication are available within the UOC classroom or not. Weekends and trips away, either for professional or personal reasons, sometimes with no Internet access, introduce delays in the decision making process, in the resolution of problems, or in the collective adherence to deadlines:

David: Hi everybody! I have been away this weekend, but I am here again. Well, I love the decision about London. If you want I also can propose Biarritz. That's the place I've been this weekend.

The above study (Blin & Appel, 2011) highlighted the pivotal role of the "hidden" curriculum in shaping language production. It showed that material-semiotic artefacts, either used or created by students (e.g. task guidelines and instructions, forum postings), as well as teacher interventions, prompted students to question their emergent collaborative practice and to re-orient the team's actions by redirecting their attention to the object and desired outcomes of the activity. Throughout the realisation of the task, the attempted deviations from planned procedures, whether successful or not, provided insights into the collective, and at times conflicting, construction of the object and into the development and consolidation of the collaborative structure of the activity system, which in turn influenced the transformation of the object of the activity into language learning outcomes.

Conclusion

This chapter aimed to provide an introduction to Cultural Historical Activity Theory, while highlighting its relevance to CMCL research. As recalled at the very beginning of this chapter, activity theory has been 'the best kept secret of academia' until relatively recently. In the last 15 years however, it has gained tremendous popularity, and credibility, in many disciplines within the social sciences.

In the context of educational research, CHAT "has shown to be fruitful for both analysing data recorded in real classrooms and designing change when trouble and contradictions become evident in these cultural settings" (Roth & Lee, 2007: 188). As discussed earlier, deviations from planned procedures such as those illustrated in the previous section, along with interpersonal or intercultural conflicts and disruptions in the work flow caused by technology breakdowns or competing activities, are manifestations of deep internal and external contradictions. The analysis of contradictions emerging in a variety of CMCL contexts (i.e. activity systems) will enable researchers and designers to better understand the complexity and dynamic nature of their mediational structure, and will thus provide directions to enhance the design of the curriculum, both "visible" and "hidden". In addition, pedagogical interventions, designed according to the principles and rules of the Developmental Work Research method (see section 0), will enable teachers and students alike, separately or together, to reflect on their own collective and individual practice, to question it, to construct and share new mediational means, and to expand the object of their language teaching and learning activity.

As scholars continue to critically examine and expand the theoretical foundations and the applications of third generation activity theory (Sannino, Daniels, & Gutièrrez, 2009; Daniels, Edwards, Engestrom, Gallagher, & Ludvigsen, 2010), CHAT is likely to offer new possibilities for thedesign and analysisof increasingly complex learning environments, where the boundaries between physical and virtual worlds, and between formal and informal learning are increasingly blurred. CHAT offers conceptual and methodological tools that can provide the basis for designing CMC learning environments and activities that will provide students with "a radically wider horizon of possibilities" (Engeström, 2001, p. 137).

References

Alm, A. (2006). CALL for autonomy, competence and relatedness. *The JALT CALL Journal*, *2*(3), 29–38.

Amory, A. (2010). Education technology and hidden ideological contradictions. *Educational Technology & Society*, *13*(1), 69–79.

Bakhtin, M.M. (1982). *Dialogic imagination: Four essays*. New edition. Austin: University of Texas Press.

Bakhtin, M.M. (1987). *Speech genres and other late essays*. Austin: University of Texas Press.

Basharina, O. (2007). An Activity Theory Perspective on student-reported contradictions in international telecollaboration. *Language Learning & Technology*, *11*, 82–103.

Blin, F., & Appel, C. (2011). Computer supported collaborative writing in practice: An activity theoretical study. *CALICO Journal*, *28*(2), 473–497.

Blin, F. (2005). *CALL and the development of learner autonomy – an activity theoretical study.* Unpublished doctoral thesis, The Open University, UK. Downloaded 1 September 2011 from <http://webpages.dcu.ie/~blinf/BlinThesis.pdf>.

Blin, F. (2004). CALL and the development of learner autonomy: Towards an activity-theoretical perspective. *ReCALL*, *16*. 377–395.

Blin, F. (2010). Designing cybertasks for learner autonomy: Towards an activity theoretical pedagogical model. In M. J. Luzón, M. N. Ruiz-Madrid & M. L. Villanueva (Eds.), *Digital genres, new literacies and autonomy in language learning* (pp. 175–196). Newcastle upon Tyne: Cambridge Scholars Publishing.

Cole, M. (1999). Cultural psychology: some general principles and a concrete example. In Y. Engeström, R. Miettinen & R. L. Punamäki (Eds.), *Perspectives on activity theory* (pp. 87–106). Cambridge: Cambridge University Press.

Coughlan, P. & Duff, P. (1994). Same task, different activities: analysis of a SLA task from an activity theory perspective. In J. P. Lantolf & G. Appel (Eds.), *Vygotskian approaches to second language research* (pp. 173–193). Norwood, NJ: Ablex.

Daniels, H. (2008). *Vygotsky and research. 1st edition.* Oxon: Routledge.

Daniels, H., Edwards, A., Engestrom, Y., Gallagher, T., & Ludvigsen, S.R. (Eds.) (2010). *Activity theory in practice.* Oxon: Routledge.

Donato R., & McCormick D. (1994). A sociocultural perspective on language learning strategies: the role of mediation. *The Modern Language Journal*, *78*(4), 453–464.

Engeström, Y. (1987). *Learning by expanding: an activity-theoretical approach to developmental research.* Helsinki: Orienta-Konsultitoy.

Engeström, Y. (1993). Developmental studies of work as a testbench of activity theory: The case of primary care medical practice. In S. Chaiklin & J. Lave (Eds.), *Understanding practice: Perspectives on activity and context* (pp. 64–103). Cambridge: Cambridge University Press.

Engeström, R. (1995). Voice as communicative action. *Mind, culture, and activity*, *2*, 192–215.

Engeström, Y. (1999a). Activity theory and individual and social transformation. In Y. Engeström, R. Miettinen & R. L. Punamäki (Eds.), *Perspectives on activity theory* (pp. 19–38). Cambridge: Cambridge University Press.

Engeström, Y. (1999b). Innovative learning in work teams: analyzing cycles of knowledge creation in practice. In Y. Engeström, R. Miettinen & R. L. Punamäki (Eds.), *Perspectives on activity theory* (pp. 377–404). Cambridge: Cambridge University Press.

Engeström, Y. (2001). Expansive learning at work: Toward an activity theoretical reconceptualization. *Journal of Education and Work*, *14*, 133–156.

Engeström, Y. (2007). Putting Vygotsky to work. The change laboratory as an application of double stimulation. In H. Daniels, M. Cole & J. V. Wertsch (Eds.), *The cambridge companion to Vygotsky* (pp. 363–382). Cambridge: Cambridge University Press.

Engeström, Y. (2008). From teams to knots: activity-theoretical studies of collaboration and learning at work. Cambridge: Cambridge University Press.

Engeström, Y. (2009). The future of activity theory: A rough draft. In A. Sannino, H. Daniels & K D. Gutièrrez (Eds.), *Learning and Expanding with Activity Theory* (pp. 303–328). New York, NY: Cambridge University Press.

Engeström, Y., Engeström, R., & Kerosuo, H. (2003). The discursive construction of collaborative care. *Applied Linguistics*, *24*, 286–315.

Engeström, Y., & Miettinen, R. (1999). Introduction. In Y. Engeström, R. Miettinen & R. L. Punamäki (Eds.), *Perspectives on activity theory* (pp. 1–16). Cambridge: Cambridge University Press.

Feldman, A., & Weiss, T. (2010). Understanding change in teachers' ways of being through collaborative action research: a cultural–historical activity theory analysis. *Educational Action Research, 18*(1), 29–55.

Gutiérrez, K.D. (2008). Developing a sociocritical literacy in the third space. *Reading Research Quarterly, 43*, 148–164.

Hakkarainen, P. (2004). Editor's introduction. Challenges of activity theory. *Journal of Russian & East European Psychology, 42*, 3–11.

Hall, R. (2001). Commentary: Schedules of practical work for the analysis of case studies of learning and development. *Journal of the Learning Sciences, 10*, 203–222.

Hardman, J. (2007). Making sense of the meaning maker: Tracking the object of activity in a computer-based mathematics lesson using activity theory. *International Journal of Education and Development using ICT, 3*. Downloaded 12 April 2009 from <http://ijedict.dec.uwi.edu/viewarticle.php?id=423&layout=html>.

Hasu, M., & Engeström.Y. (2000). Measurement in action: An activity-theoretical perspective on producer-user interaction. *International Journal of Human Computer Studies, 53*, 61–89.

Holzman, L. (2006). What kind of theory is activity theory? *Theory & Psychology, 16*, 5–11.

Il'enkov, E. V. (1977). *Dialectical logic: Essays in its history and theory*. Moscow: Progress.

Il'enkov, E. V. (1982). *The dialectics of the abstract and the concrete in Marx's 'Capital'*. Moscow: Progress.

Jahreie, C. F., & Ottesen, E. (2010). Construction of boundaries in teacher education: Analyzing student teachers' accounts. *Mind, Culture, and Activity, 17*, 212.

Jonassen, D.H. (2000). Revisiting activity theory as a framework for designing student-centered learning environments. In D. H. Jonassen & S. Land (Eds.), *Theoretical foundations of learning environments* (pp. 89–121). Mahwah, NJ: Lawrence Erlbaum Associates.

Kaptelinin, V., & Nardi, B.A. (2006). *Acting with technology: Activity theory and interaction design*. Cambridge, MA: MIT Press.

Kuutti, K. (1996). Activity theory as a potential framework for human-computer interaction research. In B. A. Nardi (Ed.), *Context and consciousness: Activity theory and human-computer interaction* (pp. 17–44). Cambridge, MA: The MIT Press.

Lantolf, J. P., & Pavlenko, A. (2001). (S)econd (L)anguage (A)ctivity theory: Understanding second language learners as people. In M. Breen (Ed.), *Learner contributions to language learning. New directions in research* (pp. 141–158). London: Longman.

Lantolf, J.P., & Thorne, S.L. (2006). *Sociocultural theory and the genesis of second language development.* Oxford; New York: Oxford University Press.

Lektorsky, V.A. (2009). Mediation as a means of collective activity. In A. Sannino, H. Daniels & K. D. Gutièrrez (Eds.), *Learning and expanding with activity theory* (pp. 75–87). New York, NY: Cambridge University Press.

Lemke, J.L. (2000). Across the scales of time: Artifacts, activities, and meanings in ecosocial systems. *Mind, Culture & Activity, 7*, 273–290.

Lemke, J.L. (2001). The long and the short of it: Comments on multiple timescale studies of human activity. *Journal of the Learning Sciences, 10*, 17–26.

Leontiev, A.N. (1978). *Activity, consciousness and personality.* Englewood Cliffs, NJ: Prentice Hall.

Lim, C.P., & Hang, D. (2003). An activity theory approach to research of ICT integration in Singapore schools. *Computers & Education, 41*, 49–63.

Lund, A. (2008). Wikis: A collective approach to language production. *ReCALL, 20*, 35–54.

Lund, A., & Rasmussen, I. (2008). The right tool for the wrong task? Match and mismatch between first and second stimulus in double stimulation. *International Journal of Computer-Supported Collaborative Learning, 3*, 387–412.

Lund, A., Rasmussen, I., & Smødal, O. (2010). Joint design for working in wikis: A case of practicing across settings and modes of work. In H. Daniels, A. Edwards, Y. Engestrom, T. Gallagher &

S. R. Ludvigsen (Eds.), *Activity theory in practice* (pp. 207–230). Oxon: Routledge.

Lund, A., & Smødal, O. (2006). Is there a space for the teacher in a WIKI? *Proceedings of the 2006 International Symposium on Wikis* (pp. 37–46). Odense: ACM Press.

McCafferty, S.G., Roebuck, R.F., & Wayland, R.P. (2001). Activity theory and the incidental learning of second-language vocabulary. *Language Awareness, 10*(4), 289–294.

Mwanza, D., & Engeström, Y. (2005). Managing content in e-learning environments. *British Journal of Educational Technology, 36*, 453–463.

Nardi, B. (Ed.) (1996). *Context and consciousness: activity theory and human-computer interaction.* Cambridge, MA: MIT Press.

O'Reilly, T. (2005). What is web 2.0: Design patterns and business models for the next generation of software. *O'Reilly Network.* Downloaded 28 February 2009 from <http://www.oreillynet.com/lpt/a/6228>.

Paavola, S., & Hakkarainen, K. (2005). The knowledge creation metaphor –An emergent epistemological approach to learning. *Science & Education, 14*(6), 535–557.

Raven, J. M. (2006). Functional organs and computer use within collaborative group projects. *Computers in Human Behavior, 22*, 981–990.

Roebuck, R. (2000). Subjects speak out: How learners position themselves in a psycholinguistic task. In J. P. Lantolf (Ed.), *Sociocultural theory and second language learning* (pp. 79–95). Oxford: Oxford University Press.

Roth, W.M. (2004). Introduction: Activity theory and education: An introduction. *Mind, Culture, and Activity, 11*, 1–8.

Roth, W.M., & Lee, Y.J. (2007). "Vygotsky's neglected legacy": Cultural-historical activity theory. *Review of Educational Research, 77*, 186–232.

Sannino, A., Daniels, H., & Gutièrrez, K.D. (2009). *Learning and expanding with activity theory.* New York, NY: Cambridge University Press.

Thorne, S.L. (2003). Artifacts and cultures-of-use in intercultural communication. *Language Learning & Technology, 7*, 38–67.

Thorne, S.L. (2005). Epistemology, politics, and ethics in sociocultural theory. *The Modern Language Journal, 89*, 393–409.

Thorne, S.L., & Black, R. (2007). Language and literacy development in computer-mediated contexts and communities. *Annual Review of Applied Linguistics, 27*, 133–160.

Thorne, S.L., & Payne, S. (2005). Evolutionary trajectories, internet mediated expression, and language education. *CALICO Journal, 22*(3), 371–397.

Thorne, S.L., & Tasker, T. (2011). Sociocultural theories and applied linguistics. In J. Simpson (Ed.), *Routledge Handbook of Applied Linguistics* (pp. 487–500). New York: Routledge.

Vygotsky, L.S. (1978). *Mind in society: the development of higher psychological processes*. Cambridge, MA: Harvard University Press.

Vygotsky, L.S (1986). *Thought and language*. Cambridge, MA: Harvard University Press.

Researching Classroom Integration of Online Language Learning Projects: Mixed Methods Approaches

PAIGE WARE & BRENNA RIVAS

The pace of growth of new technologies is exciting for foreign language instructors and researchers interested in online communication. In the last two decades, as the availability, ease, and cost-effectiveness of new technologies has grown, language instructors and researchers have added new types of media and expanded the range of audiences of what were typically confined to text-based, within-classroom studies of online communication. Language instructors and researchers today frequently create projects that allow their students to communicate through many combinations of textual, graphical, or aural media with partners distally located across several continents. Language researchers have typically examined the integration of online exchanges by conducting qualitative studies that capture how language, culture, communication, and technology merge and mix in unique, context-specific ways (c.f., Kern, Ware, & Warschauer, 2008; Thorne, Black, & Sykes, 2009).

The challenge that we undertake in this chapter is twofold: to examine the role that mixed methods research, understood as designs that combine qualitative and quantitative approaches, play in adding to the growing knowledge base forming around online language exchanges, and to examine the particular case of secondary education as a context that can benefit from mixed method approaches to research on online language learning. We begin by highlighting key features of mixed methods research and then discuss various qualitative and quantitative data collection and analysis options by drawing on examples from current research. We then turn to a discussion of the secondary classroom context as a relatively untapped area of research on online language learning and draw on illustrative examples from our two-year mixed methods study of a classroom-based, multimedia online exchange between 13-year-old students in the United States and Spain.

An Overview of Mixed Methods Research Designs

Mixed methods research designs have been an explicit focus of methodological discussion in the social sciences since the 1960s as a pragmatic avenue out of the ideological and methodological paradigm wars (Guba & Lincoln, 1994; Tashakkori & Teddlie, 1998) that pitted qualitative against quantitative research. Although a full discussion of the history and philosophy is beyond the scope of this chapter (see Tashakkori & Teddlie, 1998, for a thorough analysis), we briefly summarize a few of the key defining features of mixed methods research designs as discussed by methodologists. Our own definition of mixed methods research involves the creative combination of qualitative and quantitative data in order to address unique research questions, some of which point toward causal explanations using quantitative methods, and others which provide qualitative exploratory and explanatory information about the culturally situated, contextualized aspects of online communication.

The basic purpose of mixed methods research, as with any study, is to allow researchers to match their questions to the appropriate data collection and analysis procedures. When discussing mixed methods research, it is helpful to construe designs on a continuum from the more qualitatively- to the more quantitatively-oriented studies. Common nomenclature among research methodologists in describing mixed methods designs relies on this qualitative/quantitative distinction (Creswell, 2009; Greene, Caracelli, & Graham, 1989; Tashakorri & Teddlie, 1998). For example, study designs are frequently viewed as located on two axes: the chronological and the emphatic. Along the chronological axis, studies are either conducted sequentially, in which a purely qualitative or quantitative phase of the study comes to completion and informs the development of the second phase, or they are conducted simultaneously, in which quantitative and qualitative elements are threaded throughout the data collection and analysis phases. Along the emphatic axis, studies either give equivalent weight to both qualitative and quantitative methods, or one of the two methodological traditions is dominant (dominance is expressed by uppercase letters, QUAN, vs. lowercase, qual).

The resulting eight possible design scenarios are presented in Table 1 in a classification system that forms one of many possible taxonomies for mixed methods research (Creswell & Plano Clark, 2011; Tashakkori & Teddlie, 1998), but for the purposes of researchers new to mixed methods, this taxonomy offers a straightforward labeling system.

Table 1. Possible Design Scenarios for Mixed Methods Research

Equivalent Status Designs	**Dominant-Less Dominant Designs**
1. Sequential	1. Sequential
a. QUAL/QUAN	a. QUAL/quan
b. QUAN/QUAL	b. QUAN/qual
2. Simultaneous	2. Simultaneous
a. QUAL + QUAN	a. QUAL + quan
b. QUAN + QUAL	b. QUAN + qual

Note. Adapted from Tashakkori & Teddlie, 1998, p. 15

Mixed Methods Designs in Research on Online Language Exchanges

In post-secondary classroom contexts, foreign language and second language researchers and educators have traditionally used a qualitative lens for examining the online communication of distally located partners in synchronous and asynchronous environments. This qualitative approach relies primarily on data sources such as interviews, transcripts of interactions, surveys, and observations that can provide rich descriptive data. In online communication projects, such studies have involved a primary emphasis either on language use (Belz, 2003; Kötter, 2003; Sauro, 2009; Schwienhorst, 2002; Toyoda & Harrison, 2002; Ware & O'Dowd, 2008) or on cultural understanding (Belz, 2002; Belz & Müller-Hartmann, 2003; Furstenberg, Levet, English, & Maillet, 2001; Liaw, 2006; Menard-Warwick, 2009; Müller-Hartmann, 2000, 2006; O'Dowd, 2003; Ware, 2005; Ware & Kramsch, 2005). While these studies differ widely in their designs, with differing task designs, modes of communication, learner populations, target languages, and sample sizes (from single individuals to cohorts of classroom learners), they all share common interests in providing understandings how the nature of language teaching and learning is changing in multilingual and multimodal environments and how globalized notions of language, culture, and context intersect with local constraints of institutions and ideologies in new online realms.

In examining mixed methods research conducted in online language exchanges (see Table 2), two trends emerge. First, few studies have been designed using a mixed methods approach, likely because both mixed methods approaches and online exchanges are themselves still relatively new. Also, because online exchanges are heavily culturally and socially contextualized, qualitative designs that emphasize descriptive and exploratory studies are often preferred. Additionally, because of the cultural and social layers of context, key features of quantitative research, such as the need for standardized measures, generalizability of findings, and large sample sizes, serve as logistical as well as ideological barriers. The second trend is the predominance of simultaneous designs, which is likely due to practical reasons. Simultaneous designs allow for all data to be collected in a single semester in ways that maximize time and human resources, especially in the context of online exchanges, which typically already face scheduling constraints and challenges because they are coordinating across time zones, institutional schedules, and cultural holidays.

Table 2. Examples of Mixed Methods Research Designs from Online Language Research

Emphatic axis	**Chronological axis**	**Online Language Exchange Research**
Dominant QUAL + quan	Simultaneous	Liaw (2006). 16 EFL students in Taiwan held asynchronous reading group discussions with English-speaking partners in the U.S. Descriptive statistics were used to document the general efficiency of the system design, and content coding of the transcripts provided descriptive information about constructs of intercultural communication. Qualitative data also included semi-structured interviews.
Dominant QUAN + qual	Simultaneous	Sauro (2009). This study examined two types of CMC feedback on adult L2 English learners in Sweden using a randomized treatment and control design and pre/post/delayed-post-testing of an L2 form. The less-dominant qualitative analysis of transcripts served to inform the quantitative findings.
Dominant QUAN + qual	Simultaneous	Perez-Cañado (2010). This study examined the lexical development of first-year post-secondary students in Spain who participated in both a virtual learning environment and in a computer-mediated communication project with US American students. In a pre/post-test and control group design, results indicate greater development on quantitative mea-sures. A qualitative questionnaire was used to determine participants' attitudes at the conclusion of the semester.
Equivalent status QUAL + QUAN	Simultaneous	Ware & O'Dowd (2008). This study compared two types of peer feedback (explicit vs. implicit focus on form) on post-secondary foreign language students' (English and Spanish) attention to language form in the context of two online language exchanges (US-Spain and US-Chile) and measured language-related episodes quanti-

		tatively while also analyzing student perceptions qualitatively through surveys and interviews.
Dominant Status (QUAL/quan)	Sequential	Ware & Rivas. This study (also explored later in the chapter) took place across two years. In the first year, a qualitative-only design was completed to explore a multi-media (blogging and video exchange) online exchange between adolescent language learners in Spain and the US. These findings informed the next phase that included both qualitative and quantitative approaches to examine potential causal impacts on learner writing and cultural awareness using formal assessments, while contextualizing the project qualitative-ly with interviews and observations.

Mixed Methods Data Collection and Analysis in Online Exchanges

In this section, we focus on quantitative and qualitative data collection and analysis in online language exchanges by first addressing three main sources of data collected in online language exchange research: transcripts of interactions, surveys, and interviews. We then describe how these same data sources can be analyzed differently based on whether or not researchers use a qualitative or a quantitative approach to analysis.

Data Sources: Transcripts of Interactions, Surveys, and Interviews

Transcripts, surveys, and interviews are typical data sources in both qualitative and quantitative research of online language exchanges. Together, these data sources provide researchers with three possible points of triangulation, which refers to the process of using separate sources of information to help researchers corroborate or complicate the findings emerging from the overall analysis. The need to use some combination of at least two, if not all three, of these sources arises from the heavily situated contexts in which the data are created. For example, looking only at the transcripts of online interactions (synchronous, asynchronous, text-based or video-conferencing audiologs) between learners in two different countries would leave many context-related questions still open: what does the learner intend with a particular comment? What kinds of institutional pressures inform the learners' decisions to respond with a short rather than a long comment? What does the use of emoticons mean to a young adult in one cultural context vs. another? Bringing in additional layers of information through interviews and surveys allows researchers to interpret the interactions captured in the transcripts. In short, transcripts of the exchanges provide valuable information about the dynamic, unfolding language choices that students make, while surveys and interviews provide richly descriptive information to help contextualize any patterns or anomalies that emerge from analyzing these online interactions.

The choice of whether to triangulate transcript data with surveys, interviews, or both, depends on the ease of accessibility to the participants as well as the availability of resources. While transcripts are relatively cost-effective forms of data to collect since they are captured digitally, surveys and interviews require more time to collect, organize, and process. Surveys are typically less expensive than interviews and can be obtained using any number of online survey providers or even within the platform in which the online interaction itself takes place (Moodle, Blackboard, blogs, etc.). Surveys can include rating and ranking questions as well as open-ended items and therefore help researchers easily look for patterns within group responses.

Interviews, on the other hand, often provide essential in-depth information at the individual level that surveys rarely can capture and therefore form an indispensable tool for richly descriptive research.

However, interviews typically require either some form of face-to-face contact, which can be time-intensive to collect, and the subsequent need to transcribe interview data adds additional time burdens (Johnson & Turner, 2003). Also, because interviews are typically conducted face-to-face, online exchanges can be difficult contexts for using interviews, as participants are often located in different countries. Fortunately, Internet-based tools such as Skype, a free Internet-based tool for real-time verbal interaction, are emerging and providing new ways to conduct interview data collection at a distance. As Kendall (2008) notes, however, many of the ethical, theoretical, and methodological considerations of conducting interviews through media, rather than face-to-face, are unprecedented and therefore the object of current debate.

In sum, the three main data sources used in online language exchange research within a mixed methods approach are transcripts of the online interactions, surveys, and interviews. Researchers primarily situated within a quantitative approach might notice that data sources such as standardized assessments of gains in language or culture learning are infrequently used in the literature to date, likely because validated instruments for measuring constructs such as intercultural competence are neither commonplace nor widely embraced in the field. Researchers within a qualitative tradition might note a de-emphasis on observational data, which is an otherwise commonly used data source in classroom-based language studies, because the focus in online exchanges has most frequently been on what can be inferred from the triangulating of the interactional data along with student beliefs captured through interviews and surveys.

Data Analysis: Qualitative Approaches

As mentioned earlier, the majority of studies to date have been in the qualitative tradition, and therefore more examples from the literature can be examined for how data can be analyzed qualitatively. Analyzing transcript, survey, and interview data from a qualitative approach differs from quantitative approaches primarily with respect to two aspects: 1) how coding categories are created, and 2) how the data are reported. First, when coding data qualitatively, researchers typically use coding categories that emerge from the data; that is, they read the data multiple times, creating categories, or codes, to group similar data together, while eventually collapsing and combining these categories to make overarching statements that lead to findings. Secondly, qualitative researchers tend to report the findings from their analyses using excerpts from the raw data in the form of words rather than in numerical displays.

To analyze online exchange data qualitatively, many researchers tend to rely on discourse analysis (Belz, 2003, 2005; Kötter, 2003; Menard-Warwick, 2008; Sauro, 2009; Toyoda & Harrison, 2002; Ware, 2005; Ware & O'Dowd, 2008), content analysis (Kramsch & Thorne, 2002; Lee, 2006; Liaw, 2006; O'Dowd, 2003), and critical cultural analysis (Thorne, et al., 2009). We turn in greater depth to a few of these examples below and encourage interested readers to explore the original studies for more detailed information.

Discourse analysis of transcript data can allow for fine-grained attention to the particular choices that students make online. Belz (2003), for example, conducted a functional systemic micro-analysis of transcript data between a United States American and his two German partners by analyzing both chronologically and numerically their use of particular linguistic markers of appraisal and of epistemic modality as indexes of intercultural competence. Ware and Kramsch (2005) analyzed an episode of misunderstanding and communication breakdown across a series of online messages between a German student and a US American student by examining the two students' communicative choices through several different discourse analytical lenses, each of which offered a different interpretation of the miscommunication taking place online.

Another example of analyzing transcript data qualitatively comes from a dominant quantitative study. Sauro (2009) used transcripts to provide a qualitative component that helped explain her larger quantitative findings. She examined adult second language learners in

Sweden participating in a text-chat with native English speakers and used a pretest, posttest, and delayed posttest design via a computer-delivered assessment to focus on a particular linguistic feature (omission of the zero article on abstract noncount nouns) and found no statistically significant growth on pre/post measures. Her qualitative analysis of the transcripts allowed her to explain these findings by suggesting that the nature of feedback delivered by the US partners in the recast condition (i.e., lack of adjacency and length of recast) might have contributed to the lack of growth.

Qualitative analyses of interview and survey data are often used to help explain and contextualize transcript data. For example, O'Dowd (2003) examined interview transcripts of interactions between post-secondary learners in Spain and the US to explore possible features of the interactions that might indicate intercultural communicative competence. He also included interviews with students to assist him in contextualizing these characteristics. Ware (2005) conducted face-to-face interviews with all 21 participants in an exchange between German and US American students and used a content analysis of the interview transcripts to find several sources of tension in their online communication: different expectations and norms of communication, different social and institutional factors, and individual differences in motivation and time constraints.

Data Analysis: Quantitative Approaches

With respect to the two main points of difference between qualitative and quantitative approaches to data analysis mentioned above, quantitative researchers typically rely on codes that are assigned a priori to the phenomenon under study; that is, coding categories are first determined based on theoretical constructs or linguistic features, then raters are trained how to apply the coding system to data sources. Often, at least two raters analyze portions of the same data to achieve interrater reliability, or agreement in how they are coding, which lends support to the integrity of the data that they code independently and to the findings. Second, with respect to the reporting of the analysis, quantitative researchers utilize numerical displays to summarize their descriptive or inferential statistical analyses.

Several examples of quantitative approaches to analyzing online language exchange data are available, and the bulk of them rely primarily on descriptive statistics. Kötter (2003), for example, identified patterns of the frequency of occurrence of both negotiation of meaning and of codeswitching in his analysis of 29 German and English language students communicating in a MOO environment. Toyoda and Harrison (2002) created a typology of nine categories of text chat that initiated negotiation of meaning between native Japanese speakers and L2 Japanese speakers. Ware and O'Dowd (2008) used non-random assignment of U.S. American and Spanish post-secondary learners to two feedback conditions (e-tutoring and e-partnering) and numerically compared the type and frequency of language-related episodes and feedback strategies used in each condition.

A final example of quantitative analysis of an online language exchange illustrates how researchers can marry theoretical grounding with methodological practice to support their research questions. Liaw (2006), interested in examining intercultural learning between 16 EFL students in Taiwan and their US partners, conducted a quantitative content analysis of the students' online reading discussions. She coded for four theoretically grounded categories of intercultural competence that were created a priori based on Byram and Zarate's (1994) model of assessing intercultural competence: interest in knowing others, ability to change perspectives, knowledge about culture, and knowledge about intercultural communication. Two raters were trained to code examples of each category, and discussion of all discrepancies resolved any conflicts. She found that the students tended to write in the categories of knowledge about culture and interest in knowing others. Although there was no control group and the statistics are descriptive rather than inferential, she explicitly builds on a quantitative methodological tradition by measuring intercultural learning and by using interrater reliability to strengthen her analysis.

Secondary Education and Research on Online Language Exchanges

Despite the growing body of research at the post-secondary level, relatively little empirical work on classroom-based international online language learning has been done at the secondary level (see, however, Müller-Hartmann, 2006; Tella, 1991). Several ethnographers have documented how second and foreign language youth are using technology outside of formal classroom contexts to communicate across linguistic, cultural, geographic, and political borders and to create their online presence (c.f. Black, 2009; Lam, 2000, 2004, 2009). And within the classroom, secondary teachers have begun introducing "keypals" projects or blogging projects into their classrooms at almost every grade level, as evidenced by practitioner reports at conferences and in pedagogical journals. These class projects are a promising sign that international online language exchanges are beginning to have a presence in mainstream secondary schools, but to date such reports have typically relied on first-person accounts of interesting and successful class projects, and rarely have they explicitly focused on language learners or language learning.

The secondary environment is ripe for research, but it offers challenges and opportunities not present at the post-secondary level. Secondary students, as compared, for example, to the post-secondary population typically researched, tend to represent more diversity in their socioeconomic status, academic performance, language background, exposure and access to technology, personal accountability, experience with global communication, and motivation. Secondary teachers (in the US context, for example), compared with their post-secondary instructors, typically are constrained by a fast-paced, mandated curriculum, in which every classroom lesson must be tied to a particular standard, and they often teach over 100 students each day in short 45- or 55-minute class periods. To understand how such diverse, dynamic variables intersect with the introduction of online language learning, highly descriptive, rigorous qualitative work is necessary to understand the complex variables at play in any given context. And because of institutional demands in many secondary contexts for accountability, the introduction of such a novel technology-based project often necessitates some form of quantifiable outcome measures.

Mixed methodologies, then, are particularly well suited to studies of online exchanges in the secondary setting, as they can qualitatively capture the unique participant experience, while also examining how such projects might impact more quantifiable measures of language and culture learning. Quantitative methods, for example, can potentially capture the role that age, gender, language proficiency, socio-economic status and other identifiers might play in impacting the online exchange, while the qualitative methods offer analysis of discourse choices, stances, cultural frames of reference, contextual constraints, and individual perspectives. In this complementary interplay, the traditionally decontextualized nature of quantitative work can be contextualized through qualitative analysis, while the highly descriptive documentation of qualitative research can be triangulated with a robust understanding of larger patterns within the data.

From a practical perspective, mixed methods studies, particularly in the context of secondary education, are more likely to appeal to practitioners, administrators, and policy makers. In order to affect change, stakeholders often want to understand the practical, theoretical, budgetary, and pedagogical implications of large-scale implementation. For teachers and principals, the accountability and anxiety attached to high-stakes testing and the need for alignment to prescribed standards shape how decisions are made about which textbooks to adopt and which classroom practices to endorse. Documenting how online language learning can have positive outcomes on conventional measures of academic learning can help reassure teachers and administrators of the benefit of embracing interactive technologies. For administrators and policy makers, the quantification of outcomes on a large scale helps provide evidence of how the implementation of projects such as online language learning might generalize to other student populations across different classroom contexts.

In short, mixed methods research has the potential to appeal to a wide audience base as it both strengthens our theoretical understanding of the role that online exchanges play, as well as contributes to an empirical base in helping identify factors that promote particular types of linguistic and cultural outcomes.

Exploring an Example of a Mixed Methods Project at the Secondary Level

To illustrate an example of a mixed methods study of an online language exchange within the context of secondary classrooms, we highlight our recent study of an asynchronous multimedia exchange between 48 thirteen-year-old English as a Foreign Language (EFL) students at a secondary school in Spain and 51 native and nonnative English speakers at a secondary school in the U.S. Like much of the research reviewed in this chapter, this study was theoretically aligned with the framework of intercultural competence (Byram, 1997; Byram & Zarate, 1994) and relied on triangulated data sources of transcripts of interactions (text-based and multimedia), interviews, and surveys. As we will illustrate, we added a fourth layer to the data sources in the form of formal assessments. Qualitative research questions in this study focused on examining how an online exchange project unfolded in the particular context of secondary schools and examined student engagement, instructional roles, activity types, language use, and culture exploration. Quantitative research questions asked whether participation in such an exchange (as opposed to the control group of students who did not participate) impacted students' quality and quantity of writing as well as their performance on a researcher-created culture assessment.

Logistics

The research design took place across two years with two different cohorts of students and would therefore be labeled a sequential, dominant qualitative (QUAL), less dominant quantitative (quan) study, in which the first year (15-week session) of the project was a qualitative study that explored logistical, pedagogical, technological, and measurement issues related to the contexts of two particular English classrooms, their teachers, and their curricula. In the second year of the project (15-week session), our focus for the remainder of this section, two quantitative measures were added to the ongoing qualitative data collection and analysis in order to examine (1) the extent to which students' writing improved across conventional academic growth measures in the genre of descriptive essay writing, and (2) the degree to which students exhibited intercultural awareness vis-à-vis a control group of students on a researcher-created culture assessment.

The decision for a mixed methods design was made in large part because of the institutional demands for accountability reviewed above, particularly on the US side of the exchange. Because the Language Arts curriculum for 13-year-olds in this US school in Texas focuses on English grammar and writing, an online exchange was viewed as a way for students to use text-based and multimedia modes of presentation to organize and expand their writing. On the Spanish side of the exchange, students were enrolled in a fully bilingual K-12 English/Spanish school, so the opportunity to write in English to peers in the U.S. and to exchange cultural perspectives was viewed as a strong fit to the school's overall mission.

The logistical issues were handled primarily by the research team, rather than by the teachers, given the time demands that the research layer added to the complexity involved in setting up and maintaining an online exchange project. The research team included the primary investigator (Ware) and two doctoral graduate student researchers (Rivas in the US and Ojeda Pinar in Spain). The team organized the activities, monitored the student blogs, updated the teachers on student participation in their respective blogs on a bi-weekly basis, interviewed the students, conducted all assessments, and handled all surveys. Teachers were responsible for classroom management, grades, and assistance with collecting forms. Students exchanged weekly messages for 15 weeks across a variety of multimedia and text-based messages on prompts ranging from self-presentation to discussions of music and cultural icons. Students self-selected a partner from their classroom and were then randomly matched with two students from the partnering country. All correspondence took place through a password-protected function of Google blogs, and only the students, their teachers, and the research team had access to all blogs.

Data Collection

Table 3 provides an overview of which data were collected, aligns each data type with its function, and provides examples of the prompts or questions used to elicit the data. Qualitative data sources included monthly surveys to monitor students' views, one-on-one and focal group interviews with students and teachers to develop more in-depth understanding of their experiences, and a database of all online interaction, which consisted of text-based blog postings and comments and short student-produced multimedia movies. Quantitative data sources were collected on both the participating students as well as on a control group of non-participating students at the beginning and at the end of the exchange in the form of two measures: 1) a pre/post timed writing assessment to measure growth in writing fluency and idea development; and 2) a post-only culture assessment to measure differences between participating and non-participating students' abilities to write messages that demonstrated intercultural awareness.

Table 3. Qualitative and Quantitative Data Sources in the Secondary Study

Data Source	Function of Data Source	Example of Prompts & Questions
Surveys (qualitative)	*Monitor students' experiences through open-ended questions *Provide information about patterns at the group level about satisfaction, motivation, and learning	"What do you hope to learn in this online exchange?" "Write down at least two things you have learned about your partner."
Interviews (qualitative)	* Provide in-depth contextual understandings of individuals * Trace individual perceptions across time and within different contexts with focal students	"In what ways do you use technology to communicate in out-of-school contexts?" "Which of the activities have you enjoyed the most and what did you learn from it?"
Online interactions (qualitative)	* Understand how students interacted across various prompts and through various media * Explore which types of activities generated which types of linguistic functions, engagement levels, and cultural exploration	"Activity 3: Create a short 'survival guide' for your partner; if they came to your school, what slang would they have know to survive? Also—what cultural saying can you teach them? Are there cultural sayings that you think are 'typical' for Americans/Spanish?"
Writing measures (quantitative)	* Measure gains in conventional aspects of writing (fluency and idea development)	"Describe a typical day in your life on a weekday. You have 10 minutes to plan your essay and 20 minutes to write it."
Culture assessment (quantitative)	* Measure potential differences between participants and a control group on degrees to which responses demonstrate intercultural learning	"Imagine that your partner asks you about some of the stereotypes of the United States. She or he wants to know if it is true, for example, that all Texans are cowboys, like they have seen in the movies. What would you write?"

Data Analysis

A discussion of the complete analysis is beyond the scope of this chapter, so we instead highlight examples from each approach, first qualitative then quantitative, to illustrate how each offers a unique lens for understanding one aspect of the project. The particular construct we feature examines the skills of interpreting and relating, taken from Byram's model of intercultural communicative competence (1997). A qualitative analysis of the transcripts of online interaction, for example, allows us to explore the linguistic and semiotic choices that students made during the exchange and to consider whether those choices reflected an ability to interpret their culturally situated context and to relate it to their partners. This type of analysis is iterative and often proceeds by first developing specific codes to describe the content of particular excerpts from the transcripts, then by examining ways in which codes overlap and converge in the interest of developing overarching categories that group together similar types of excerpts. Table 4 provides three examples of the first wave of qualitative coding, in which transcripts were examined for instances that demonstrated students' attempts to interpret and relate information for their partners, and codes were assigned to capture the different ways in which this was accomplished.

Table 4. Qualitative Analysis: Skills of Interpreting and Relating in the Online Transcripts

Examples from Online Transcripts	Codes
* El horno no está para bollos -> The oven is not for muffins It's not the best moment for do something. For example, you've failed a lot of exams, so it isn't the best moment to ask your parents if you can do a party. In this situation you can use "El horno no está para bollos". –student in Spain	*Translates cultural saying and relates with example
Religion! Racial religion may be the worst! People think that just because were African American than all of us are so into religion or all of us are Baptist! But its so not true! I'm a Christian. Many folks are nondenominational and that's basically when its like multiple cultures mixed in one bunch! Then some people just don't like the word religion at all. They just don't care for nothing! But I do! –US student	*Describes and interprets stereotype within cultural context *Relates the stereotype to self (personalizes)
This picture [cartoon of the statue of liberty holding a hamburger and Coke] shows how people see the U.S. because they have so many fast food places which is actually true, but we are learning how to make it better. –US student	*Chooses and interprets image re-presenting cultural ster-eotype

In a second wave of this iterative qualitative analysis, we look for patterns to emerge in how students attempt to interpret and relate information. From these three codes, for example, we might anticipate overarching categories to start emerging such as "interpreting stereotypes" and "relating examples to self and cultural others."

Turning to an example of a quantitative analysis, we examine the use of a culture assessment administered to the participating students and to a control group of non-participating students in the US. Quantitatively, the use of a control group on this assessment allows us to make inferences about the degree to which students who participated in the exchange demonstrated skills of interpreting and relating vis-à-vis a control group. The culture survey features 8 open-ended items, each one envisioning a hypothetical online partner from Australia who poses a question or scenario to the students. For example, one question asks how the student would react to a particular stereotype, while another asks what a picture of Barak Obama means to them and to other US Americans. In both of these sample items, the students wrote responses, and two trained raters coded the responses on a scale according to the degree to which the response reflected the skills of interpreting and relating (i.e., provides cultural information, offers contextual explanation, and demonstrates audience awareness). Table 5 provides examples of responses to an item from the survey that asked students to respond to their partners' question about the stereotype of all Texans being cowboys.

Table 5. Quantitative Analysis: Skills of Interpreting and Relating in the Culture Survey

Rated high	**Rated low**
Well, in movies it might show that all texans are cowboys. But that is so not true. There are many cities where you will never see a cowboy. Texas has many cultures, and being a cowboy isn't the only one.	No not everyone is a cowboy.
No, its not true because not all texans look like cowboys. In fact many of us have never worn that clothes before. Many people that live in texas are not even white there are many cultures and races.	I'm not a cowboy. Haven't seen any either

The above example illustrates just two extremes from a range of student responses to this particular item about stereotypes. Coders were trained to rate items high if they were in line with Byram's model (1997) of "skills of interpretation and relation": a) acknowledged that stereotypes are common; b) put a particular stereotype into a different perspective for the partner; and c) provided additional information on what Texans can be like. The response on the left, rated high, for example, shows an acknowledgement of the source of the stereotype, refutes it in informal language ("so not true"), and provides additional information about people in Texas. The responses rated lower tended to be a simple refutation: "No not everyone is a cowboy."

The contrast between these two types of high and low responses is, in many ways, precisely what we hoped the cultural exchange might help shift for students—helping them imagine other ways of engaging with the larger world and providing concrete examples of what kinds of communicative choices might shift them in one direction or the other. So, from a mixed methods research perspective, the use of a culture assessment with participating students and with a control group of non-participating students allows for inferences to be made about whether or not participating in such an online language exchange actually impacted students' skills of interpreting and relating cultural information. Such inferences, in the context of the qualitative analysis, provide an important triangulating function for data analysis.

Conclusion

In this chapter, we have discussed common elements of mixed methods research designs, provided an overview of the use of such designs in online language exchange research, and focused on a study within the secondary education context to explore one particular mixed methods design. We have argued that the secondary context can benefit from blending the theoretical underpinnings and practical applications of both qualitative and quantitative designs. While researchers can spend years developing expertise in one type of design and may ground themselves in the strengths of their analysis, mixed methods designs encourage collaboration and respect for the unique contribution of each research methodology. Online language exchanges can be seen through multiple lenses, allowing for different types and levels of analysis.

The particular design of a mixed methods project depends not only on the research questions under investigation, but also to some degree on the level of training and expertise of the researchers involved. Each tradition of inquiry, whether qualitative or quantitative, is grounded at the ideological level in a set of values and worldviews, and at the methodological level in a set of tools, techniques, and terminology. Most researchers require years of training to follow only one of these methodological paths, and many graduate programs therefore must emphasize training in one methodology over the other to cultivate experts within a particular methodological tradition. For individual researchers to develop expertise and gain experience in both can take many years and rely on working within larger teams (see Creswell & Plano Clark, 2011). Novice researchers interested in mixed methods research might then consider first focusing on developing expertise in one tradition of inquiry and continually look for opportunities to apprentice themselves on teams that weave together both strands of research. In the end, the excitement surrounding advances in multimedia communicative capabilities, coupled with the unique analytic potential of mixed methods research, present promising opportunities for new avenues of research in online language exchanges and intercultural communication.

References

Belz, J. A. (2002). Social dimensions of telecollaborative language study. *Language Learning & Technology, 6*(1), 60–81.

Belz, J. A. (2003). Linguistic perspectives on the development of intercultural competence in telecollaboration. *Language Learning and Technology, 7*(2), 68–117.

Belz, J.A. (2005). Corpus-driven characterizations of pronominal dα-compound use by learners and native speakers of German. *Die Unterrichtspraxis / Teaching German, 38*(1), 44–60.

Belz, J. A., & Müller-Hartmann, A. (2003). Teachers as intercultural learners: Negotiating German-American telecollaboration along the institutional fault line. *The Modern Language Journal, 87*(1), 71–89.

Black, R.W. (2009). Online fanfiction, global identities, and imagination. *Research in the Teaching of English, 43*(4), 397–425.

Byram, M. (1997). *Teaching and assessing intercultural communicative competence.* Clevedon, England: Multilingual Matters.

Byram, M., & Zarate, G. (1994). *Définitions. Objectifs et evaluation de la competence socioculturelle* [Definitions, objectives and evaluation of socio-cultural competence]. CC LANG 94 (1). Strasbourg: Council of Europe.

Creswell, J. W. (2009). *Research design: Qualitative, quantitative, and mixed methods approaches* (3rd Edition). Thousand Oaks: Sage Publications.

Creswell, J.W., & Plano Clark, V. (2011). *Designing and conducting mixed methods research.* Thousand Oaks, CA: Sage Publications.

Furstenberg, G., Levet, S., English, K., & Maillet, K. (2001). Giving a virtual voice to the silent language of culture: The CULTURA project. *Language Learning & Technology, 5*(1), 55–102.

Greene, J.C., Caracelli, V. J., & Graham, W.F. (1989). Toward a conceptual framework for mixed-method evaluation design. *Educational Evaluation and Policy Analysis, 11*(3), 255–274.

Guba, E. G., & Lincoln, Y. S. (1994). Competing paradigms in qualitative research. In N. K. Denzin & Y. S. Lincoln (Eds.), *Handbook of qualitative research* (pp. 105–117). London: Sage.

Johnson, R.B., & Turner, L.A. (2003). Data collection strategies in mixed methods research. In A. Tashakkori & C. Teddlie (Eds.), *Handbook of mixed methods in social and behavioral research* (pp. 297–319). Thousand Oaks, CA: Sage.

Kendall, L. (2008). The conduct of qualitative interviews: Research questions, methodological issues, and researching online. In J. Coiro, M. Knobel, C. Lankshear & D. Leu (Eds.), *Handbook of research on new literacies* (pp. 133–150). Mahwah NJ: Erlbaum.

Kern, R., Ware, P., & Warschauer, M. (2008). Network-based language teaching. In N. V. Deusen-Scholl & N. H. Hornberger (Eds.), *Encyclopedia of language and education, 2nd Edition, Vol. 4: Second and foreign language education* (pp. 281–292). New York: Springer.

Kötter, M. (2003). Negotiation of meaning and codeswitching in online tandems. *Language Learning & Technology, 7*(2), 145–172.

Kramsch, C., & Thorne, S. (2002). Foreign language learning as global communicative practice. In D. Block & D. Cameron (Eds.), *Globalization and language teaching* (pp. 83–100). London: Routledge.

Lam, W. S. E. (2000). L2 literacy and the design of the self: A case study of a teenager writing on the Internet. *TESOL Quarterly 34*(3), 457–482.

Lam, W. S. E. (2004). Second language socialization in a bilingual chat room: Global and local considerations. *Language Learning & Technology, 8*(3), 44–65.

Lam, W.S.E. (2009). Multiliteracies on instant messaging in negotiating local, translocal, and transnational affiliations: A case of an adolescent immigrant. *Reading Research Quarterly, 44*(4), 377–397. dx.doi.org/10.1598/RRQ.44.4.5.

Lee, L. (2006). A study of native and nonnative speakers' feedback and responses in Spanish American networked collaborative interaction. In J. Belz & S. Thorne (Eds.), *Internet-mediated intercul-*

tural foreign language education (pp. 147–176). Boston: Heinle & Heinle.

Liaw, M-L. (2006). E-learning and the development of intercultural competence. *Language Learning & Technology, 10*(3), 49–64.

Menard-Warwick, J. (2009). Comparing protest movements in Chile and California: Interculturality in an Internet chat exchange. *Journal of Language and Intercultural Communication, 9*(2), 105–119.

Müller-Hartmann, A. (2000). The role of tasks in promoting intercultural learning in electronic learning networks. *Language Learning & Technology, 4*(2), 129–147.

Müller-Hartmann, A. (2006). Learning how to teach intercultural communicative competence via telecollaboration: A model for language teacher education. In J. Belz & S. Thorne (Eds.), *Internet-mediated intercultural foreign language education* (pp. 63–84). Boston: Heinle & Heinle.

O'Dowd, R. (2003). Understanding 'the other side': A qualitative analysis of intercultural learning in a Spanish-English e-mail exchange. *Language Learning & Technology, 7*(3), 118–144.

Perez-Cañado, M-L. (2010). Using virtual learning environments and computer-mediated communication to enhance the lexical competence of pre-service English teachers: A quantitative and qualitative study. *Computer-Assisted Language Learning, 23*(2), 129–150.

Sauro, S. (2009). Computer-mediated corrective feedback and the development of L2 grammar. *Language Learning & Technology, 13*(1), 96–120.

Schwienhorst, K. (2002). Evaluating tandem language learning in the MOO : Discourse repair strategies in a bilingual Internet project. *Computer-Assisted Language Learning, 15*(2), 135–146.

Tashakkori, A., & Teddlie, C. (1998). *Mixed methodology: Combining qualitative and quantitative approaches.* Thousand Oaks, CA: Sage.

Tella, S. (1991). *Introducing international communications networks and electronic mail into foreign language classrooms: A case study in Finnish senior secondary schools.* Helsinki, Finland: Yliopistopaino.

Thorne, S., Black, R., & Sykes, J. (2009). Second language use, socialization, and learning in Internet interest communities and online gaming. *Modern Language Journal, 93*, 802–821.

Toyoda, E., & Harrison, R. (2002). Categorization of text chat communication between learners and native speakers of Japanese. *Language Learning & Technology, 6*(1), 82–99.

Ware, P.D. (2005). "Missed" communication in online communication: Tensions in a German-American tele-collaboration. *Language Learning & Technology, 9*(2), 64–89.

Ware, P.D., & Kramsch, C. (2005). Toward an intercultural stance: Teaching German and English through telecollaboration. *The Modern Language Journal, 89*(2), 190–205.

Ware, P.D., & O'Dowd, R. (2008). Peer feedback on language form in telecollaboration. *Language Learning & Technology, 12*(1), 43–63.

Acknowledgements

The authors would like to thank the National Academy of Education/Spencer Post-Doctoral Grant for funding the research project used as an example mixed methods study. We would also like to thank Borja Ojeda Pinar, graduate student at the Universidad de Jaén, for his dedication and expertise to the project on the Spanish side of the exchange.

Section II: Key Areas of Research: Tasks, Culture, Multimodality and Virtual Worlds

Researching Multimodal Communicative Competence in Video and Audio Telecollaborative Encounters

MELINDA DOOLY & MIRJAM HAUCK

> Research is the process of going up alleys to see if they are blind.
> Marston Bates, 1906–1974 (American writer)

Research in areas as diverse as educational psychology, applied linguistics, sociolinguistics, anthropology, sociology, communication and didactics (to name a few) has undertaken increasingly more complex investigations into the roles of language, literacy and learning, especially as education in today's society falls under rising scrutiny. Among the key issues are the purpose of and appropriate approach to language and literacy education in a world dominated by technological advances. The need for a different, new type of literate citizen is often highlighted in public discourse as well as among academics.

> [T]he challenges that we face today in education are daunting […]. The world becomes more complex and interconnected at a lightning-fast pace, and almost every serious social issue requires an engaged public that is not only traditionally literate, but adept in a new, systemic literacy. (Seely Brown, 2008: xi)

As Kramsch (2006) argues, educational needs of today go beyond knowing how to communicate meanings; learners must come to understand the process of meaning-making itself. This implies sophisticated competence in the manipulation of symbolic systems -including the many variants of discursive modalities (spoken, written, visual, and electronic). Learners must be able to interpret meaning from discourse features, or as Kramsch (2006: 251) has put it, students must have "symbolic competence".

These considerations foreground the issue of modality in communicative competence (which is the baseline of most foreign language teaching approaches in the EU) and bring out the importance of how these competences must be taught (for more on communicative competence see Canale & Swain, 1980; Pica & Doughty, 1985; Savignon, 1997; Council of Europe (COE), 2001).

Researchers interested in studying language, literacy and communication have become more and more aware of the importance different semiotic modes hold as an integral part of meaning-making. This applies in particular to investigations of meaning-making in online interactions where different technological affordances provide various modalities for communicating. Key theorists in multimodality, Kress and van Leeuwen, define multimodality as

> […] the use of several semiotic modes in the design of a semiotic product or event, together with the particular way in which these modes are combined – they may for instance reinforce each other […], fulfil complementary roles […] or be hierarchically ordered. (2001: 20)

Of course, multimodality is and always has been part of meaning making; throughout history humans have used more than just written or spoken words to communicate. However, within Western society, especially in the context of education, there has been a "dominance of writing as the means of communication and representation" (Kress, 1998: 58). Still, this has been changing over recent decades, especially as the use of image has gained ground. In a large part, the shift from books to screens has contributed to this development, moving us "from print to post-print text cultures" (Lankshear, 1997: 1). Kress (2003: 1) talks about a "revolution in the uses and effects of literacy and of associated means for representing and communicating at every level and in every domain."

Early work by the New Literacy Studies movement[1] and by the New London Group gave a significant impetus to the study of mul-

1 This is a group of independent but linked researchers, in a large part coming out of work by Gee, Street, Heath, Barton and Hamilton who specifically

timodality in literacy and language learning. This work has highlighted the need to try to capture the complexity of 'real' literacy practices in contemporary society and through technological innovation so that these practices can be understood within their broader social context. These literacy practices have been called the 'new communicative order' (Kress & van Leeuwen, 1996; Lankshear, 1997; Street, 1998). This new communicative order is related to how new social practices of communication in many different domains (work, education, home, entertainment) are becoming increasingly more blurred and consist of many different simultaneous modalities. (For instance, a professional designer working from home may work with an interconnected designing platform, engage in a chat with avatars in virtual worlds during an online seminar and answer personal and professional emails from her Blackberry, all at the same time).

Thorne, Black and Sykes (2009) underscore the influence the New London Group has had on research perspectives in language education and multimodality.

> Over a decade ago, the New London Group (1996) put forth a manifesto that called for a broadening of traditional language-based approaches to literacy teaching and learning to acknowledge and accommodate emergent literacy practices catalyzed by "the multiplicity of communications channels" (…). (Thorne, et al., 2009: 804)

Language educators have begun to integrate the concept of this new communicative order (and the inevitable multimodality that accompanies it) into their teaching, as is reflected in COE's *Common European Framework of Reference for Languages: Learning, Teaching and Assessment* (CEFR) (2001). Many teachers now recognise that words, images, sound, touch and other salient features of communication

---

looked at literacy as a social practice. The notion of "new literacies" stems from work by Lankshear and Knobel in association with new communicative environments. Their work draws from both the New Literacy Studies and the New London Group (a team of academics looking at literacy practices in the new millennium).

are all part of a wide spectrum of communicative practices and competences; in other words, language learning involves far more than 'knowing the language'.

In this context the benefits of Computer-Mediated Communication in language learning have been outlined in many of the latest studies, for instance as part of language socialization (Crystal, 2001; Lam, 2004; Thorne, 2003, 2008) or learner interaction (Smith, 2003, 2004; Schwienhorst, 2004; O'Rourke, 2005), to mention only a few areas of research. Thorne, et al., (2009) argue that CMC in virtual worlds and Massively Multiple Online Games (MMOGs) can promote many assets associated with language learning.

> [...] natural and unscripted interaction, reciprocal alterations in expert status, explicit self-correction and other-correction at the level of linguistic form, extensive repair sequences, development of an emotional bond, and exhibition of motivation by both parties for learning the other's language. (Thorne et al., 2009: 811)

Similar arguments can be posed for CMC in formal language classrooms. The application of 'telecollaboration' in language teaching and learning has a growing number of supporters, perhaps most significantly in blended learning environments, as it is seen as a means of achieving similar positive assets as those listed by Thorne et al. (above). (See Belz, 2003; O'Dowd & Ware, 2009; Dooly, 2010; Guth & Helm, 2010; Helm & Guth, 2010; Furstenberg & Levet, 2010 for more in-depth discussion.) In other words, in conjunction with the call for research in new literacies emerging from the relevance of Web 2.0 in everyday life, there is an evident need for investigation in Multimodal Communicative Competence (MCC) in telecollaborative language learning.

The Need for Research in MCC

As daily interactions in formal and informal language learning have switched to more online modes, researchers have underlined the mediating role of teacher, peers, setting, language, and technology (Lantolf, 2000) and in particular have begun to focus on communicative practices that are based on technological mediation (García-Carbonell, Rising, Montero, & Watts, 2001; Abrams, 2006; Belz & Thorne, 2006; Chun, 2008; Thorne & Reinhardt, 2008; Zheng, Young, & Wagner, 2009; Furstenberg & Levet, 2010).

Developments in CMC have brought about a move from mainly text chat and conferencing to multimodal environments that go beyond written language use (Stockwell, 2007; Panichi & Deutschmann, this volume). Audio-conferencing as well as desktop video-conferencing applications are increasingly used as platforms for communication, especially in the context of telecollaboration. The tools available (e.g. Skype, NetMeeting, Elluminate, Breeze, FlashMeeting, Second Life, Active Worlds, Wimba, Huddle and DimDim[2]) are environments with different modes for representation and communication including spoken and written language, visual and graphic systems, spatial systems and body language.

Such environments help bridge the distance between learners across time zones and geographical space and foster meaning-making in multiple modalities, including oral communication and interaction (Hampel, 2006). New modes of communication can be explored by learners and teachers together, for example, the use of emoticons (Negretti, 1999), icons such as social tagging (Godwin-Jones, 2006; Maggio, Bresnahan, Flynn, Harzbecker, Blanchard, & Ginn, 2009), or avatars (Schneider & von der Emde, 2000).

Given the impetus of CMC in education, it is difficult not to concede that learners' needs and teaching designs are affected by the

2 All the tools mentioned in the chapter were available when the book went to press.

omnipresence of "the decentred, multimedia character of new electronic media", which is inevitably more complex "than the processes involved in working with pre-computer, linear text" (Warschauer, 1999: 11). To begin with, there is a need for different types of reading (reading for gist, scroll reading, conceptually linking different texts available through hyperlinks, etc.), not to mention the knowledge needed for diverse navigational aspects (Pegrum refers to "hypertext literacy" (2009: 38)). Added to this list are the additional modalities available in Virtual Environments (VEs) or Virtual Worlds (VWs) where communication can be text-based (instant messaging and text chat) or may also draw on gestural, visual, proxemic and deictic non-verbal modalities.

As Ciekanski and Chanier (2008) point out, learners' interaction in multimodal settings affects both their focus and their engagement within the learning process – the telecollaborative task may prioritise fluency over accuracy, for instance. This suggests the need for further research into telecollaborative language teaching and learning strategies and how teachers design telecollaborative exchanges. It has been argued elsewhere (Hauck, 2010) that among the various forms of learning, computer supported collaborative learning is particularly well suited to raising awareness of online modes and meaning making and to fostering the development of multimodal literacy.

Learning possibilities are especially evident in telecollaboration, due to the close link between collaborative learning and second language acquisition through a communicative teaching approach (Allford & Pachler, 2007; Dooly, *in press*). Collaborative learning and the Communicative Teaching Approach (CTA) are now well-established precepts for language teaching (see Johnson & Johnson, 1989; Johnson, Johnson, & Holubec, 1993; Chen, 1999, Kessler, 1992, McCafferty, Jacobs & Da Silva Iddings, 2006). Consequently, collaborative learning between distanced partners is of growing interest for researchers and provides a backdrop for research into multimodal literacy in telecollaboration (e.g. Simpson, 2005; Örnberg Berglund, 2009a; Thorne et al., 2009; Develotte, Guichon, & Vincent, 2010). Inevitably, the general communicative competences that are integral to telecollaborative language learning underscore the urgent need for research in multiple practices and multiple modality competences.

Carrying out Research in Multimodality

A first step for research is deciding upon the investigative method to be adopted for exploring specific research questions. Research methods can be classified in various ways but they are often heuristically divided between qualitative or quantitative methods. Of course, a research design, e.g., how the chosen method is applied, may actually combine both qualitative and quantitative approaches (mixed methods; see Ware & Rivas, this volume). See also Reinhardt (this volume) for an in-depth discussion of theoretical and analytical frameworks applied to CMC research.

Briefly, quantitative methods rely on numerical data (e.g. surveys or questionnaires, sampling) to consider 'how many' and 'how often' in regard to a particular phenomenon. The principal aim is to classify specific features, count them and perhaps compare them with other numerical data in order to create statistical models that explain what has been observed in the study. For instance, a researcher might use quantitative statistics to find out which emoticon is most favoured by a certain profile of users or how often chat is used during a videoconference during telecollaborative interaction.

The use of quantitative data may mean the omission of contextual detail. Researchers using quantitative data must be aware of issues such as statistical significance, inappropriate statistical inference, inaccurate measurement or scaling, interferences in sampling, and problems with missing data (Maxim, 1999). For more information on quantitative research see Black (1999); Morgan, Reichert & Harrison (2002) and Neuman (1997).

Qualitative methods aim to provide a detailed description of what is being studied. They may encompass many different types of approaches, ranging from case studies to recording of interactions in the participants' everyday situations (versus laboratory settings). Data is typically in the form of words (e.g. transcriptions), images (e.g. screenshots) or objects (e.g. students' output). Here, the researcher can be the object of study; for instance a teacher may videotape and log all his exchanges with students while online to observe how multimodal features shape the communication during the interaction (practitioner research, Lamy & Hampel, 2007). Another productive approach to research in MCC is action research (AR) – a form of self-reflective enquiry undertaken by participants in social situations in order to improve their own practices and to gain more insight into what is going on in the whole process. (See Carr & Kemmis, 1986; Stringer, 2007, for more information on AR.) To give an example, a researcher-teacher interested in observing (and ultimately improving) the quality of instruction-giving in video-conferencing may implement action research, drawing on qualitative data of different phases of instruction-giving and instruction-interpretation.

Some researchers (Dörnyei, 2007; Allwright & Hanks, 2009) have criticized the action research approach and argue that it is too limiting. These authors have suggested a move to exploratory practice or inclusive practitioner research instead (see also Kemmis & McTaggart, 2000 on participatory action research). Allwright and Hanks (2009: 145) drawing on Allwright (2003) conclude:

> Third-party research in general cannot meet our purposes, and practitioner research, the form of AR [action research], has not yet taken us far enough away from the third-party model to overcome these limitations. […] The first two parties for research on education are the teachers and the learners. (Allwright & Hanks, 2009: 145)

They remind us that language learning and teaching and research are social processes and call for learners to be treated as "key practitioners" without excluding teachers. Instead, both should be considered "'practitioner colleagues' with the teacher playing a collegial role in helping learners develop as researchers of their own practices and as practitioners of learning" (Allwright & Hanks, 2009: 146).

This highlights the importance qualitative data can make in providing rich, contextualised descriptions of the observed features of the study; such approaches focus on process rather than outcomes and are inductive (the researcher builds from abstractions, theories and observations). Observation is the principal means of data collection. Hence, this type of research tends to be time-consuming and cannot be applied to widely dispersed contexts. Researchers must be aware of issues such as organization and management of large amounts of data, difficulties in data coding and the need to control researcher bias. For more information on qualitative research see Silverman (1993, 2000) and Neuman (1997). For detailed explanations of research in online communication, see Lamy & Hampel (2007).

Compiling a Corpus: The Complexity of Multimodal Data

The way in which the researcher collects and organises the data will depend on the type of research being carried out and the focus of the research question(s). It is assumed that the reader of this chapter is more likely to be interested in carrying out primary research (based on original data) than secondary research (based on secondary sources from other research). Thus, we begin by looking at data collection.

A principal question for researchers interested in multimodality is what may be considered researchable data, especially considering that multimodal data is complex and diverse (and more so in the context of telecollaboration, particularly if the exchange involves the use of a mix of asynchronous and synchronous online tools, with distanced partners). The following screenshots (taken from some readily available conferencing applications such as *FlashMeeting* (figure 1), *Elluminate* (figure 2) exemplify the degree of complexity of such data.

(In all the images, the names of participants have been changed or removed and permission to publish visual data obtained.)

Figure 1. FlashMeeting (<http://flashmeeting.e2bn.net/>)

In *FlashMeeting* one user speaks at a time, taking the 'video slot' on the left hand side while others are visible as 'low-refresh' thumbnails on the right. The others can queue to speak, and take the video slot. At the same time public text chat can be seen by all users and various other features are available such as icons (for example a green tick or a red cross for voting or to express agreement or disagreement as well as a question mark to signal that further information is required), an onscreen whiteboard (hidden behind the "xtra" tab) and shared urls (behind the "url" tab).

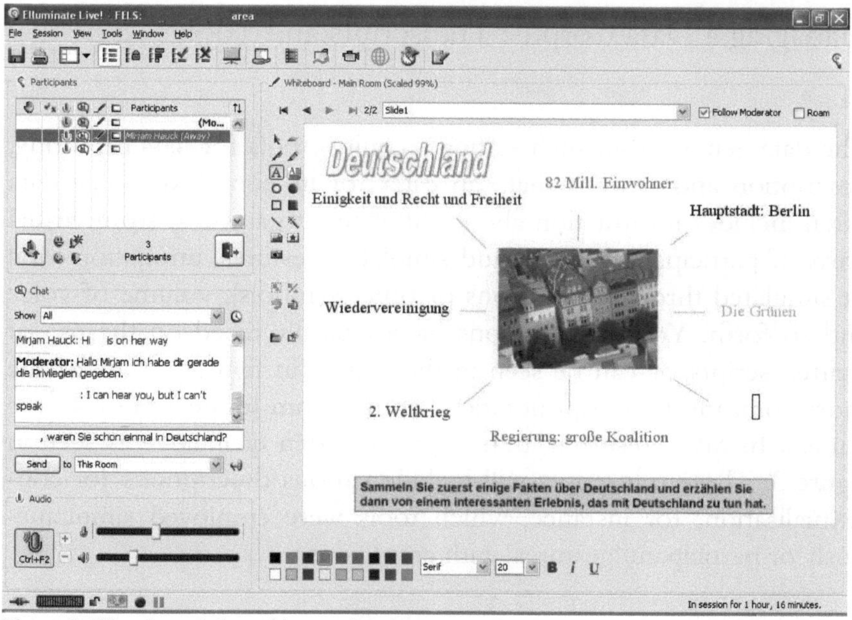

Figure 2. Elluminate (<http://www.elluminate.com>)

In *Elluminate* up to six participants can engage in simultaneous talk. As in *FlashMeeting,* learners and teachers can work together in real time (and *in situ* negotiation of meaning-making inevitably takes place) through audio-conferencing and tools for the exchange of graphical and textual data. The whiteboard is for writing and drawing and also allows users to upload images which can then be jointly manipulated. It is also possible to embark together on a Webtour.

The text chat provides space for additional synchronous textual input, again both bi- and multidirectional. In addition, the system allows users to create their own virtual "rooms" with all of the above functionalities where they can meet in pairs or small groups. Up to six participants can also switch on their webcams at any time during an online session. In short, conferencing applications offer researchers numerous possibilities of multimodal data.

Managing a Data Corpus: Transcripts and Tools

The data generated in such settings requires tools for data capturing, description and analysis that can cater for its complexity. The data often includes information about entrance into and exit from virtual areas of participation, visual and simulated gestures, intonation (oral or simulated through emoticons or other symbols), volume of voice and so forth. Yet, transcriptions have typically relied on the use of written scripts, as can be seen in the extract in figure 3. One of the more common transcript notations comes from Jefferson (2004); see Annex. In MCC research, transcripts are often qualitative as seen in figure 3. These transcripts will include various descriptions for contextualisation, for instance, which tools were employed simultaneously or participant 'gestures' with emoticons.

Transcription May 2, 2004

Part	Date	Time	Film clip	Participants
1	2/5//2004	00:00:05 - 00:19:52	Project 020504.avi	Michael, Anna, Russ, Sangi, Marta, Teresa, Jacques, Martina, Elena

turn id	start time	actor	audio	text chat	vote	other tools	comments
audio55	00:10:31	Russ	ich hab (miraus noch so eine streckung) angeklickt es war eigentlich angeklickt weil - audio (was alle macht) ich habe so eine komplizierte soundcard (1,5)				
audio56	00:10:41	Marta	ok (na bei) also ich - höre dich gut Russ - überhaupt möchte ich gern zu allen du sagen ist das in ordnung bitte mal ein tick für mich - yes oder no **(v2)** man kann unten wählen **(v3)** (1,5) **(v4) (v5)** (1)				
vote2		Anna			yes		
vote3		Russ			yes		
vote4		Teresa			yes		
vote5		Martina			yes		
audio57	00:10:55	Marta	ok (2) **(en10)** jetzt kommt Ilona Ilona ich hab gerade gefragt ob ich zu allen du sagen darf (3) kannst du vielleicht mitwählen **(en11)** ja oder nein yes oder no (2) **(t3)** kann man unten (1,5) links anklicken (4) neben wipe da gibt es einmal yes und einmal no>				Marta gives instructions on how to use the votes.
entrance10		Elena					

Figure 3. Example of a transcript from a session in Lyceum (names of participants have been changed)

There are applications that have readily available features for compiling data from telecollaborative exchanges. These applications often render quantitative transcripts. In figure 4, it is possible to see the communication of eight participants in a 59-minute session. The diagram in this illustration shows the overall pattern of tool use in one particular session. The diagram includes information on participants using the audio channel, text chat, emoticons, voting buttons, and the queuing button. The top row represents everyone's audio contributions, while the other rows represent each participant and their contributions via the audio channel (indicated by bars of different lengths) and the other tools.

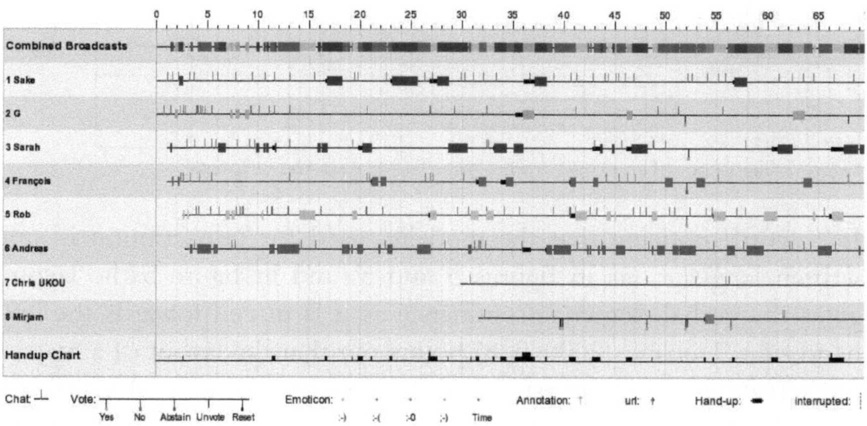

Figure 4. *Flashmeeting* transcript (automatically generated by the system after a session)

Typically, the researcher designs the transcript recording according to the research focus. Figure 5 shows the interaction in a telecollaborative exchange that took place in an internet-based audio-graphic conferencing environment called *Lyceum*. The platform provides multiple synchronous audio channels as well as synchronous text chat and several shared graphical interfaces. The transcription incorporates the temporal sequence of the session (columns) while also describing spatial elements (rows). The researcher may decide to use quantitative and qualitative transcripts. In figure 5, the interrelation between the modes has been given more prominence by concentrating less on detailed audio transcription and more on the diversity of modalities used by those who took part in the interaction.

Transcription June 20, 2004

Part	date	time	Film clip	Participants
1	20/6/2004	00:05:53 - 00:24:58	ARC Projekt 200604.avi	Students 1-5, Native speakers (NS), informants 1 & 2, Researchers (Angie & Lisa)

turn id	start time	actor	audio	text chat	vote	other tools	comments
audio1	00:05:53	Raquel	hallo - guten morgen guten abend (1,5)				
audio2	00:05:57	Lisa	hallo guten morgen guten abend (4)				
audio3	00:06:02	Eva	und hier auch hallo (3) **(a1)** (2)				
away1		Phil					
audio4	00:06:10	Raquel	oh jetzt ist Phil verschwunden - ehm - Elisa und Angie scheinen noch in den Lobby zu sein (1,5) denn warten wir vielleicht nur kurz es ist glaube ich auch gerade erst - zehn (en1) oder elf beziehungsweise - was ist es in Australien fünf oder sieben? (4) (en2)				
entrance1		Elisa					
entrance2		Angie					
audio5	00:06:29	Raquel	hallo Elisa (3)				
audio6	00:06:32	Elisa	(...) (2)				Emanuele is inaudible
audio7	00:06:37	Raquel	Elisa - wir können dich nicht hören ehm (1) versuchst mal noch mal (3)				
audio8	00:06:43	Elisa	(...) **(v1)**(6)				
vote1		Raquel			no		
audio9	00:06:52	Raquel	ich weiß nicht ob du so ein mikrofon hast wo du die lautstärke - regulieren kannst ehm am mikrofon - versuch das mal (1,5) sonst musst du vielleicht ehm (2) in die (1) also raus aus Lyceum und die audio level (so) stellen (5) **(l1)** (3)				

Figure 5. Transcript of an extract from a recording of a session in *Lyceum*

It is worth noticing that the modality used for transcription is still written language (as in figures 3 and 5) and in figure 5 the layout gives the verbal element prominence as it is placed towards the left hand side. Thibault (2000: 318) points out that the layout of a matrix may create a false impression within Western traditions of visual literacy, because what is being placed on the left is doubly privileged by giving it both temporal and logical priority.

For researchers, this brings up the question of whether language-based techniques are the appropriate tool for analysing multimodal data and if not, what kinds of tools are required? The need to research contextualised discourse events realised through evolving technologies has given further impetus to recording audio and visual data. It is now possible to record interactions both in formal as well as informal contexts and transcribe them in ways that take close account of the social context. Currently, there are several resources available for automatically collecting data from online interaction such as Camtasia or Screenjelly (see figure 6)

Figure 6. Example of student activity captured by Screenjelly

There are also several Computer Assisted Qualitative Data Analysis Software (CAQDAS) packages available such as Elan, Transana, Nvivo, ATLAS.ti, MAXqda, HyperRESEARCH and QUALRUS which allow researchers to store and analyse multimodal data in a systematic fashion.

When it comes to organising and analysing the data (as well as the reporting of findings) written and spoken language are still usually the centre of interest, especially in telecollaborative language learning settings. Yet, on their own, written and spoken language provide only partial evidence. Modalities of communication such as intonation, gestures, gaze, etc. are often still described in their relation to spoken and written language and not as separate meaning making and communication modes in their own right. As a result data is often lost in translation or its status is reduced to context (Flewitt, Hauck, Hampel, & Lancaster, 2009).

It is, therefore, recommended to start from generally recognised protocols and then to adapt them as needed. At the same time, these adaptations must be meticulously noted and a key provided when results are analysed and published, along with a contextualisation of the data setting. "The transcription literature across three decades has emphasized the need for researchers to be explicit about transcription" (Davidson, 2009: 46).

Of course, if the researcher hopes to encompass the complexity of the data, and therefore to record qualitative differences in how body, gestures, voice and other modalities are used within the social and technological settings of the interaction, then a more complex notation system may be necessary. This need has been recognised by many high-profile researchers and has resulted in multidisciplinary projects (e.g. TalkBank) that propose the integration of high-level interface (for instance in Java) that stores annotation data as XML.

Increased capacity for multiple-level annotation and easily captured online data are two aspects that can make the task of researchers working on multimodality in telecollaboration "much easier than their non-networked colleagues" (Lamy & Hampel, 2007: 183) but these features do not necessarily help the researcher "to understand the meaning-potentials of the resources as precisely and as explicitly" as possible (Kress, 2003: 24). Nor can these technologies "automatise all the processes" (Lamy & Hampel, 2007: 183). Again, the necessity of a reliable notation system comes to fore:

> What is transcribed depends on the research context and on what the researcher is trying to find out, but transcriptions must be recognised as reduced versions of observed reality, where some details are prioritised and others are left out. (Flewitt, et al., 2009: 45)

In the case of multimodal research the need for combining new forms for transcripts is patent since transcriptions of language must also include transcription of action (Norris, 2002, 2004) and social context. Researchers have recognised the challenges of translating data from one medium to another, especially when trying to reproduce the richness of video images. Innovative approaches are becoming more common: Norris (2002, 2004) describes and illustrates the data through step-by-step images. Kendon (2004) uses simple line drawings based on video freeze-frames, with dialogue written beneath them; Rogoff (2003) makes pictorial representations taken from screenshots; and Goodwin (2004) employs a similar method that includes gesture descriptions in the drawings. Plowman and Stephen (2008) have integrated technology for creating comic strips to represent specific events in their data.

Clearly, there are many tools available that facilitate data compilation and data management. Researchers interested in studying some aspect of MCC are encouraged to explore different avenues, guided by the underlying research questions while acknowledging their influence on: a) choice of tool(s) for data capturing, and b) the approach to transcribing and representing the data and thus –irrevocably– the analysis and the findings.

Another important factor to consider is the question of anonymisation of the participants. Inevitably, the use of screenshots or similar representations implies a visual identification (even when the names of participants are changed). The researcher must consider carefully whether the disclosure of visual data is ethical and should endeavour to always have permission to record and use visual images. Technology for changing facial features may be employed; however, again, this may affect the research itself –especially if the focus is on eye contact, facial gestures, etc. The use of visual and audio data with young students is especially problematic –and this is precisely a key area where research in telecollaboration might make a valuable contribution. Bearing all of these questions and issues in mind will help the researcher decide which tool is most suitable for capturing and managing the data needed.

Analysing Multimodal Data

We have seen that there is now an ample range of technological tools for data collection and new data analysis resources have become widely available and affordable. However, the underlying logic of data categorisation in these software packages may be, by its very nature, biased towards coding. Such bias can shape the processes and outcomes of data analysis. For instance, some of the coding schemes in these packages are hierarchical, and most impose a linear, time-oriented format on transcripts. And inevitably, these tools do not interpret or analyse the data.

Researchers must consider which is the best way to analyse and summarise the data in a time efficient manner. They may be starting out with a pre-existing analytical framework (e.g. the application of content analysis to text chat according to Herring's (2007) proposed coding scheme). Or they may devise their own framework. In the case of a new or derived framework, the researcher should strive to make their analysis 'trail' as detailed and auditable as possible.

In the case of MCC research, it is almost inevitable that any established research position will be 'altered' to take into account new modes of communication that are not usually considered in face-to-face situations. For instance, Örnberg Berglund (2009b) takes an ethnographic perspective to study disrupted turn adjacency and communicative coherence. However, unlike traditional ethnographic studies, MCC does not necessarily require physical access to the subjects of the study. This implies careful consideration of how to contextualise the study since the research may only have 'partial' access to the study participants. Moreover, the use of multimodal communication with online tools blurs the lines between disrupted turn adjacency and technological 'hiccups' that would not be present in face-to-face conversation analysis.

In another example, Satar's original approach (thesis in process) analyses every aspect of multimodal data to find evidence of 'social presence' in language learner interactions via Desktop Video Conference (DVC), and uses Atlas.ti (fig. 7).

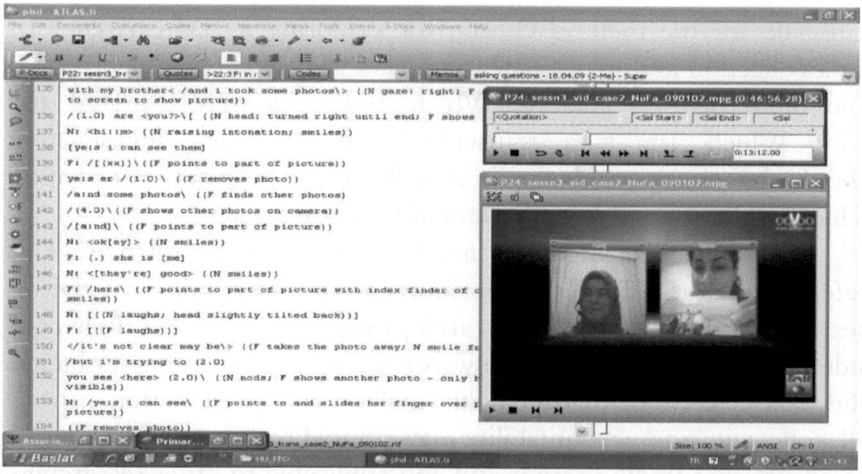

Figure 7. Screenshot of the use of Atlas.ti (<http://www.atlasti.com/>) (Permission given to publish visual data)

Linking visual interactions with the relevant transcription allows triangulation of different types of data. Another example of multiple data sources is the work done by Develotte, Guichon, and Vincent (2010). Their work focuses on how language teachers learn to teach using Skype, focusing on how the participants use their webcams and other multimodal resources during the pedagogical interaction. The study combines the use of screen capture recordings and semi-guided interviews with teacher trainees, thus merging online and face-to-face data.

Multimodal audio-video data may not even 'belong' to the 'real' world. Researchers interested in the development of effective language learning environments in Virtual Worlds often employ audio and video for capturing multimodal data. Combining traditional ethnographic studies with conversation analysis of Virtual Worlds can help educators understand learner participation that goes beyond learners' voiced interaction (see Panichi & Deutschmann, this volume).

Analysis of qualitative data can be through random sampling, but a clear rationale for the choice of data inclusion must be provided. For instance, in the case of research in MCC, a clear rationale of why a particular mode has been featured should be given along with a rationale for the method chosen for exploring it. Transparency of data collection and management are also vital: how were data stored and then used for analysis? Which modalities were captured and why? Which data were transcribed and why? The investigation should be clearly contextualised and all the relevant information which might affect the results should be made explicit.

Researcher reflexivity has not been mentioned until now. This refers to a clearly delineated positioning (and description) of the researcher's role in the whole research process. It implies carefully considering and acknowledging how researcher presence may influence the data collection, management, analysis and presentation. Above all, reflexivity and accountability may compel the researcher to strive to ensure that findings are useful and applicable to other researchers and educators in the field.

Research into Multimodal Communicative Competences is complex and challenging. At the same time, there is promise of exciting, innovating horizons for future researchers willing to explore expanding parameters of communication that is opening up, exponentially, with each new generation of language learners.

References

Abrams, Z. (2006). From theory to practice: Intracultural CMC in the L2 classroom. In L. Ducate & N. Arnold (Eds.), *Calling to CALL: From theory and research to new directions in foreign language teaching* (pp. 181–209). San Marcos, TX: Computer Assisted Language Instruction Consortium.

Allford, D., & Pachler, N. (2007). *Language, autonomy and the new learning environments.* Bern; Oxford: Peter Lang.

Allwright, D. (2003). Exploratory practice: rethinking practitioner research in language teaching. *Language Teaching Research*, *7*(2), 113–141.

Allwright, D., & Hanks, J. (2009). *The developing language learner.* Houndmills: Palgrave Macmillan.

Belz, J. (2003). From the special issue editor. *Language Learning & Technology, 7*(2), 2–5. Downloaded 30 July 2010, from <http://llt.msu.edu/vol7num2/speced.html>.

Belz, J., & Thorne, S. (Eds.) (2006). *Internet-mediated intercultural foreign language education.* Boston: Thomson Heinle.

Black, T.R. (1999). *Doing quantitative research in the social sciences: an integrated approach to research design, measurement, and statistics.* London: Sage.

Örnberg Berglund, T. (2009a). Multimodal student interaction online: an ecological perspective. *ReCALL, 21*(2), 186–205.

Örnberg Berglund, T. (2009b). Disrupted turn adjacency and coherence maintenance in Instant Messaging conversations. *Language@Internet 6*(2). Downloaded 30 July 2010 from: <http://www.languageatinternet.de/articles/2009/2106>.

Canale, M., & Swain, M. (1980). Theoretical bases of communicative approaches to second language teaching and testing. *Applied Linguistics, 1*(1), 1–47.

Carr, W., & Kemmis, S. (1986). *Becoming critical. Education, knowledge and action research.* Lewes: Falmer.

Chen, H. (1999). A comparison between cooperative learning and traditional, whole-class method—teaching English in a junior college. *Academic Journal of Kang-Ning, 3*, 69–82.

Ciekanski, M., & Chanier, T. (2008). Developing online multimodal verbal communication to enhance the writing process in an audio-graphic conferencing environment. *ReCALL, 20*, 162–182.

Council of Europe (COE) (2001). *Common european framework of reference for languages: Learning, teaching and assessment (CEFR).* Cambridge: Cambridge University Press.

Crystal, D. (2001). *Language and the internet.* Cambridge: Cambridge University Press.

Chun, D. (2008). Computer-mediated discourse in instructed environments. In S. Magnan. (Ed.), *Mediating discourse online* (pp. 15–45). Philadelphia: Benjamins.

Davidson, C. (2009). Transcription: Imperatives for qualitative research. *International Journal for Qualitative Methods*, *8*(2), 1–52. Downloaded 07 July 2010 from <http://ejournals.library.ualberta.ca/index.php/IJQM/article/viewFile/4205/5401>.
Develotte, C., Guichon, N., & Vincent, C. (2010). The use of the webcam for teaching a foreign language in a desktop videoconferencing environment. *ReCALL 22*(3), 293–312.
Dooly, M. (2010). Teacher 2.0. In S. Guth & F. Helm (Eds.), *Telecollaboration 2.0: Language, literacies and intercultural learning in the 21st century* (pp. 277–303). Bern: Peter Lang.
Dooly, M. (in press). Promoting competency-based language teaching through project-based language learning. In M. Pérez Cañado (Ed.), *Competency-based language teaching and learning.* Amsterdam: John Benjamins.
Dörnyei, Z. (2007). *Research methods in applied linguistics.* Oxford: Oxford University Press.
Flewitt, R., Hauck, M., Hampel, R., & Lancaster, L. (2009). What are multimodal data and transcription? In C. Jewitt (Ed.), *Handbook of Multimodal Analysis* (pp. 40–54). London: Routledge.
Furstenberg, G., & Levet, S. (2010). Integrating telecollaboration into the language classroom: Some insights. In S. Guth, & F. Helm (Eds.), *Telecollaboration 2.0: Language, literacies and intercultural learning in the 21st century* (pp. 305–336). Bern: Peter Lang.
García-Carbonell, A., Rising, B., Montero, B., & Watts, F. (2001). Simulations/gaming and the acquisition of communicative competence in another language. *Simulation & Gaming*, *32*, 481–491.
Godwin-Jones, R. (2006). Emerging technologies. Tag clouds in the blogosphere: Electronic literacy and social networking. *Language Learning & Technology*, *10*(2), 8–15. Downloaded 18 October 2010 from <http://llt.msu.edu/vol10num2/emerging/default.html>.
Goodwin, C. (2004). A competent speaker who can't speak: The social life of aphasia. *Journal of Linguistic Anthropology*, *14*(2), 151–170.

Guth, S., & Helm, F. (2010). Introduction. In S. Guth & F. Helm (Eds.), *Telecollaboration 2.0: Language, literacies and intercultural learning in the 21st century* (pp. 13–35). Bern: Peter Lang.

Hampel, R. (2006). Rethinking task design for the digital age: A framework for language teaching and learning in a synchronous online environment. *ReCALL*, *18*(1), 105–121.

Hauck, M. (2010). The enactment of task design in telecollaboration 2.0. In M. Thomas & H. Reinders (Eds.), *Task-based language learning and teaching with technology* (pp. 197–217). London & New York: Continuum.

Helm, F., & Guth, S. (2010). The multifarious goals of telecollaboration 2.0: Theoretical and practical implications. In S. Guth & F. Helm (Eds.) *Telecollaboration 2.0: Language, literacies and intercultural learning in the 21st century* (pp. 69–106). Bern: Peter Lang.

Herring, S. C. (2007). A faceted classification scheme for computer-mediated discourse. Downloaded 16 June 2008 from *Language@Internet.* <http://www.languageatinternet.de/articles/2007/761>.

Jefferson, G. (2004). Glossary of transcript symbols with an introduction. In G. H. Lerner (Ed.), *Conversation analysis: Studies from the first generation* (pp. 13–31). Amsterdam/Philadelphia: John Benjamins.

Johnson, D. W., & Johnson, R. T. (1989). *Cooperation and competition: Theory and research.* Edina, MN: Interaction Book Company.

Johnson, D. W., Johnson, R. T., & Holubec, E. J. (1993). *Cooperation in the Classroom (6th edition).* Edina, MN: Interaction Book Company.

Kemmis, S., & McTaggart, R. (2000). Participatory action research. In N. K. Denzin & Y.S. Lincoln (Eds), *Strategies of qualitative enquiry* (pp. 336–396). Thousand Oaks, CA: Sage.

Kendon, A. (2004). *Gesture: Visible action as utterance.* Cambridge: Cambridge University Press.

Kessler, C. (1992). *Cooperative language learning: A teacher's resource book.* Englewood Cliffs, NJ: Prentice Hall.

Kramsch, C. (2006). From communicative competence to symbolic competence. *The Modern Language Journal, 90*(2), 249–252.

Kress, G. (1998). Visual and verbal modes of representation in electronically mediated communication: the potentials of new forms of text. In I. Snyder (Ed.), *Page to screen: Taking literacy into the electronic era* (pp. 53–79). London: Routledge.

Kress, G. (2003). *Literacy in the new media age*. London: Routledge.

Kress, G., & van Leeuwen, T. (1996). *Reading images: The grammar of visual design*. New York: Routledge.

Kress, G., & van Leeuwen, T. (2001). *Multimodal discourse: The modes and media of contemporary communication*. London: Arnold.

Lam, W.S.E. (2004). Second language socialization in a bilingual chat room: Global and local considerations. *Language Learning & Technology, 8*, 44–65.

Lamy, M-N., & Hampel, R (2007). *Online communication in language learning and teaching*. Basingstoke: Palgrave Macmillan.

Lankshear, C. (1997). *Changing literacies*. Buckingham: Open University Press.

Lantolf, S. (2000). Introducing sociocultural theory. In J. P. Lantolf (Ed.), *Sociocultural theory and second language learning* (pp. 1–26). Oxford: Oxford University Press.

Maggio, L.A., Bresnahan, M., Flynn, D.B., Harzbecker, J., Blanchard, M., & Ginn, D. (2009). A case study: using social tagging to engage students in learning medical subject headings. *Journal of the Medical Library Association, 97*(2), 77–83.

Maxim, P.S. (1999). *Quantitative research methods in the social sciences*. New York; Oxford: Oxford University Press.

McCafferty, S.G., Jacobs, G.M., & Da Silva Iddings, A.C. (2006). *Cooperative learning and second language teaching*. Cambridge: Cambridge University Press.

Morgan, S.E., Reichert, T., & Harrison, T.R. (2002). *From numbers to words: reporting statistical results for the social sciences*. Boston; London: Allyn and Bacon.

Negretti, R. (1999). Web-based activity and SLA: A conversation analysis research approach. *Language Learning & Technology, 3*(1),

75–87. Downloaded 18 October 2010 from <http://llt.msu.edu/vol3num1/negretti/>.

Neuman, W.L. (1997). *Social research methods: qualitative and quantitative approaches* (3rd edition.). Boston: Allyn and Bacon.

Norris, S. (2002). The implication of visual research for discourse analysis: Transcription beyond language. *Visual Communication*, *1*(1), 97–121.

Norris, S. (2004). *Analyzing multimodal interaction: A methodological framework*. New York: Routledge.

O'Dowd, R., & Ware, P. (2009). Critical issues in telecollaborative task design. *Computer Assisted Language Learning*, *22*(2), 173–188.

O'Rourke, B. (2005). Form focused interaction in online tandem learning. *CALICO Journal*, *22*(3), 433–466.

Pegrum, M. (2009). *From blogs to bombs: The future of digital technologies in education*. Perth: University of Western Australia Press.

Pica, T., & Doughty, C. (1985). The role of group work in classroom Second language acquisition. *Studies in Second Language Acquisition*, *7*, 233–48.

Plowman, L., & Stephen, C. (2008). The big picture?: Video and the representation of interaction. *British Educational Research Journal*, *34*(4), 541–565.

Rogoff, B. (2003). *The cultural nature of human development*. New York: Oxford University Press.

Savignon, S.J. (1997). *Communicative competence. Theory and classroom practice. Texts and contexts in second language learning*. NY: McGraw-Hill, Inc.

Schneider, J., & von der Emde, S. (2000). Brave new (virtual) world: Transforming language learning into cultural studies through online learning environments (MOOs). *ADFL Bulletin*, *32*(1), 18–26.

Schwienhorst, K. (2004). Native-speaker/non-native speaker discourse in the MOO: Participation and engagement in a synchronous text-based environment. *Computer-Assisted Language Learning*, *17*, 35–50.

Seely Brown, J. (2008). Foreword. Creating a culture of learning. In T. Iiyoshi & M.S. Vijay Kumar (Eds.), *Opening up education. The collective advancement of education through open technology, open content, and open knowledge* (pp. xi–xvii). Cambridge MA: The Carnegie Foundation for the Advancement of Teaching, MIT Press.

Simpson, J. (2005). Conversational floors in synchronous text-based CMC discourse. *Discourse Studies, 7*(3), 337–361.

Silverman, D. (1993). *Interpreting qualitative data: methods for analyzing talk, text, and interaction.* London: Thousand Oaks, CA: Sage.

Silverman, D. (2000). *Doing qualitative research: a practical handbook.* Thousand Oaks, CA: Sage.

Smith, B. (2003). Computer-mediated negotiated interaction: An expanded model. *Modern Language Journal, 87*, 38–57.

Smith, B. (2004). Computer-mediated negotiated interaction and lexical acquisition. *Studies in Second Language Acquisition, 26*, 365–398.

Stockwell, G. (2007). A review of technology choice for teaching language skills and areas in the CALL literature. *ReCALL, 19*(2), 105–120.

Street, B. (1998). New literacies in theory and practice: What are the implications for language in education? *Linguistics and Education, 10*(1), 1–24.

Stringer, E. T. (2007). *Action research: A handbook for practitioners* (3rd edition). Newbury Park: Sage.

Thibault, P. (2000). The Multimodal transcription of a television Advertisement: Theory and practice. In A.P. Baldry (Ed.), *Multimodality and multimediality in the distance learning age* (pp. 311–85). Campobasso: Palladino Editore.

Thorne, S. L. (2003). Artifacts and cultures-of-use in intercultural communication. *Language Learning & Technology, 7*(2), 38–67.

Thorne, S. L. (2008). Mediating technologies and second language learning. In J. Coiro, C. Lankshear, M. Knobel & D. Leu. (Eds.), *Handbook of research on new literacies* (pp. 417–449). New York: Lawrence Erlbaum.

Thorne, S. L., Black, R. W., & Sykes, J. M. (2009). Second language use, socialization, and learning in internet interest communities and online gaming. *The Modern Language Journal, 93*, 802–821.

Thorne, S. L., & Reinhardt, J. (2008). "Bridging activities," new media literacies and advanced foreign language proficiency. *CALICO Journal, 25*, 558–572.

Warschauer, M. (1999). *Electronic literacies: Language, culture, and power in online education.* Mahwah, NJ: Lawrence Erlbaum Associates.

Zheng, D., Young, M., & Wagner, M. (2009). Negotiation for action: English language learning in gamebased virtual worlds. *Modern Language Journal, 93*, 489–511.

The Classroom-Based Action Research Paradigm in Telecollaboration

ANDREAS MÜLLER-HARTMANN

In telecollaborative projects, "internationally-dispersed learners in parallel language classes use Internet communication tools such as e-mail, synchronous chat, threaded discussion and MOOs [...], in order to support social interaction, dialogue, debate and intercultural exchange" (Belz, 2003: 2). Telecollaborative learning environments are characterized by complex interrelations between structural aspects, such as institutional affordances and constraints and aspects of agency. This broad "ecological context of telecollaboration and language learning and language use in telecollaboration" represents a complex research field (Belz, 2002: 62). In this contribution we will look at the potential of the case study design in action research, and activity theory as possible research approaches in telecollaboration. In terms of research questions, the focus here will be on the development of teachers' competences, such as intercultural communicative competence, multimodal competence, and teaching competences, which they need to design, organize and teach telecollaborative projects.

Research on telecollaboration is mostly done by researchers who do not come as outsiders to the research process, but who, while being researchers, are also the practitioners who are actually responsible for the telecollaborative learning environment and who, while pursuing diverse research questions, also look at the development of their own practice (e.g. Belz & Müller-Hartmann, 2003; O'Dowd, 2006). Consequently, when trying to improve one's practice, a pedagogic approach to research is needed which includes all participants, the teacher-researcher as well as the learners. This classroom-based research approach pursues a research perspective that closely links research, teaching, and learning. The action research (AR) paradigm is especially helpful in this regard, since teachers themselves are central to the research process trying to improve their own practice (Burns, 1999; Edge, 2000; Allwright & Hanks, 2009). At the same time AR contributes to educational theory building so that other teachers can also profit from it.

Due to the complex interrelations of this environment and its agents, which involves teachers and learners and the different roles they fill, the tasks that structure the telecollaborative exchange, the computer as a multimodal tool, and the impact the sociocultural context has on the agents and the task-as-process, all variables cannot be controlled. A case study approach will allow the researcher "to learn what is happening" in the research field by observing and exploring over a longer period of time "the context as an essential part of understanding the phenomenon under investigation", here the telecollaborative project (Nunan & Bailey, 2009: 158, 162; see also Yin, 2003). Through its holistic approach to collecting and triangulating data from different perspectives, the case study approach allows a rich contextualization of the processes, which is crucial to understand what is happening.

While the case study approach provides a clear frame for the research context, activity theory (AT) helps the researcher to deal with the rich contextualized data of the case, analyzing the data from different perspectives to understand the complex processes taking place in telecollaboration (Engeström, 1999; Lantolf & Thorne, 2006). AT, the modern development of sociocultural theory, provides us with categories for structuring such fields of human interaction and for mapping "the complexities of social practice in educational settings" (Thorne, 2004: 57).

In the following we will first present the potential of the case study approach when engaging in AR before we look at how competences of pre-service teachers can be developed in a telecollaborative project between two university teacher education seminars, one in Germany and one in the U.S., as an example of a research question focussing on telecollaboration. Finally we will show how AT helps the teacher-researcher to understand the complex interrelations between human agents, computer tools and the sociocultural context and how it supports analyzing the data in light of the research question.

Doing Classroom-based Qualitative Research Using Case Studies

Researching and improving telecollaborative teaching environments must take place in the very context these projects are located in. To do this we need to take the conditions in which teaching and learning takes place – the classroom and the people who act in it – seriously. From empirical studies (see Freeman & Johnson, 1998; Schocker-v. Ditfurth, 2001; Johnson, 2009) we know that a mere transmission of knowledge and ideas developed in other contexts will not necessarily lead to more effective practice, and that we need to focus on the teachers or teacher-researchers to improve classroom learning, helping them to become change agents in their professional field. As Freeman and Johnson (1998) have pointed out:

> the core of the knowledge base must focus on the activity of teaching itself; it should center on the teacher who does it, the contexts in which it is done, and the pedagogy by which it is done. (1998: 397)

Consequently we need to develop educational theories of practice in close collaboration with pre- and in-service teachers within the different contexts they work in. Research, therefore must take place in school and university classrooms, and not in laboratory settings (see Ellis, 2003: 333; Eckerth, 2008: 35). In terms of task-based language teaching (TBLT), Skehan states:

> (T)here is an urgent need to relate task-based research to pedagogic situations. (...) task research needs to be conducted within pedagogic contexts, to establish whether or not the research findings have relevance for classroom reality. [...] we need to make progress in understanding what the role of the teacher can most effectively be, as well as how relevant insights on tasks can be incorporated into teacher training. (2007: 298)

The same argument has been put forward by CALL researchers. In their call for a normalization in CALL research, Chambers and Bax (2006) argue for a broader sociocultural research paradigm, stating that we "need more description of the learners, settings, and events in [CALL] contexts" (Huh & Hu in Chambers & Bax, 2006: 467); and we especially "need a better understanding of how exactly all of these factors interact and operate in real pedagogical contexts" (Chambers & Bax, 2006: 466–67, see also Hampel, 2006; Müller-Hartmann & Schocker-v. Ditfurth, 2008). When pursuing this kind of research:

> offering a broad and balanced analysis of the various factors and their interaction, it could have a local impact, in that it could lead to the better use of CALL in the research settings themselves. It could also have a wider impact, in that it could illuminate the ways in which these factors could be managed in other contexts. (Chambers & Bax, 2006: 467)

Consequently, to understand the contexts and the processes involved we need to look at the classroom from the perspectives of the participants themselves, the learners – here pre-service teachers – as well as the teacher-researcher(s), which makes a largely qualitative research design necessary. Qualitative researchers study phenomena in their natural settings, attempting to make sense of, or to interpret phenomena in terms of the meaning people bring to them (Denzin & Lincoln, 2000). Considering the larger sociocultural context, ethnographic research, as one form of qualitative research, takes a "holistic perspective in conducting research", looking at the "local meanings of action, as defined from the actors' point of view", i.e. an emic point of view (Davis, 1995: 433). The same is true for AR. As to data collection:

> an interpretive qualitative study utilizes interviews, observations, and other forms of data collection within the time frame necessary for gaining an understanding of the actors' meanings for social actions (an emic perspective). (ibid.)

In this interpretive stance to research, triangulation of data on the basis of qualitative and quantitative approaches is crucial, as Denzin points out, providing a quality control strategy of the data. "The goal of multiple triangulation is a fully grounded interpretive research approach. Objective reality will never be captured. In depth-understanding, not validity, is sought in any interpretive study" (Denzin, 1989: 246, see also Dörnyei, 2007: 43–44). As Huberman and Miles phrase it:

> triangulation is less a tactic than a mode of inquiry. By self-consciously setting out to collect and double-check findings, using multiple sources and modes of evidence, the researcher will build the triangulation process into ongoing data collection. (1994: 438)

The case study approach provides the frame for the triangulation of data from the emic perspective including the sociocultural context. "A case is a 'bounded instance' [...] whether those boundaries are physical (a certain school site, a child), or temporal" (as in a telecollaborative project over a semester) (Nunan & Bailey, 2009: 161). In terms of research approach, case studies are "methodologically speaking (...) a 'hybrid' in that almost any data collection and analytical methods can be used" (ibid.: 157). Other characteristics of case studies are their longitudinality, the multiple perspectives, and the triangulation of data. The phenomenon in the case study "is studied in context, focussing on observation, description, inference and interpretation, all important facts of ethnographic and practitioner research" (ibid.: 162), thus grasping especially well the complexity of telecollaborative projects. By providing extensive presentation of primary data (see the appendices for examples) and by triangulating these different data sources, case studies offer a rich description of the phenomenon's context. The issue of contextualization is crucial because:

> each human case is complex, operating within a constellation of linguistic, sociolinguistic, sociological and other systems, and the whole may be greater than – or different from – the sum of its parts. (Duff, 2008: 37).

Various research studies on the teacher role in CALL in general and telecollaboration in particular have pursued such a research approach, using interviews, observation, reflective conversations, focus group discussions, and in-class discussion activities to explore the teacher's role when using computers (Lam, 2000; Nunan & Wong, 2005; Hartnell-Young, 2006). Researching telecollaborative learning environments in pre-service teacher education, both Fuchs (2006: 93–108) and O'Dowd (2006: 100–104) used ethnographic and case study approaches to establish data triangulation through participant observation, pre-and post-course questionnaires, email and chat transcripts as well as other forms of learner data. And Belz and Müller-Hartmann (2003: 72) presented "a self-reflective case study" of their "development as teacher-learners of telecollaboration in telecollaboration." These last three qualitative research studies also incorporated an AR approach since these teacher-researchers tried to improve their future practice of telecollaboration with the help of their studies.

Researching Your Own Classroom – Action Research and Exploratory Practice

The action research approach has had a long tradition in classroom-based research (see Altrichter & Posch, 1990; Burns, 1999; Edge, 2000; Allwright & Hanks, 2009). As Nunan and Bailey clarify:

> the term classroom research refers to research conducted in classrooms – regardless of who does it or what methods are used. Action research, in contrast, is an actual research method, in that it involves a codified sequence of steps. (2009: 19)

In AR teachers turn researcher, combining the two roles in one person, creating new educational knowledge. AR is self-reflective, allowing teacher-researchers to better understand and possibly change their classroom practices (see Carr & Kemmis, 1986: 220). According to Nunan and Bailey, AR comprises the following steps:

> We define action research as a systematic, iterative process of (1) identifying an issue, problem, or puzzle we wish to investigate in our own context; (2) thinking and planning an appropriate action to address that concern; (3) carrying out the action; (4) observing the apparent outcomes of the action; (5) reflecting on the outcomes and on other possibilities; and (6) repeating these steps again. (2009: 227)

These steps also structure our case study (see below). For an example of this cyclical nature of AR of a telecollaborative case study at secondary school level, see Jackstädt and Müller-Hartmann, (2001). While usually being low-scale in terms of size and interference in classroom processes, AR nevertheless "involves systematic collection of data [...] and analysis of qualitative data and description of events and processes" (Benson, 2001: 282).

There are also pitfalls to this research approach as Dörnyei (2007) has shown. He points out that "teachers usually lack (a) the time, (b) the incentives, and (c) the expertise or professional support to get meaningfully engaged with research" (pp. 191–192). But he also suggests a solution when he says that "the most obvious place to start [AR] would be in pre-service and in-service teacher training courses" (ibid.: 194), so that future teachers start early to develop an appropriate research attitude for their professional context. This is where Allwright and Hanks (2009) pick up the baton, and develop a specific approach to AR that makes handling AR more conducive to teachers' and learners' needs and thus more feasible. Their criticism of AR is similar to that of Dörnyei's. They see three major problems:

- The continuing influence of the third-party model;
- the consequent focus on the teacher, risking the potential marginalization of the learner;

- the focus on change and improvement, rather than on understanding (Allwright and Hanks, 2009: 142).

Sometimes AR is abused by outside researchers (third-party model), relegating teacher and learners to the position of "research subjects, providers of data and not practitioners in their own right at all" (Allwright & Hanks, 2009: 143). For examples of truly collaborative research projects between teachers and researchers see Ulichny and Schröder, 1996; or Jackstädt and Müller-Hartmann, 2001. Allwright and Hanks also argue that the focus of AR on changing and improving practitioners' practice "has led to an undermining of the crucial role of understanding in research" (ibid.: 144). They above all expect AR "to develop our general understandings of learners and also to enable learners to develop their understandings, and so develop as practitioners of learning" (ibid.: 142). They stress that teachers "need particular understandings that are directly appropriate to their unique situations, not high-level generalisation" (ibid.: 146).

Allwright and Hanks (2009) propose a different kind of practitioner research which they call exploratory practice (EP). "EP will take us beyond the third-party model methodologically, will not marginalize learners, will prioritize learner understandings that are ultimately 'too deep for words'" (ibid.: 149). The difference between action research and exploratory practice is the intention the teacher-researcher pursues with his or her research.

> AR starts out as an intention to change in order to solve a problem, or at least to introduce an innovation. EP starts out with an intention to try to understand, rather than change. (Allwright and Hanks, 2009: 172–173)

One decisive characteristic of EP is the "use of familiar classroom activities as investigative tools" because "good research itself can be good pedagogy. The point of EP is not to get research done, but to get teaching done well, in a way that fosters the development of understanding in and among all the participants" (Allwright & Hanks, 2009: 154). This will not only reduce the workload of the teacher-researcher, but it will produce interesting data from the emic perspective. Allwright and Hanks call these activities "potentially exploitable pedagogic activities" (2009: 155). They suggest a whole gamut of activities for data generation, establish principles for the suitability of these activities, and make suggestions of how to adapt activities to use them for data generation. (ibid.: 193–198).

When looking at the telecollaborative case study below, two levels have to be differentiated. In the teacher education seminar, the two course instructors pursue an EP approach to their research, i.e. first of all trying to understand the complex processes when developing pre-service teachers' competences through 'pedagogic activities'. At the same time, learners develop a stance of reflective practice which allows them to eventually do practitioner research themselves in their future professional contexts (see Lamy & Hampel, 2007: 174–177, for a valuable ethical guide to practitioner research). Lamy and Hampel support this process when they say that "trainee teachers need to experience the online classroom as their students will experience it, to reflect on it and also to observe more seasoned peers" (ibid.: 73–74). By using an EP approach to teacher learning, we try to instill an attitude of professional development as a continuous process of action and reflection.

Having elaborated on the general approach to classroom-based qualitative research methodology, we now present the research context the research question for our case study grew out of (identifying the issue). Then the research field and the project will be described before we move on to the steps of data collection (planning and carrying out an appropriate action) and finally data analysis (observing and reflecting on the outcome of the action) with the help of activity theory.

Identifying an Issue – How to Develop Teaching Competences in Task-based CMC?

The role of the teacher is crucial in initiating, developing and monitoring telecollaborative exchanges for language learning. This creates multiple demands on the teachers. They need to develop competences in the central areas of multiliteracy or multimodal competence (Cope & Kalantzis, 2000), Intercultural Communicative Competence (ICC) (Byram, 1997), and Task-Based Language Teaching (TBLT), i.e. teaching competences (Samuda & Bygate, 2008; Raith, 2010; Müller-Hartmann & Schocker-v. Ditfurth, 2011), to effectively implement technology into their teaching. One central aim of teacher education programs is to provide technology-rich learning environments to allow pre-service teachers to develop these competences (Belz & Thorne, 2006; Hubbard & Levy, 2006; Kassen, Lavine, Murphy-Judy, & Peters, 2007).

Multiliteracy or Multimodal Competence

During the last decade we have moved through several literacy models that include the use of technology – from computer or information literacy to electronic literacy to multiliteracy (Warschauer & Shetzer, 2000: 172–173; for an overview on comprehensive literacy skills see Pegrum, 2009, chapter 3; see also Dooly and Hauck, this volume). Multiliteracy, which has been developed by the New London Group (Cope & Kalantzis, 2000) since 1996, is one of the most comprehensive literacy models to date, because it integrates individual human agency with larger societal structures. In the concept of multiliteracy there is a constant interplay between individual agency and social, economic, historical and political structures that determine the various discourses and hence, human agency, but which are also changed through human activity. The New London Group argues that the development of literacy needs to incorporate the multifaceted discourses that a potentially global participation enables learners to engage in, because of the unrestricted access to texts on the internet and the multimodality of this text universe (Luke 2000: 73; Hauck, 2010). Kress (2003) has called this competence multimodal competence or multimodality. The New Media Consortium (2005: 8) has defined this new kind of literacy as "a set of abilities and skills where aural, visual, and digital literacy overlap." At the same time these multimodal texts are culturally grounded. When learners engage with them while communicating with other learners world-wide, they need to develop ICC to negotiate linguistic and cultural differences.

The task of the teacher is to help learners navigate these intertextual environments and support them in developing these skills through a task-based approach that is learner- and problem-oriented. As Hauck summarizes:

> the challenge for telecollaborative partners is therefore threefold: engaging with meaning making via multiple modes in a new, online culture while depending on limited written and /or oral proficiency in another language. (2010: 227)

Hampel and Stickler (2005) have suggested a pyramid of skills which teachers need to develop multimodal competence. The skills described on the first three levels of this pyramid cover basic ITC competences, specific technical competences when using software, and the skill of dealing with constraints and possibilities of the medium. In terms of language teaching, they point out on levels four and five of their pyramid that teachers need to be able to turn "an online environment into a platform where communicative competence can be developed" which "is dependent on a sense of community and trust" (ibid.: 318). At the same time they stress that "interaction in an online environment can be achieved through task design" (ibid.: 318; see also Hampel, 2006). On the last two levels of the skills pyramid teachers need to be able to provide creativity and choice as well as to develop their own teaching styles. The research focus here is on levels one through four.

Intercultural Communicative Competence (ICC)

Teachers do not only need competences in facilitating communicative competence, but also ICC, which comprises attitudes of openness and curiosity, intercultural knowledge, skills of discovery and interaction, skills of relating and interpreting oral and written texts, and last but not least critical intercultural awareness to help turn learners into intercultural speakers (Byram, 1997). Consequently language teachers need to become "intercultural speaker[s]" themselves, i.e. they need to develop the capacity of establishing relationships, managing dysfunctions and mediating" in telecollaboration before they will be able to support learners in the process (Byram, 1997: 31–32; see Müller-Hartmann, 2006). The ISTE National Educational Technology Standards also include this competence:

> teachers develop and model cultural understanding and global awareness by engaging with colleagues and students of other cultures using digital age-communication and collaboration tools. (NETS-T, 2008)

Task-Based Language Teaching Competence (TBLT)

A third area of competence is TBLT, something Hampel and Stickler's (2006) skills pyramid also incorporates. During the last ten years TBLT has been established as one of the central approaches to learning and teaching a foreign language, and it has been widely researched from psycho-linguistic and sociocultural perspectives (Ellis 2003; Van den Branden, 2006; Van den Branden, Van Gorp, & Verhelst, 2007; Samuda & Bygate, 2008; Müller-Hartmann & Schocker-v. Ditfurth, 2011). TBLT has also become an important teaching and research approach in telecollaboration, as these environments generate authentic communication, using real-world tasks to involve learners in meaningful negotiation (Müller-Hartmann 2000; O'Dowd & Eberbach, 2004; Hampel, 2006; O'Dowd, 2006; Müller-Hartmann & Schocker-v. Ditfurth, 2008; Thomas & Reinders, 2010).

Raith (2010) has developed a competence model for teaching TBLT which comprises the three areas or phases of (1) introducing tasks, i.e. motivating learners to get involved with the tasks, of (2) accompanying and supporting the task process, and (3) of reflecting the task process. In the telecollaborative case study below we especially focus on the first two phases which among others also incorporate the more specific competences of:

- A: Introducing tasks: The teacher

  (...) can introduce the task in a way that task demand and task support are balanced so that they actively participate in the task process.

  (...) can explain the tasks in a way that learners immediately understand the purpose, product and procedure of the task.

- B: Supporting the task process: The teacher

  (...) can support processes of meaning negotiation in the task process

  (...) can motivate learners to fully engage in accomplishing the task. (Raith, 2010: 151–153)

Having identified the issue or research question of our exploratory practice endeavor, we would like to present the research field, before we show how activity theory allowed us to discover instances of these diverse competence developments in our case study.

Planning and Carrying Out an Appropriate Action – A Telecollaborative Case Study

The context of this case study is a telecollaborative project between two teacher education seminars at the University of Education in Heidelberg (UE) and Columbia University (CU) in New York City that took place from October–December 2007. On the content side the aim of the project seminar was to develop pre-service teachers' teaching competences in TBLT, while also developing ICC and multiliteracy when engaging in CMC with their partners abroad. This case study represents the first cycle of a research project that is organized according to EP characteristics. In the fall of the academic year of 2008/9 the next research cycle followed implementing the research findings from the first cycle in a new telecollaborative project.

Throughout the project pre-service teachers worked together in inter-institutional teams of four or five students. The UE students, who were working on an M.A. degree for teaching EFL in primary or secondary school, were younger than the CU students who were working on an M.A. in TESOL, and who had already taught a number of years in various contexts. Quantitative data from pre-course questionnaires showed that learners in both classrooms brought different levels of technical competences to the exchange. We worked with Moodle, using the forum and wiki as main tools. The project was task-based and the tasks were structured in the following way:

1. Introductory task – getting to know each other and comparing institutional contexts to become aware of affordances and constraints in both contexts (time structure, workload, assessment procedures).
2. Two practice tasks – discussing TBLT principles on the basis of theoretical texts, analyzing and re-designing American ESL and German EFL textbook tasks: Evaluating (and re-writing) grammar and integrated skills task in light of TBLT principles.
3. Final task (this task was assessed at CU): a) designing a lesson plan for an integrated skills task sequence and b) designing a cultural awareness-raising task.
4. Peer evaluation of final task – inter-institutional team 1 evaluated the final task product of inter-institutional team 2, team 2 of team 3, etc.

Students were given substantial feedback on all task designs by the two instructors. These tasks were instrumental as "potentially exploitable pedagogic activities" in allowing students to develop TBLT teaching competences while at the same time providing data to gauge their competence development in this area and others (Allwright & Hanks, 2009: 155–157). The same approach was partially used in terms of assessment procedures. While the CU instructor used formative assessment (for example, CU students received a grade for their final task), UE students were summatively assessed in form of a portfolio that focused on their learning process, i.e. the development of their teaching competences. Additionally a reflection tool was used to allow UE students to reflect on the telecollaborative project, while at the same time generating important emic data to understand students' motivation and actions. In this magnifying glass (MG) task, each student created a mind map based on his/her experiences in the project (see appendix, part C). They chose one critical incident from their mind map that was especially interesting or surprising and put this under the MG, i.e. they turned the paper around and drew a picture of that incident inside the form of a large MG, literally, and also figuratively putting the critical incident under the MG to look more closely at it. This was achieved by prohibiting the students from writing into the picture. When all MGs had been put up on the board, students described, speculated about, and discussed the intended meaning of the pictures. This procedure ensured a discussion of all the salient issues and enabled students to learn about their peers' experiences, thus working through their own experiences and putting them into a larger frame.

The data sources in this project were:

- Pre-questionnaire on computer competence and learners' expectations (closed and open questions)
- Notes of participant observation
- Posts in the forums
- Text generation for the tasks in the wikis
- Mind maps and MGs
- Group discussion of MGs
- Post-questionnaire on learners' experiences in the project (open questions)

- Portfolios of the students who needed credit for this class
- E-mail exchange between the two instructors

Having used pedagogic activities, such as tasks, portfolios, and the MGs, to collect data for triangulation, the next step requires establishing a theoretical framework that will help understand the interrelations among the various data pools. Activity theory is the most promising approach when analyzing complex data sets that integrate emic perspectives with the sociocultural context.

Observing the Outcome of the Action – Activity Theory as a Tool to Analyze the Data

To reduce complexity we will look at the different data sets of one inter-institutional team of four students (Tim and Jie from CU, and Olga and Anna from UE). In terms of the task-in-process we focus on the UE classroom, trying to understand how learners developed the targeted competences.

Human activity is seen as the central unit of analysis in AT that allows us to study "different kinds of human practices as development processes" (Lantolf & Thorne, 2006: 209). The graph represents one educational activity system (AS), i.e. the case study of our telecollaborative project. As can be seen in the graph, all aspects of AT are interrelated, influencing each other. After having briefly described the three levels of the AS, the different categories will be applied to the project data (for a detailed analysis of AT see the contribution by Blin in this book).

Level I

The three levels of the AS define and influence human behaviour in different ways, but at the same time these different perspectives focus on one event, which in this case is constituted by the activities learners engage in as a result of the tasks (level II) they use in the project. Tasks are mediated through the available mediational means (level I), the foreign language English (for most of the learners), tools, such as the computer and its applications (Moodle, wikis, fora), and conceptual tools such as TBLT that mediate the learning process. Before focusing on the central level II, let us consider the wider sociocultural context, developed by Engeström (1987, 1999), of level III.

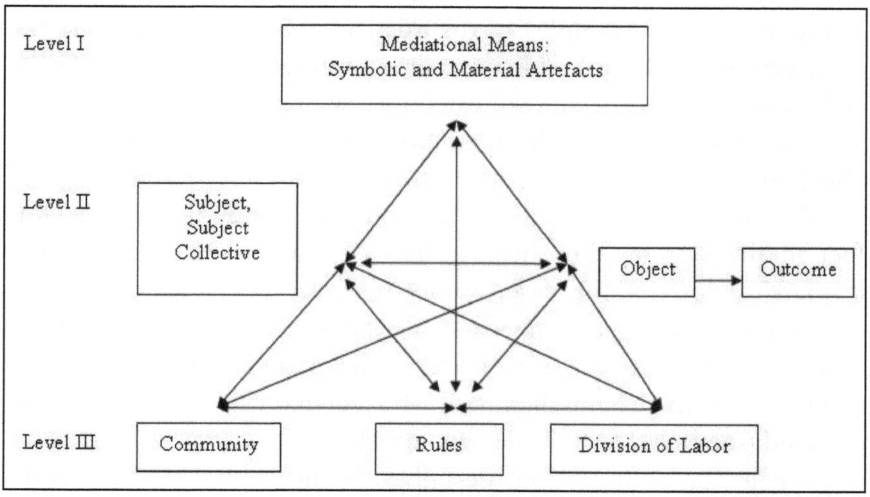

Figure 1. Activity system (based on Engeström 1999)

Level III

The learners and the instructor we focus on form part of a culturally and historically specific community, a German university FL classroom which forms part of a wider educational setting, the university and its pre-service teacher program. UE and CU learners come from different cultural backgrounds and they bring different professional experiences to the project, thus forming two different communities. These communities are governed by different rules and norms which have developed historically and institutionally and which have an impact on the classroom level, and with that on the actions of level II. Rules of politeness, for example, play a decisive role in intercultural task negotiation. If these rules are not adhered to, intercultural misunderstanding and the breakdown of communication can ensue (see Ware, 2005; O'Dowd, 2006; O'Dowd & Ritter, 2006). While both instructors adhered to a task-based approach, the rules of the CU course foresaw a higher workload and different assessment procedures (see above). In the AS this influenced students' motives and thus their actions and the task outcomes on level two (see below). These are typical examples of affordances (both classes pursue the same professional goal) and constraints (difference in age and experience, assessment procedures), categories we know from research on telecollaboration (Belz & Müller-Hartmann, 2002; O'Dowd & Ritter, 2006). By analyzing the interrelations between the different levels of the AS, the researcher can identify nodes of contradictions or conflict in the system, thus helping him or her to better understand learners' actions in the case. Some of these contradictions can be dealt with, engaging in a process of expansive learning (Engeström, 1987) for the next research cycle, while certain institutional constraints, such as the misalignment of academic calendars, cannot be changed (see Belz & Müller-Hartmann, 2003).

Finally, division of labor describes the horizontal level of working together in the classroom, i.e. "the actions and interactions among the members of the community" (Thorne, 2004: 58), and "the vertical division of power and status" (Engeström, 1993: 67). This comprises the social roles and cultural identities of learners and teachers as well as the hierarchical relationships between them. A change in hierarchical relations takes place, for example, if peer evaluation, as in our last task, plays an important role in the assessment approach, having learners and instructor share power. The horizontal level of the division of labor is important because telecollaborative projects are usually characterized by intensive collaborative group work. The division of labor in the inter-institutional teams is a crucial aspect of task instructions and task sequencing and influences the instructor's role as facilitator and monitor of the learning process.

Level II

This level is particularly important because it represents the processes on the classroom level. The subject is the instructor and the subject collective the learners. Learners in the language classroom (community) possibly share the same goal or object, in our case, developing TBLT, ICC, and multiliteracy competences. Engeström explains that

> the object refers to the 'raw material' or 'problem space' at which the activity is directed and which is moulded or transformed into outcomes with the help of physical and symbolic, external and internal tools. (1993: 67)

This means that teachers design and sequence tasks with the help of technology to engage learners in the process of learning, the outcome of which are the aforementioned competences. In terms of EP, the pedagogical approach to teaching TBLT is the 'raw material' that needs to be looked at from the emic perspective of its participants, as it is here that learning is organized and takes place.

In AT, an activity is not the same as a task that learners engage in. Coughlan and Duff explain that:

> an activity [...] comprises the behaviour that is actually produced when an individual (or group) performs a task. It is the process, as well as the outcome, of a task, examined in its sociocultural context. (1994: 175)

This distinction is important, since it describes the role of pedagogic tasks in the larger frame of an activity. In this AS the participants learn how to teach TBLT as well as to navigate the telecollaborative project, developing ICC and multiliteracy in the process (object). Both teachers and learners, pursue a specific object when designing and negotiating tasks on the basis of computer tools. This process is facilitated by the teachers through a more or less strict task sequence. When looking at the object of the activity system, or 'problem space', we can distinguish three levels of human behavior that represent different analytical perspectives on one event, the activity level (contextualizing framework = developing competences), the actions (goal-oriented behavior = analyzing and redesigning textbook tasks), and the operations (automatized or habituated actions using tools, such as wiki or forum). As Lantolf and Thorne (2006) explain, we could simply say that activity (1) asks why something is done (and therefore refers to what motivates learners' involvement in an activity); action (2) describes what takes place (and therefore refers to the goal or product of an activity); and operations (3) say how it is carried out (and therefore refers to the process and the conditions under which something is done). Translated into TBLT, this means that teacher and learners may have different motives in their activities of developing TBLT competences and multiliteracy. Some learners might want to learn about TBLT, others might be mainly interested in the international encounter to develop intercultural friendships, while still other learners might focus on task completion, ignoring their partners' attempts at further socializing (see O'Dowd, 2006). Collecting data from the emic perspective allows to understand learners' motives and with that objects. In the AT discourse different objects thus orient learners' behavior in the classroom, and manifest themselves in different forms for different participants at different times (Blin, 2004: 383).

Reflecting on the Outcomes – Results of the First Action Research Cycle

In the appendix excerpts from the different data sources (A–D) of this case study are provided (we suggest to read the data first before continuing with the analysis here). What do we learn from the analysis? In the following we look at different nodes of the activity system from the emic perspective of the Olga-Anna/Jie-Tim inter-institutional team with a specific focus on Olga to show how the triangulation of different data sets, triggered through 'exploitable pedagogic activities', help understand the processes of competence development. AT with its three levels and interrelated nodes provides the frame for the analysis. In presenting the results we focus on one competence field, looking at one node of the AS. Nevertheless, it will become clear that the competence areas are as interrelated as the nodes of the AS are.

Before looking at the negotiation of tasks, a word about the team structure (community/division of labor) is in order. There seems to be a clear distribution of leadership positions in the team. While Olga assumes a leadership position in terms of establishing the working procedure (A 6–11 and 33–35), Tim does so in terms of group cohesion, pulling the team together in a difficult moment (A 44–46). He does this very nicely by commenting on his own emotional state/perspective. This is a form of horizontal or even intra-team vertical division of labor (level III), since both head their local teams in terms of the object (achieving a positive task outcome (level II) which can only be achieved by establishing team leadership and cohesion, (see Müller-Hartmann & Schocker-v. Ditfurth, 2008, pp. 26–33). In the local UE team we find a clear horizontal division of labor between local partners (D 1–33, C->Feelings).

Multiliteracy Competences

While multiliteracy comprises various competences, we focus here on the mediational means or tools, i.e. the first three levels of Hampel and Stickler's skills pyramid (2006). The learners brought different IT competences to the project. While Olga likes the wiki (D 56–59) and uses it easily for task 4 (A 30), Tim has major problems with the wiki (A 31–32) and Jie never used it. Consequently, on the habitual operational level Olga and Anna handle all the tools of the Moodle system well, whereas Tim has major problems. Olga also realizes the potential or affordance of these mediational means for the team's task negotiation process. She points out that with the help of the wiki the team can work on the same page (D 55–56), thus negotiating their textual products. Olga also realizes that the forum allows for transparent communication in the community or subject group (D 75–77). She suggests an additional forum to support local team work processes (D 34–36). At the same time she realizes that this might clash with rules because the rule of using such a forum could lead to some students not talking freely (D 39–41). Relating the three levels of the AS to each other clearly shows the potential of this research tool to understand learners' agency in the sociocultural context of this specific case. By using these tools to negotiate task processes, Olga and Anna not only develop multimodal competences, but they also realize the potential of these tools for the task process, developing TBLT competences in the process. For example, Olga suggests a chat to facilitate the negotiation of tasks, thus facilitating the action on level II by way of an additional web 2.0 tool. The interrelated nodes of the AS nicely show how multiliteracy competences can possibly influence team processes and with that successful task completion.

TBLT Competences

By realizing the potential of the mediational means for task negotiation, Olga and Anna develop TBLT competences in Raith's (2010) second phase, supporting the task process. They reflect about the affordances of specific tools to support the negotiation of meaning and content, and oral language production by suggesting the chat tool. They also develop competences for the first task phase (introducing tasks), which again is connected to multimodal competence. To allow learners to engage with a task, task clarity is decisive. Tim, for example, did not even find the task at the top of the moodle site, showing the challenge he is confronted with in terms of navigating a learning platform. Olga tells him where to find the task (A 4–5). Olga also decides to put the final version of Task 1 into a new forum post to make it more visible. She uses mediational means to make the outcome transparent on the organizational level. Task clarity is not always established in the project (B 6–7) and task instructions cause confusion (D 100–101). In the last task, task clarity is an issue, causing Tim to be really frustrated (A 36–38). This also creates a conflict because Jie does not accept criticism (see below under ICC). Task clarity thus has an important effect on the activity or object. As Olga realizes task negotiation can be supported through task clarity, i.e. by providing clear instructions (B 6–7, C-> Organisation->Later in school). Olga also develops the competence of balancing task demands and task support. In the post-questionnaire she comments on the division of labor, especially as regards the last task, since she was not happy with the fact that her team always had to work out the final task product (B 2–5). Instead she wishes for a more efficient way to organize the division of labor by checking the workload distribution, and by providing lots of guidance (B 10–11, 20–22, C -> organisation -> in school). Olga also suggests an additional forum to support the local team work process (D 34–36), since rules for making a certain number of posts can support task negotiation. She suggests having the learners provide comments regularly on the team work from an early stage on (B 11–12). This and predefining several deadlines could provide important task support in Olga's eyes (D 46–47). That way the teacher can monitor the work process. With that Olga also develops competences on the third level of Raith's model (2010), reflecting tasks. By monitoring the task process through a forum she is able to engage in formative assessment of the team's working habits.

Intercultural Communicative Competences

In the course of the project Olga realizes that it is crucial to establish a positive team relationship and with that trust in the community and for that a personal level needs to be established between partners. Olga suggests that this can be achieved, for example, through a chat at the beginning of the project, intensifying the getting-to-know phase (D 92–95, C -> Organization -> Project). She is clearly thinking here on the attitudinal level of Byram's ICC model (1997), helping learners to open up to each other, becoming curious. She also becomes aware of the fact that the teacher has to keep the object of her students in mind, taking into consideration their expectations, ideas, and fears (D 94–95). The same thing applies when looking at their multimodal competence. Olga and Anna realize that some aspects of team cohesion are not being realized because the potential of the learning platform to support team cohesion by using pictures is not used. Their suggestion in this regard is not picked up by their partners (A 86–88).

In terms of the skill of interpreting and relating, the whole group creates a lot of positive face throughout the project, establishing social presence and thus trust by thanking each other, or taking leave at the end of the project (A 17–22, 59–63). This can be seen in the exchange between Olga and Tim when they finalize task 2 (A 17–22), and also when Olga criticizes Tim in task 4 and he accepts her methodological suggestions (A 48–58).

Missing task clarity and a certain degree of inability to navigate the learning platform lead to a critical incident (A 39–43) and with that to critical cultural awareness on Olga's side. "To sum up, I learned that negotiation also means to realize when team partners do not want to discuss their work any further and to respect and accept this" (D 67–69). In terms of pragmatic rules, she also reflects about the difficulty of how direct one should be when addressing problems with the partners, when they provided an unsatisfying product in task 4 (D 51–54).

While ICC seems to be located predominantly on level III of the AS, since issues of community, division of labor and rules strongly influence communication in the team, data also shows that the mediational tool (level I) is crucial in understanding students' competence development.

Conclusion – Learning for the Next Research Cycle

The analysis of the excerpts from the triangulated data of this one inter-institutional team shows the potential of the AT approach to understand – in the sense of exploratory practice – the complex processes at work when pre-service teachers develop competences. Based on this understanding a new action research cycle can be designed which integrates some of the findings from this analysis, such as spending more time on the introduction of the technical tools to allow learners to use them to their full potential in the task negotiation process.

The various "potentially exploitable pedagogic activities" (Allwright & Hanks, 2009: 155–157), such as the tasks themselves, the portfolios and the MGs, have generated the necessary data for understanding the processes and interrelations among learners, teachers, tools, and the sociocultural context in this AR case study. At the same time, by taking the learners seriously, they allowed pre-service teachers to develop their various competences as well as a reflective mode, enabling them to participate in and profiting from the data collection processes. Using an exploratory practice approach we interfered as little as possible in the classroom processes by using activities or tasks for data generation that form a central part of the course program. And as can be seen in the students' comments, they understood the model function of these pedagogic activities they were supposed to have for their future teaching. After the discussion of the MG many students commented on its usefulness for the secondary foreign language classroom to help learners reflect about project experiences.

While the technical tools, such as wiki and fora, automatically produce important data, the more reflective tasks of the project, such as the evaluation of the other teams' products in the final task, the MG and the discussion of the results, as well as the portfolio are central to gaining in-depth insights into learners' thought processes. The last two exploratory practices can be adapted to the kind of data that is needed. The MG task, for example, helps the teacher-researchers as well as the learners to discover critical incidents because the learners have to make a choice when putting a feeling or incident under the magnifying glass. The portfolio is especially helpful to gather data about the learning process and the development of competences because you can decide on the frame. In this case, for example, learners were asked among other things to decide on their best task and explain why they consider it especially well designed (TBLT competences), the collaboration in their local and their inter-interstitutional team (ICC), and in how far the project contributed to their professional development (multiliteracy, ICC, TBLT).

Last but not least we also need to consider quantitative data in the sense of the mixed method design (Dörnyei, 2007), because when triangulating data in the case study, quantitative data provides us with important data from the pre-questionnaires about learners' technical competences – and here Tim rated the lowest in the CU team – allowing us to use the full potential of AT to establish all of the interconnections. It is through this approach, by triangulating data from different (emic) perspectives that we can understand the processes that are involved on the classroom level in telecollaborative projects and to help future teachers to become reflective practitioners and with that possible future teacher-researchers themselves.

References

Allwright, D., & Hanks, J. (2009). *The developing language learner.* Houndmills: Palgrave Macmillan.

Altrichter, H., & Posch, P. (1990). *Lehrer erforschen ihren Unterricht. Eine Einführung in die Methoden der Aktionsforschung.* [*Teachers research their own teaching. An introduction to the methods of action research*]. Bad Heilbrunn: Julius Klinkhardt.

Belz, J. A. (2002). Social dimensions of telecollaborative foreign language study. *Language Learning & Technology, 6* (1), 60–81.

Belz, J. A. (2003). From the Special Issue Editor. *Language Learning & Technology, 7* (2), 2–5.

Belz, J. A., & Müller-Hartmann, A. (2002). Deutsch-amerikanische Telekollaboration im Fremdsprachenunterricht – Lernende im Kreuzfeuer der institutionellen Zwänge. [German-American telecollaboration in foreign language teaching – learners caught in the crossfire of institutional constraints]. *Unterrichtspraxis, 35*(1), 72–82.

Belz, J. A., & Müller-Hartmann, A. (2003). Teachers as intercultural learners: Negotiating German-American telecollaboration along the institutional faultline. *The Modern Language Journal, 87*(1), 71–89.

Belz, J. A., & Thorne, S. L. (Eds.) (2006). *Internet-mediated intercultural foreign language education.* Boston: Thomson Heinle.

Benson, P. (2001). *Teaching and researching autonomy in language learning.* Harlow: Longman.

Blin, F. (2004). CALL and the development of learner autonomy: Towards an activity-theoretical perspective. *ReCALL, 16*(2), 377–395.

Burns, A. (1999). *Collaborative action research for English language teachers.* Cambridge: Cambridge University Press.

Byram, M. (1997). *Teaching and assessing intercultural communicative competence.* Clevedon: Multilingual Matters.

Carr, W., & Kemmis, S. (1996). *Becoming critical: Knowing through action research.* London: The Falmer Press.

Chambers, A., & Bax, S. (2006). Making CALL work: Towards normalisation. *System, 34*(4), 465–479.

Cope, B., & Kalantzis, M. (for the New London Group) (Eds.) (2000). *Multiliteracies. Literacy learning and the design of social futures.* London and New York: Routledge.

Coughlan, P., & Duff, P. (1994). Same task, different activities: Analysis of a SLA task from an activity theory perspective. In J. Lantolf & G. Appel (Eds.), *Vygotskian approaches to second language research* (pp. 173–191). Norwood, NJ: Ablex Publishing Company.

Davis, K. A. (1995). Qualitative theory and methods in applied linguistics research. *TESOL Quarterly, 29*(3), 427–453.

Denzin, N. (1989). *The research act (3rd edition).* Englewood Cliffs: Prentice Hall.

Denzin, N., & Lincoln, Y. (Eds.) (2000). *The handbook of qualitative research.* Thousand Oaks, CA: Sage.

Dörnyei, Z. (2007). *Research methods in applied linguistics.* Oxford: Oxford University Press.

Duff, P. A. (2008). *Case study research in applied linguistics.* New York: Lawrence Erlbaum Associates/Taylor & Francis.

Eckerth, J. (2008). Task-based language learning and teaching – Old wine in new bottles? In J. Eckerth, & S. Siekmann (Eds.), *Task-based language learning and teaching. Theoretical, methodological, and pedagogical perspectives* (pp. 13–46). Frankfurt: Peter Lang.

Edge J. (Ed.) (2000). *Action research. Case studies in TESOL practice series.* Alexandria, VA: TESOL.

Ellis, R. (2003). *Task-based language learning and teaching.* Oxford: Oxford University Press.

Engeström, Y. (1987). *Learning by expanding. An activity-theoretical approach to developmental research.* Helsinki: Orienta-Konsulat.

Engeström, Y. (1993). Developmental studies of work as test bench of activity theory: The case of primary care medical practice. In J. Lave & S. Chaiklin (Eds.), *Understanding practice: Perspectives on activity and context* (pp. 64–102). Cambridge: Cambridge University Press.

Engeström, Y. (1999). Activity theory and individual and social transformation. In Y. Engeström, R. Miettinen & R.L. Punamäki (Eds.), *Perspectives on activity theory* (pp. 19–38). Cambridge: Cambridge University Press.

Freeman, D., & Johnson, K. E. (1998). Reconceptualizing the knowledge-base of language teacher education. *TESOL Quarterly, 32*(3), 397–417.

Fuchs, C. (2006). *Computer-mediated negotiation across borders. German-American collaboration in language teacher education.* Frankfurt: Peter Lang.

Hampel, R. (2006). Rethinking task design for the digital age: A framework for language teaching and learning in a synchronous online environment. *ReCALL, 18* (1), 105–121.

Hampel, R., & Stickler, U. (2005). New skills for new classrooms. Training tutors to teach languages online. *Computer Assisted Language Learning, 18*(4), 311–326.

Hartnell-Young, E. (2006). Teachers' roles and professional learning in communities of practice supported by technology in schools. *Journal of Technology and Teacher Education, 14*(3), 461–480.

Hauck, M. (2010). The relevance of multimodal communicative competence in telecollaborative encounters. In S. Guth, & F. Helm (Eds.), *Telecollaboration 2.0. Language, literacies and intercultural learning in the 21st century* (pp. 219–248). Bern: Peter Lang.

Hubbard, P., & Levy, M. (Eds.) (2006). *Teacher education in CALL.* Amsterdam: John Benjamins Publishing Company.

Huberman, A.M., & Miles, M. (1994). Data management and analysis methods. In N.K. Denzin & Y.S. Lincoln (Eds.), *Handbook of qualitative research* (pp. 428–444). Thousand Oaks: Sage.

International Society for Technology in Education (ISTE) (2008). *The ISTE national educational technology standards (NETS-T).* Downloaded 28 June 2010 from <http://www.iste.org/Content/NavigationMenu/NETS/ForTeachers/2008Standards/NETS_T_Standards_Final.pdf>.

Jackstädt, H., & Müller-Hartmann, A. (2000). Virtual encounters in the English language classroom: Intercultural learning through e-mail projects in foreign language teaching. In J. Edge (Ed.), *Action research* (pp. 117–128). Alexandria, VA: TESOL.

Johnson, K. E. (2009). *Second language teacher education. A sociocultural perspective.* New York: Routledge.

Kassen, M. A., Lavine, R. Z., Murphy-Judy, K., & Peters, M. (2007). *Preparing and developing technology-proficient L2 teachers.* Computer Assisted Language Instruction Consortium (CALICO), Texas State

University, San Marcos, Texas. USA. Downloaded 28 June 2010 from <https:www.calico.org/page.php?id=411>.

Kress, G. (2003). *Literacy in the new media age.* London: Routledge.

Lam, Y. (2000). Technophilia vs. technophobia: A preliminary look at why second language teachers do or do not use technology in their classrooms. *Canadian Modern Language Review, 56*(3), 389–420.

Lamy, M.-N., & Hampel, R. (2007). *Online communication in language learning and teaching.* Houndsmill: Palgrave Macmillan.

Lantolf, J., & Thorne, S. (2006). *Sociocultural theory and the genesis of second language development.* Oxford: Oxford University Press.

Luke, C. (2000). Cyber-schooling and technological change: Multiliteracies for new times. In B. Cope & M. Kalantzis (Eds.), *Multiliteracies: Literacy learning and the design of social futures* (pp 69–91). New York: Routledge.

Müller-Hartmann, A. (2000). The role of tasks in promoting intercultural learning in electronic learning networks. *Language Learning & Technology, 4*(2), 129–147. Downloaded 28 June 2010 from <http://llt.msu.edu/vol4num2/muller/default.html>.

Müller-Hartmann, A. (2006). Learning how to teach intercultural communicative competence via telecollaboration: A model for language teacher education. In J.A. Belz & S.L. Thorne (Eds.), *Internet-mediated intercultural foreign language education* (pp. 63–84). Boston: Thomson Heinle.

Müller-Hartmann, A., & Schocker-v. Ditfurth, M. (2008). Research on the use of technology in task-based language teaching. In A. Müller-Hartmann & M. Schocker-v. Ditfurth (Eds.), *Aufgabenorientiertes Lernen und Lehren mit Medien: Ansätze, Erfahrungen, Perspektiven in der Fremdsprachendidaktik [Task-based learning nd teaching with media: Approaches, experiences and perspectives in foreign language teaching]* (pp. 11–64). Frankfurt: Peter Lang.

Müller-Hartmann, A., & Schocker-v. Ditfurth, M. (2011). *Task-supported language teaching.* Paderborn: Schöningh.

New Media Consortium (2005). *A global imperative: The report of the 21st century literacy summit.* Downloaded 31 July 2009 from <http://www.nmc.org/pdf/Global_Imperative.pdf>.

Nunan, D., & Bailey, K. M. (2009). *Exploring second language classroom research. A comprehensive guide.* Boston: Heinle.

Nunan, D., & Wong, L. (2005). Innovation and change: Information technology and in-service teacher education. In C. Davison (Ed.), *Information technology and innovation in language education* (pp. 195–227). Hong Kong: Hong Kong University Press.

O'Dowd, R. (2006). *Telecollaboration and the development of intercultural communicative competence.* Berlin: Langenscheidt.

O'Dowd, R., & Eberbach, K. (2004). Guides on the Side? Tasks and challenges for teachers in telecollaborative projects. *ReCALL, 16*(1), 5–19.

O'Dowd, R., & Ritter, M. (2006). Understanding and working with 'failed communication' in telecollaborative exchanges. *CALICO Journal, 23*, 623–642.

Pegrum, M. (2009). *From blogs to bombs: The future of digital technologies in education.* Perth: University of Western Australia Press.

Raith, T. (2010). *Kompetenzen für aufgabenorientiertes Fremdsprachenunterrichten. Eine qualitative Untersuchung zur Ausbildung von Fremdsprachenlehrkräften.* [*Competences for task-based foreign language teaching. A qualitative research project focussing on the education of foreign language teachers*]. Frankfurt: Peter Lang.

Samuda, V., & Bygate, M. (2008). *Tasks in second language learning.* New York: Palgrave Macmillan.

Schocker-v. Ditfurth, M. (2001). *Forschendes Lernen in der fremdsprachlichen Lehrerbildung.* [*Learning by doing research in foreign language teacher education*]. Tübingen: Narr.

Skehan, P. (2007). Language instruction through tasks. In J. Cummins & C. Davison (Eds.), *International handbook of English language teaching. Part I* (pp. 289–301). New York: Springer.

Thomas, M., & Reinders, H. (2010). *TBLT and technology.* Philadelphia: John Benjamins Publishing Company.

Thorne, S. (2004). Cultural historical activity theory and the object of innovation. In O. St. John, K. van Esch & E. Schalkwijk (Eds.), *New insights into foreign language learning and teaching* (pp. 51–70). Frankfurt: Lang.

Ulichny, P., & Schoener, W. (1996). Teacher-researcher collaboration from two perspectives. *Harvard Educational Review, 66*, 496–524.

Van den Branden, K. (2006). *Task-based language education. From theory to practice.* Cambridge: Cambridge University Press.

Van den Branden, K., Van Gorp, K., & Verhelst, M., (Eds.) (2007). *Tasks in action: Task-based language education from a classroom-based perspective* (pp. 32–67). Newcastle: Cambridge Scholars Publishing.

Warschauer, M., & Shetzer, H. (2000). An electronic literacy approach to network-based language teaching. In M. Warschauer & R. Kern (Eds.), *Network-based language teaching: Concepts and practice* (pp. 171–185). Cambridge: Cambridge University Press.

Ware, P. D. (2005) "Missed" communication in online communication: Tensions in a German-American telecollaboration. *Language Learning & Technology, 9*(2), 64–89. Downloaded 28 June 2010 from <http://llt.msu.edu/vol9num2/ware/default.html>.

Yin, R. (2003). *Case study research: Design and methods (3rd edition).* Thousand Oaks, CA: Sage Publishing.

Appendix 1: Parts A – C

Part A: Data from the forum of group 10 over the course of the project (October 23rd, 2007 – December 20th, 2007)

Task 2 (analyzing and designing grammar task)

Tim (Nov. 7th): What are these 5 comments connected to? (principles of grammar teaching Olga had sent) What are the questions that you were answering?

Olga (Nov. 7th): The questions we answered are posted at the very top of the forum list in moodle – it's Task 2.

Olga (Nov. 10th): Well, concerning the "choices" you talked about Tim, I think first we should agree on concentrating on the present progressive only because this is what the task says (explains working procedure of how to come to a result in the group) Or should we rather set up a time for a chat, so that we can talk about the task more easily?

Olga (Nov. 11th): Thanks for the edited version, Tim! It's good that you added the "Express yourself" task. I guess we must have overlooked it. I tried to add the task into the other categories as well (context, purpose...) Would you mind having a look again? And how do you like the chart?

Tim (Nov. 11th): Thanks for your work Olga!! The chart looks wonderful. I reread the whole thing again, and when I got to part 5, I made some changes. I put it together with a variety of options and some follow-up. If you'd rather not keep the changes I made, we can go back to version 2.

Olga (Nov 12th): Thanks for your additional parts, Tim! I think we could post the document as our final version now. [...]. I'll post it in a new forum topic, so that the document can be identified as final version more easily. Good work guys.

Task 3 (analyzing and designing reading tasks)

Olga (Nov. 20th): As our work is still going to continue for a little while, it would be really nice for us to know how you look. So, why haven't you added a picture to your profiles? [...] This would be much nicer than just talking to a smiley and a name.

Task 4 (comparing textbook tasks/ designing lesson plan – focus on reading tasks again)

Olga (Nov. 27th): I posted my contributions to task 4 in Wiki.

Tim (Nov. 30th): I looked at the wiki this morning and it was empty. What is a wiki anyway?

Olga & Anna (Dec.4th): Unfortunately, we had to redo the task that you did because you didn't work with the principles at all. Please work on task 4 step 1–5 today. Make sure you use the PPP structure.

Tim: Wow, I really messed up. This whole assignment has been so confusing and again, I just realized what you two were asking us to do in class last night.

Olga (Dec. 5th): Unfortunately I have to say that I don't like the idea of splitting up the different principles and using only one principle for each task.(...) Also I think you did not really analyse your tasks.

Jie (Dec. 6th): Please check my document again and you'll see that I did not SPLIT the principles for any single task.

Tim (Dec. 6th): Hey Group. I sense a certain amount of end of the semester frayed nerves. I know mine are. Let's try to get beyond the nerves and just get on with the task.

Olga (Dec. 13th): Thanks for the document. It is very detailed – looks good to me. During reading task: [...] I don't think it is good to prohibit the use of dictionaries. I mean, they could use an English-English dictionary to work out the meaning of unknown words. How should the students be able to explain something they don't know if they are not allowed to use materials to make sure they are on the right rack? And what exactly is the product of this task? A list of weak explanations on the board? I think instead it would be nice to have each group telling a short summary of their passage.

Tim (Dec. 14th): Olga you bring up some very good points. I made a few changes by incorporating some of your ideas and making my methods a bit clearer. Let me know if it looks OK to you.

Olga & Anna (Dec. 18th): Thank you for your work. We wish you a Merry Christmas and a happy New Year.

Tim & Jie (Dec. 18th): Thanks to you as well for all of your hard work!! Und ein Froehliche Weihnachtszeit und eine gluecklisches Neues Jahr (I hope I didn't butcher that too badly…)

Part B: Olga's post-questionnaire (summary) (right after the project on Dec. 22nd)

I was absolutely satisfied with the content of our final product, however I was not happy about the division of labor in the group and with the development of the final version. It always seemed to be our job to work out the final document and there were several misunderstandings during the working process for this task.

I learned that it is necessary to give very clear task instructions in order to make the tasks as definite as possible. This can be applied in my own classroom teaching with the help of appropriate preparation and several checks of the actual formulation of the task. Furthermore, I experienced the importance of checking that the students' work is equal on both sides. This could be realized by having the students giving comments on the group work regularly, beginning at an early stage already.

I definitely feel motivated to use such a project in my own teaching. It is a great opportunity to get in touch with native speakers and to learn about a different culture. All learners should be trained in using the provided facilities to communicate, such as Wiki.

From this project I learned how to evaluate and redesign tasks effectively. Furthermore, I could improve the ability to put myself in the students' situation to find out if a task is appropriate or not. The teachers should check the working processes in the groups right from the beginning. The learners should be given some rules of how to communicate, e.g. how to react if there was an annoying incident.

Part C: Magnifying glass (individual brainstorming – January 2008)

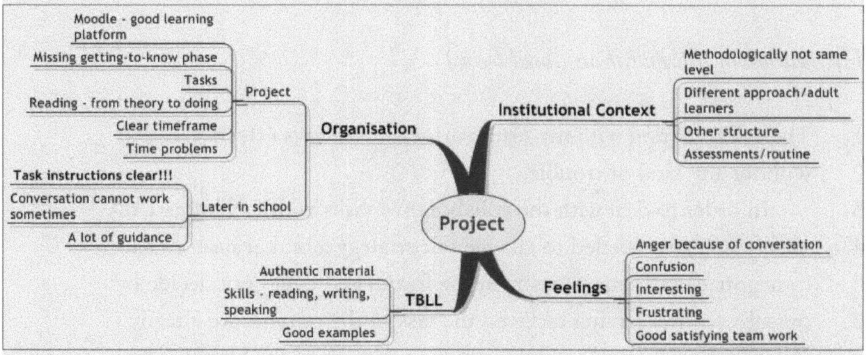

Appendix 2: Part D

Part D: Olga's Portfolio (this was handed in March 2008)

Evaluation of collaboration (local team)

The collaboration with my team partner was always effective and without any kind of trouble.

In order to deal with the collaborative tasks with Columbia University (CU) we needed to change our strategy a bit because we had to negotiate with our partners in the forum and could not decide by ourselves. After having received the task in the seminar we already started to work on our contributions so that we were able to post them in the forum right away if it was our turn. This was supposed to make it easier for our partners because then they already had something to look at when they attended their seminar.

During the week, everybody posted their ideas in the forum and I only needed to contact my local partner when there was a problem. To me it was very positive that we always decided together on how to answer posts, which implied misunderstandings concerning the content, and we wrote our replies together during the seminar. This way of collaboration made it possible for us to discuss first if we both interpreted the CU reactions identically and then both of us could think about what to answer in order to formulate an appropriate reply. I think that this method is very important since it could happen that a person misinterprets a post and therefore might overreact, which would cause further problems.

Another positive experience was the subdivision of tasks in my local team with the aim of arranging the parts of a task so that everyone had the same amount of work to do. We always made equal contributions to tasks, whether working individually at home or together in class. I also enjoyed that we were able to learn from each other while solving the assignments because if one person could not come up with an answer the other person was able to help, which had a great learning effect. Collectively, I was very pleased with the work of my local team since we tried to keep in touch as much as possible and thus we were able to be very flexible. This highly depends on the students' willingness to work and to engage with the whole project.

One possibility that comes to my mind in order to improve cooperation would be the introduction of another forum in Moodle for the work of the teams in class. This would be a possibility for the instructor to check if the working process is going alright or if there are any problems, like one-sided work or difficulties in time management. Of course, such a forum could also influence cooperation in a negative way because some students might not be able to talk feely then and will feel controlled and moreover this would be additional work for the instructor. However, it could be possible to arrange part of the working process in such a forum, so that the students do not need to use it all the time, but perhaps for certain parts of a task.

Another important point to improve the effectiveness of teamwork is the predefinition of several deadlines for parts of a task, so that it becomes clear to everyone when the work should be started, which means that the problem of students who put their work off until the last minute can be avoided.

PH Heidelberg – Columbia U Teams (contribution to professional development)

To me, it was difficult then to decide if we should tell our partners that they did not do their job very well, and that we could not accept their version. Such situations helped me to develop a sense for the right amount of directness which will be very helpful for my further career as a teacher.

The tool called "Wiki" in Moodle was very helpful for negotiation because we could work on one single page without having to open new forum topics and could directly comment on passages which needed to be discussed. Despite these possibilities sometimes it was hard to negotiate because in my group there were several misunderstandings concerning the task instructions which caused confusion. In a few situations I also had the impression that the CU team did not want to negotiate since they had their own ideas, and did not take our comments into consideration or simply did not reply to our comments anymore. In my opinion, this is not very sensitive because a person should at least tell her/his reasons for not taking a suggestion into consideration. To sum up, I learned that negotiation also means to realize when team partners do not want to discuss their work any further and to respect and accept this.

Furthermore, I developed an idea about how to formulate suggestions for improvement without having the other person feeling offended, which is very important and I also learned that negotiating a common focus is the essential basis for effective group work. The communication channels I preferred for negotiation were the forum and Wiki. I liked the forum because everybody could see what the others wrote, so the communication between all group members stayed clear and traceable.

Wiki would have been a great tool as well, however our CU team was not really able to work with it due to a lack of knowledge about how to use it properly. So communication stopped suddenly and they continued posting comments in the form, which was ok for us though.

I was a little surprised about the friendliness in their final mail after all the problems in task 4 and had to smile about their attempt to write in German. To me, this message showed that they might have liked to know a little more about our culture although they always kept a certain distance, since they never showed pictures of themselves and misspelled our names, which actually symbolizes a little indifference. Probably, the context in which this project was placed did not leave any room for them to show more interest since they simply had a lot of work to do and furthermore received grades for their work, which is an additional stress. Therefore I think it is essential to create a good personal level by using a chat at the beginning of the a project so that the groups know each other and can deal with problems more easily.

Summary: Criteria for E-mail Projects

Initiation: Talking about the students' expectations before the project as well as a discussion about fears, obscurities or possible problems which could occur during the project.

Support:

If possible, arrange a chat at the beginning of the project.

Offer possibilities for the students to create a personal level with their partners as this is the basis for effective group work.

Create meaningful tasks by applying TBLL-principles.

Always give clear task instructions and include deadlines for handing in the final version as well as parts of the task.

Provide an early check of the working processes in the groups.

Provide possibilities for peer evaluation before the project is done so that there is a chance to work on problems.

Teacher intervention in a group's working process should only happen in extreme cases (great communication problems; insult).

Provide possibilities for the class to check the results of other groups and to compare own work with work of others.

Language Learning in Virtual Worlds – Research Issues and Methods

LUISA PANICHI & MATS DEUTSCHMANN

Virtual worlds are increasingly being used for educational purposes and for language education in particular. They are not only appealing platforms for distance language education and useful complements to face-to-face or classroom-based language education, but they are also being used for informal learning outside institutional settings.

Although teaching in virtual worlds represents one of the more recent developments in online education, this mode of teaching is paradoxically often closer to traditional face-to-face teaching than many other forms of online education (through a Learning Management System (herein LMS), for instance). Virtual worlds are, for example, highly reliant on synchronous communication and times and places for meetings have to be organised just as in real life (RL) education. Further, the physical appearance of students and teachers through avatars will affect our first impressions of each other (just as they would in a physical classroom). Similarly, the design of the physical (digital) space may influence the learning event, just as the choice of arrangements of desks in a classroom, for example, may do. Since most virtual worlds are more or less open, we can also get unexpected visitors joining an event just as someone may knock on the classroom door.

Of course, many features are different too: you cannot fly or teleport yourself in RL, and you cannot change your appearance or gender at the press of a button, and you certainly cannot build a new university building in an afternoon. Nevertheless, we argue that virtual worlds represent a different type of online learning situation from LMS-based environments, therefore meriting special attention when it comes to the potential for research. Note here, however, that many virtual worlds such as Second Life® (SL) are also being integrated into LMS environments through tools such as SLOODLE (integrating Moodle and SL) and through the new generations of viewers, which allow efficient two-dimensional (2D) integration of content into the three-dimensional (3D) world of SL.

This chapter will illustrate some of the environmental features of virtual worlds that make them particularly attractive to practitioners interested in carrying out research into language learning and teaching as well as telecollaborative activities involving SLA. We will also try to illustrate some of the specific challenges that need to be considered when conducting language research in virtual world environments. One of these includes ethical issues, where the representation of the self through an online alter ego is creating the need for new ethical considerations on questions such as online privacy and security, and learners' personal data disclosure (cf. Sadler, 2008; Wang & Heffernan, 2010). Finally, we will attempt to give a brief overview of current research into language learning in virtual worlds and propose areas of potential future research.

Virtual worlds as closed or open environments

Virtual worlds, such as Second Life®, are often open environments. In this case human interaction and human language encounters of the more spontaneous informal kind are easy to observe first hand as an avatar. In other words, the researcher is free to observe human interaction as it would occur in more or less public places like the street or the local square or in a university cafeteria, for example, or any other location where people meet spontaneously. Other situations in Second Life® are more orchestrated or programmed, and people come together because they have made an arrangement to do so. This includes the case, for example, of structured learning events in SL, where students and teachers gather together in the same location at the same time in order to participate in an educational event just as they would on any other distance education platform for synchronous communication or in a face-to-face classroom or lecture theatre. These encounters can theoretically take place anywhere in the open space of SL, but more commonly they do so in a more sheltered educational space, which has often been built by the educational institution providing the learning event. Indeed, many educational bodies own and build their own spaces so that they have control over the activities and the identity of users in that specific space.

In virtual world environments of this kind, restrictions to access to certain spaces can be put into place so that the privacy of the learning event and community is established. In addition to this, Second Life®, for example, until recently made available a 'teen grid', which was a different grid to the main world, and to which the owners and creators of SL, Linden Lab, had greater levels of control over content and the entry of end-users. Many educational bodies opted for the teen grid of SL for education with users aged 13 to 17[1].

Other virtual worlds such as Activeworlds and OpenSim enable the end user to create, tailor and host a private virtual world on their own server. In other words, an educational institution can gain access to a private world which carries with it all the main design features of virtual worlds but which is not open to the general public. In this sense the virtual world can be defined as "closed." Here access is only available to students and educators who have been identified by the educational body that has contracted the virtual world and which has total control and responsibility over access, privacy and security. In this sense, this type of virtual worlds hosts a closed community which is predetermined by an educational body.

1 Unfortunately, following the lowering of the access age from 18 to 16 for SL and changes to the rating of SL environments, Linden Lab has shut down the Teen Grid. However, the Teen Grid remains a good example of how virtual worlds can be used successfully with children and young adults.

In view of the above, it is fair to say that virtual worlds offer a variety of contexts for educational observation: from informal learning and interaction in naturalistic open environments, to more structured learning in controlled and sometimes closed learning environments. Obviously, the range of possibilities on the scale open-closed (and informal and formal learning) described above has consequences for research design and research ethics.

Virtual Worlds as Environment for Telecollaborative Activities

In some respects virtual worlds are ideal for telecollaboration. As mentioned above, they often constitute open, publically available environments accessible to anyone with the required hardware and bandwidth. This obviously facilitates logistics in a telecollaborative project (given that the technical requirements and skills are met of course). In addition, the three-dimensional make-up of virtual worlds adds to the sense of presence and the feeling that you are actually in the same space adding to group bonding. There are other affordances which make virtual worlds such as Second Life® particularly interesting for telecollaboration. Not only do they cater for various modes of Computer-Mediated Communication, henceforth CMC (see section below), but they also allow students to manipulate and create digital objects together in the learning environment.

There are examples of successful telecollaborative projects which have exploited this affordance. *The Centre for Computing* (CCH) at King's College London and *Informatica Umanistica* (InfoUma) at Pisa University, for example, ran a project whereby students collaborated in creating representations of culturally important historical buildings (the Tower of London and the Leaning Tower of Pisa). One of the motivations for the project in addition to the specific curricula goals of the involved partners was that "students have the opportunity to learn about different cultures and acquire language skills" (Bani *et al.* 2009: 127). These ambitions correspond closely to Belz's (2003) definition of telecollaboration as the use of different types of Internet communication tools in order to support social interaction, dialogue, debate, and intercultural exchange between internationally-dispersed learners in parallel language classes.

Virtual worlds can also be used in telecollaborative activities as environments for exploration. In the course *Business Talking* given by Linnaeus University, Sweden in collaboration with University of Central Missouri, USA, Swedish students are designated American "buddies", who show them around various locations in Second Life® at the start of a course. The American students all attend a course on Cyber culture and are experienced SL users. In this way, the Swedish "newbies" are introduced to the culture of SL, as well as being exposed to the target language and American native speakers.[2]

As is the case with all telecollaboration, one of the main challenges is designing meaningful activities that are relevant to all partners involved. As pointed out by several authors (Dooly, 2008; O'Dowd & Ritter, 2006; Belz & Muller-Hartmann, 2003), careful planning needs to precede a telecollaborative activity so that socio-institutional factors as well as individual factors that may sabotage a fruitful collaboration are taken into consideration in the planning stage. Using virtual worlds as a tool for collaboration may involve added challenges in this respect. Firstly, the fact that virtual worlds are largely a synchronous environment means that extra attention has to be paid to time differences and differences in the academic calendars between the partner universities. Secondly, if students are working from computers on-campus there may well be technical aspects such as security matters related to fire-walls and security settings that have to be considered prior to a collaborative event. A third consideration to be taken into account is that virtual worlds are in general synchronous environments where several different activities may be

2 For a more thorough description of the Business Talking course, see Richardson (n.d.) <http://avalonlearning.pbworks.com/w/page/7682802/Business-Talking>.

taking place at the same time and in the same area. A virtual world learning space is, in other words, much harder to manage and monitor than a traditional on-line conferencing system such as Adobe Connect, for example, which may lead to problems when it comes to assessment, documentation and data collection.

Given the complex nature of the learning environments, planning and close monitoring of course activities are of great importance in virtual world telecollaboration. Here the developer/researcher may benefit from using theoretical models to help structuring this work. In course trials under the EU-funded AVALON project,[3] for example, Activity Theory was used both in the planning and evaluation stages of the course in order to highlight different aspects which were affecting the motivation and engagement of students (Molka-Danielsen & Deutschmann, 2009).

The Environment from a Researcher Perspective

In this section we discuss a number of issues that are relevant from a more practical research perspective. These include the types of data that are retrievable from virtual world environments, data collection methods, as well as technical and attitudinal factors that may affect learners' observed behaviour.

Affordances for Communication and Types of Language Data

In language education, virtual worlds are used as a CMC platform particularly suited for synchronous voice and chat communication. Most worlds have built-in voice chat that can accommodate simultaneous conversations of groups of up to approximately 30 partici-

3 <http://avalonlearning.eu>.

pants. Text chat is another synchronous communicative affordance, and most worlds have built in tools for saving and retrieving chat logs. The potential for multimodality in communication is further enhanced by private text and voice IM (instant messaging) that also tend to be default communicative features of most virtual world environments. This, of course, complicates matters from a data collection point of view, as one is never fully aware of all the potential private conversations that may be going on parallel to the public communication. Virtual worlds also allow for asynchronous written communication through the use of notecard messages that can be sent to individuals and groups.

In addition to this, and unlike other online CMC platforms, the 3D rendering of the environment coupled with the building features available to all users, as well as the representation of the self via an avatar, mean that a wide range of non-verbal communicative channels are also available to the user. For example, most worlds include non-verbal default communicative gestures where scripts for events such as "bowing", "blowing a kiss", "yawning" or "clapping" are activated through a simple click. In addition, performative non-verbal communication such as giving someone a present or physical positioning (whether one is close or far from one's interlocutor, for example) may impact on the communicative process. Similarly, the building or creation of spaces, the use of artefacts and the modelling of the avatar will influence communicative processes, as well as open up the possibilities for aesthetic communication.

In other words, "communication" in virtual worlds in a broader sense is a complex issue involving (a) synchronous and asynchronous multimodal linguistic communication, where both public and potentially private communication can take place simultaneously; (b) non-verbal communication through gestures and body positioning; and (c) aesthetic communication through the representation of self both in terms of appearance via one's avatar, i.e. the 3D rendering of oneself, and the use of personal space. In addition to this, the design of the 'space' may also influence communicative processes.

Another consideration for researchers to be aware of is the intra-world culture in terms of narrative framework and rules. To illustrate this compare, for example, World of Warcraft, for which there are strict and narrow game rules and narratives against those with looser narrative frameworks (e.g. Second Life® as a freer environment with fewer defined rules and structures). This in-world cultural variable will obviously influence the design of any learning and/or research activity allocated to the specific world. For example, in World of Warcraft, a learning event may have to be built into a gaming narrative and the students may be entering as "trolls", "orcs", "dwarfs" or "blood elves" and carry with them a long history of "local" culture, including language norms.

This raises the following questions: What channels of communication, and which environmental features that may influence these are of interest to the researcher? Should the entire communicative event be recorded (i.e. verbal, non-verbal and representational forms of communication)? What are the implications of taking one or two isolated communicative functions out of their original context? How much of the in-world culture needs to be taken into consideration? To what extent are avatar histories and personal stories relevant to the discussion of research outcomes? There are no simple answers to these questions, as they will differ depending on the individual research question and the resources available to the researcher. It is important, though, that these questions be raised at an early stage of the research process so that a reasonable balance can be achieved between the need to research a specific area or answer a specific research question and the wealth and complexity of information that is available. The decision of what data is of interest will also impact on the data collection procedures, and more specifically on what recording devices and methods are chosen.

In some of our own research, for example, we focussed on how supportive moves made by the teacher encourage learners to engage with language, what type of linguistic behaviour in the learners leads to engagement in others, and how the affordances of the virtual world environment affected these (Deutschmann & Panichi, 2009a).

Here we chose to limit ourselves to spoken discourse and we focussed specifically on supportive moves, (i.e. when active listening is being signalled linguistically through acknowledgments, minimal responses such as *uhu* and *aha* and follow-up questions). We were interested in how this type of linguistic behaviour affected turn-taking and student participation. Accordingly, we recorded all the lessons and measured floor space for each student as well as the turn-taking patterns, but we only needed to transcribe the specific parts of the conversations which included supportive moves. In this way, we could rationalise the data collection. Based on the analysis of this data we could conclude that the supportive linguistic behaviour of teachers was important in increasing learner activity in a virtual world environment and that this was particularly true in the early stages of a course.

Observing and Recording Data in Virtual Worlds

The choice of which data to record will, as suggested in the previous sections, depend not only on what is of interest to a researcher but also on what time and financial resources are available. On the simplest level we have the retrieval of chat logs, for which most virtual world environments have built-in functions. This public chat data may need to be complemented with voice recordings, in which case there are a number of free software options that work directly with the computer's sound card, such as Audacity (which works both for Macs and PCs). In addition, many virtual worlds have default tools for capturing images (and if they do not, simple screen capture is an obvious option), and it may well be the case that the purely linguistic content of communicative events (written and/or spoken) coupled with still images to describe the environmental setting is good enough to record the necessary observational data for a research project. If this is the case, recording empirical data is relatively straightforward. However, note that exact time references need to be reported when recording voice and chat separately so that these communicative modes can be matched at a later date. If we as researchers need to go further and record other events in the environment, things become more complex.

Unfortunately, to date, most of the virtual worlds that are popular for education to do not have their own built-in recording system, so all recordings of virtual world events require the use of external recording software on one's own computer. There are several programmes on the market that will allow for the recording of events in virtual worlds and, as expected, different systems require different programmes. Here the two main options are: programmes that merely capture the visuals, creating a movie which can later be matched with audio recording and chat files (programmes such as Jing or Screen Flow in combination with Audacity or Sunflower, for example) or software which captures both audio and images (Fraps, Camtasia or Camstudio, just to mention a few). Although often preferable, one should be aware of the complications of using software that captures both sound and images simultaneously.

Firstly, note that it is often impractical to record via screen capture programs while interacting with other avatars in the environment from the same computer which is recording the event. Most screen capture programs do not allow simultaneous recording of in and out sound, and thus the only practical way of capturing sound and images during an event is to have a second person present through a so-called "dummy avatar", whose sole task is to follow the events and to record them through his/her computer screen capture software. For those researchers that are also teachers of the learning event, one thus needs to bear in mind that two avatars and two computers will usually be necessary, and when movement is involved it is difficult to coordinate both the avatars and still focus on participating in the events going on.

Secondly, it is often tricky to get settings right for the recording of sound and images, so it is advisable to do test runs prior to the event to check that all systems are functioning correctly and that the correct in and out audio-channels are being recorded. From experience, we can note that it is extremely frustrating to record 90 minutes of crucial research data only to find that sound was not captured because the external speakers, rather than the head-set output was being recorded! Finally, one should also be aware of the fact that recording sound and images usually renders extremely large files (often in excess of several gigabytes) and researchers will need to ensure that the computer which is being used for data collection is up to the task.

When considering data collection in virtual worlds we must also be aware of their three-dimensional nature. For example, when recording through a dummy avatar it is only that avatar's angle of perception that is recorded. This may be problematic in such cases in which many conversations are going on in different locations of an environment. The sound in worlds such as Second Life® simulates real life sound behaviour in terms of volume and distance, so that avatars can hear each other more loudly when close and more faintly when far apart, and not at all when very far apart. Also note that chats are also only recorded when avatars are relatively close to each other, so that there may be several parallel chats going on at different locations of an educational space.

As is the case with the recording of face-to-face language learning events, recordings are thus primarily limited to teacher-group activities. If learners break up into smaller groups and move to other locations for pair work and are out of sound reach or in a soundproof area that is out of local chat reach and out of sight within the virtual world, then their activities and sound will not be recorded. Learner activity can however be tracked by asking students to save copies of their individual chats or instant message exchanges. Recordings of their voice chat and performance within the environment will not be recorded unless students themselves record what happens to their avatar via their individual computers with the appropriate screen capture technology. Note, however, that snapshots are a feature of many virtual worlds and can be used as student documentation of the places they have visited and the activities they have carried out together with a post-narrative of the student-led event.

Virtual world educational events can also be observed via the researcher/observer's avatar as direct observation, as one would do if one were observing a face-to-face lesson. Here a simple notepad might be the only extra equipment necessary. In direct observation, the observer/avatar can also be a "living" part of the environment and can move around with the students and teachers and interact with them if required by the research design. Finally, it is important to note the potential impact on the social dynamics that observation and/or recording (via an interactive or dummy avatar) may have (cf. observer's paradox, Labov, 1972: 209). Since participants should always be informed that they are being recorded or observed, such effects in a virtual world are comparable to the impact that an observer or a video camera might have in face-to-face learning and teaching situation. However, it might also be argued that the presence of an "observer" avatar is more discreet than that of an observer in a classroom since no recording devices are visible. However, we would argue that this feature of "discreetness" should not be taken as a green light for not informing the research subjects (see also the section on *Ethical issues and copyright* below).

User Technical Ability and Environmental Impact

A crucial aspect to bear in mind when observing avatar verbal and non-verbal behaviour in the environment is that of "user technical ability", "emotional comfort" and "technical factors", and the impact that these may have on what we observe in the virtual world. It may thus be erroneous to draw conclusions about the communicative intentions of a user based solely on the observed behaviour in the environment. Firstly, unlike face-to-face communication in which we are all more or less versed and which we have been developing since birth, it cannot be taken for granted that learners in virtual worlds are at ease in the communicative setting and in full control of the expressive potential of the environment. The fact that a student is not responding to chat messages may thus be a result of inability to operate the tool, rather than a disinclination to communicate. Secondly, even experienced users come up against technical problems with sound transmission, and the impact of such technical aspects on the communicative event also needs to be considered. Here again, silence, for example, may be the result of a dysfunctional microphone rather than shyness.

As a researcher, it is therefore often necessary to include information about the learners and their experience of the environment in the research design. In addition, disruptive technical failings need to be noted. In a sense it can be argued that the development of communicative competence in virtual worlds is similar to the development of communicative competence in the foreign language. For language learners in virtual worlds, the communicative situation is doubly critical: they are required to communicate in a language which is not their own and in an environment in which they are often complete novices.

In the research we have conducted to date we have thus tried to complement recording of data with questionnaires and surveys aimed at providing us with information about learner profiles in terms of technical competence and attitudes towards the environment (Deutschmann & Panichi, 2009a; Deutschmann, Panichi, & Molka-Danielsen, 2009). In addition, we have often felt the need to conduct complementary interviews (face-to-face or in software such as Skype), where students have a chance to talk about issues such as technical failures, etc. A pre-requisite for such complementary data collection is that one makes sure that one knows how to reach participants outside the virtual world, something which may seem obvious, but which is easily forgotten as we often primarily tend to identify our research subjects through their avatar alter egos.

Collecting this type of data often reveals hidden aspects that may be of interest to the researcher. For example, in one recent study (Deutschmann, Molka-Danielsen, & Panichi, 2011) post-course questionnaires revealed that one of the things students felt was missing from the technical initiation in the course was information about how to improve the appearance of their avatar. This was not mentioned during the actual course but could have improved engagement and the feeling of comfort of the students (who wants an ugly avatar after all?). As teachers, we just assumed that no complaints meant that things were fine. We had not considered the potential importance of the avatar in identity construction in collaborative virtual world environments, an aspect which opens up an entire new field of potential research.

Ethical Issues and Copyright

Because of their nature, virtual worlds challenge research ethics in many exciting ways. In this section we will limit ourselves to a discussion of the special ethical dilemmas raised by virtual worlds: namely privacy, avatar identity and consent, and copyright, while taking more or less for granted the general ethical issues of any Internet research and domain-specific research. However, we have collected here a few of the most general and common recommendations for which there would seem to be a certain degree of consensus in the educational community and which it makes sense to discuss with reference to virtual worlds.

There are three layers of ethical issues to be considered when conducting research in virtual worlds, e.g. the Association of Internet Researcher's – AoIR – Ethics Guide 2002.[4] The first layer is made up of general research concerns, which are relevant for all research into language learning: participant informed consent and appropriate use of the research data collected. More specifically, issues that may be relevant are: form of consent (in writing, orally), and legal age of consent. These issues are addressed in many of the most commonly available research guides in the social sciences in general and in the field of Second Language Research more specifically (for a recent

4 <http://www.aoir.org/reports/ethics.pdf>.

review of resources, see Thomas, 2009; for a comprehensive overview see Mackey & Gass, 2005). As with all research in the social sciences, the main recommendation is that there be no harm to the participants deriving from the research and that, if possible harm is identified, measures be taken to minimise that risk.

In addition to this, there are ethical issues which are general for online communication (Capurro & Pingel, 2002) and online and Internet research. For example, the Association of Internet Researchers Guide on Ethics (Ess & the AoIR ethics working group, 2002) underlines how the distinction between public and private spaces is often blurred. The researcher needs to pay attention to the "perception" of private and public as experienced by the research *subject* and it should not necessarily be based on the researchers' perception or general assumptions. In addition to this, the researcher needs to consider the venue where the human interaction in taking place (in our case, virtual worlds) and consider its specific expectations of privacy, either implied or made explicit in policy statements, for example. Last but not least, the AoIR Guide (2002) also talks about the need for a multidisciplinary and multicultural approach to ethics in the internet/global age where it cannot be assumed that what is perceived to be "ethical" in one domain or research culture and/or national culture is necessarily so in another.

To sum up, the following recommendations can be made when evaluating the ethics of research into virtual words. All of the following need to be taken into account: the researcher's discipline policy, the researcher's institutional policy, the venue's policy as well as national policy. As the AoIR Guide (2002) points out, since the Internet is a cross-national resource, national legal and privacy legislation of the research country and the countries under whose jurisdiction the subjects come are also areas which can be of concern when carrying out online research.

The final and third tier of ethical issues are those which arise from the specific venue, in our case virtual worlds, and will be discussed in the sections below.

Privacy and Observation in Virtual Worlds

What is unique about virtual worlds compared to videoconferencing, for example, is that they often give a *false sense of privacy* to the user and the researcher. One needs to bear in mind that, unless in specific closed or protected areas, all activity in multi-user virtual worlds is public in the sense that, just as you would walking down the street in real life or if someone walked into a room unannounced, you can be seen and overheard by others/avatars in that world. In addition to this, it is also relatively easy to "spy" on other avatars: for example, the user viewer can be used to home in on a specific conversation, even in a closed space, and you can hover over avatars without them being aware of it.

From an educational perspective, this perceived anonymity and privacy may be positive, for example in language education, where this can lead to students expressing themselves more openly or being more adventurous and taking greater initiative than they would in a face-to-face classroom. At the same time, preliminary investigations (Panichi, Deutschmann, Bryan, & Richardson, 2008) into the learner's affective experience of virtual worlds indicate that the opposite may also be true: some (inexperienced) students in virtual worlds often feel challenged and intimidated by the complexity of the environment and will shy away from interaction with other avatars. In addition to this, our preliminary investigations also indicate that some experienced virtual world gamers fail to be able to take virtual worlds seriously for "academic learning" or the learning of a foreign language and are hesitant to engage with others in the environment to this end. In this sense, degrees of *user perceived sense of protection* afforded by the use of an avatar and degrees of *user perceived sense of environmental appropriateness* for the task at hand may also be a factor the researcher may want to bear in mind.

Indeed, the AoIR Ethics Guide (2002) goes as far as to suggest that cultural differences in the perception of privacy be also considered alongside individual differences. In view of this, it would seem appropriate to recommend that individual reaction to the environment be taken into consideration as an ethical issue and that comfort and ease in and tolerance and acceptance of the environment should not be taken for granted by the researcher.

Further, from a researcher perspective, the false sense of privacy in observing human interaction may actually be one of the greatest ethical pitfalls for researchers. This characteristic, i.e. that in a way some virtual worlds are actually like a 24/7 online window onto spontaneous human interaction and behaviour, makes research into human behaviour in naturalistic settings highly attractive whatever the research focus (psychology, linguistics, anthropology, marketing, etc). (psychology, linguistics, anthropology, marketing, etc). In addition to this, the fact that human interaction can be more or less covertly observed and recorded either via an avatar of via a strategically placed object or avatar positioning makes observation and research not only easy but extremely time- and cost-effective as well.

Last but not least, the fact that people may feel freer in virtual worlds than in face-to-face contact is also interesting for research. As a result of this, yet also in addition, researchers may also want to bear in mind the effect the specific virtual world has on the avatar/user which might be different to that in another online platform or in face-to-face interaction (indeed this is a research angle in itself). For example, the representation of self via an avatar can lead to a *false sense of impunity* as some students/residents may perceive their avatars to be free of social and behavioural norms which are in place in our societies and will behave in ways that are offensive to others or perceived as being intrusive of personal space.

In response to this, there has been an increasing awareness by some virtual world providers and the educational community that virtual world behaviour needs to be regulated by the same norms that govern "real life". Linden Lab, the owners and providers of Second Life®, for example, have developed an increasingly detailed series of policies addressing privacy and user-created content (see the section on *Intellectual property and copyright* below). By the same token, consensus in the educational community is very much moving towards an understanding that virtual worlds are an extension of reality in terms of emotional response to human interaction and its affective dimension (Carter, 2010; Panichi, Deutschmann, & Molka-Danielsen, 2010). Indeed, this is one of the main reasons virtual worlds are considered such a powerful platform for online and distance education and telecollaboration in the first place. In accordance with this view, the most prominent recommendation made by the SL Association of Researchers (2010) is not surprisingly that researchers should treat virtual world research in the same way as real life research is treated. And, as mentioned in the section above, the fact that research should not violate the legal requirements for privacy protection enforced in the countries under whose jurisdiction the research and the subjects find themselves (at the time of the research and beyond?) (AoIR Ethics Guide, 2002, p. 7) thus places research ethics in a much greater playing ground than one may initially be aware of.

Avatars and Identity

It can be argued that, while avatars, user identity and the relationship between the two is one of the most exciting and powerful dimensions of virtual worlds for education in the humanities and languages, it is also one of the most challenging areas for research in virtual worlds. Not being able to identify one's subjects and the transformation of identity that is possible in the 3D world means for researchers that there will be ambiguity in gaining consent. Whose consent is received? That of the user or that of the avatar? Where is the process of getting consent carried out, in the actual venue or in another platform? (See also the section below on *Avatars and informed consent*). Furthermore, there may be additional problems related to the interpretation of results when the user's sex, age, language background, etc. are hard to identify. However, the tracing of user identity is an ethical problem which exists in Internet-based and online research in general. Capurro and Pingel (2002) state that one of the main ethical dilemmas of Internet research indeed arises from the *tension* between the proper object of research, i.e. online existence, and bodily existence.

An additional consideration may be made about the *researcher's* avatar and what we might want to call the *observer avatar paradox*. Indeed, it can be argued that the observer's paradox in real life is actually magnified in virtual worlds, where not only the observer might influence the outcome of the observation but so might the observer's avatar. It would make sense to recommend, perhaps, that the avatar of an observer and teacher/researcher be as unobtrusive as possible. Researchers may want to think carefully about how to create/dress their avatar with specific reference to the environment they will be investigating, the cultural norms of the subjects under observation and the topic of their research.

Finally, as many researchers and educational practitioners in virtual worlds know (i.e. Carter, 2009; Lim, 2009; Molka-Danielsen & Deutschmann, 2009; Deutschmann & Panichi, 2009b), virtual worlds are often experienced as a real physical, emotional, creative and artistic space by users and there is often a lot of emotional investment made by users in the creation of an avatar warranting caution to be exercised in interaction with them and all other user- generated content. Researchers may also want to bear this in mind in particular in view of recent recognition of copyright in user-generated content by some virtual world providers, as will be discussed in the section below on *Intellectual property and copyright.*

Avatars and Informed Consent

Informed consent is a term which appears consistently in the literature and conversations about research ethics. Examples of research in virtual worlds which has made use of informed consent can be found in the research carried out by the authors. In Deutschmann *et al.* (2009) and Deutschmann & Panichi (2009a) we recorded all lessons we taught in SL as part of two Academic English courses we ran with students formally enrolled with our institutions. The implications of this in terms of ethical research issues is that informed consent for participation was easy to access and was clearly structured within both our institutional settings and the domain of our research discipline. Students initially were informed in writing (and they agreed in writing) that all lessons would be recorded for language education research purposes prior to the course commencement and that greater information about the scope of the research would be provided to them at the end of the course. The consent form explained that the full scope of our research could not be revealed to them until the end of the course so as not to influence the outcome of the research. Upon completion of the course, students then went through a second phase of written informed consent where the specific scope and purpose of the research was made clear to them.

In addition to this, as our focus was to analyse student and teacher discourse, we only looked at records of the text chat and listened to recordings of our lessons where all avatars were identified as real life students and both avatar and real life identity were kept anonymous. In our research structure, student avatars were perceived by all participants as an extension of a real life individual and were treated with the same level of privacy and anonymity as participants in classroom research which is video recorded. In other words, our research did not involve subjects that were not enrolled within our institutions, and classes took place on educational islands which did not attract other virtual world residents and where we were able to keep a record of who was in our vicinity during lessons. In addition to this, all students involved in the research had no previous knowledge of the virtual worlds and had created an avatar purely so that they could attend our courses (i.e. we did not have to deal with avatar history and in-world status issues of the end-user avatar).

In ongoing research we have been involved in under the EU-funded project AVALON for the development of language learning scenarios in virtual worlds, we have, however, had to extend our written consent form to include issues such as privacy rights of avatars and consent about the use of photos and recordings where avatars are identifiable. This is because we collected data of all activity under the project (not only voice and text chat) and because many of the participants in our programmes were not necessarily easy to trace through our institutions nor were they necessarily residents in nations with similar privacy legislation. Indeed, many course participants under the AVALON project were recruits directly from Second Life® activities under the project that did not necessarily take place on islands where we were the estate or land owner (see the section below on *Intellectual property and copyright*).

Capurro and Pingel (2002), however, in their discussion of ethical issues in online communication research go on to question what is actually meant by "informed consent" and, along similar lines of argument as the AoIR Guide (2002), also raise the issue of the *medium of consent*. Where does consent occur? On which platform? Via email? In writing or orally? And this brings us back to the discussion about avatar identity in the section above. When can we consider consent to be delivered? Via the avatar in the virtual world or via the avatar's user identity on another platform? These are all questions we feel that researchers should bear in mind when addressing informed consent in virtual worlds.

Intellectual Property and Copyright

Several virtual worlds have explicit written policy to deal with the increasing complexity of intellectual property and copyright surrounding the use of virtual worlds. Second Life®, for example, has the following policies with which the researcher should be familiar: *Second Life Terms of Service*, *Snapshot and machinima policy*, *Intellectual Property policy*, *Second Life Community Standards*, *Guidelines on Using Linden Lab's Trademarks*.

These policies will inevitably lead the researcher to want to verify, for example, who is in the vicinity during recording or observation in-world, to want to know whose voice and chat is being recorded and to determine whether an unidentified avatar's name is visible in a recording. These policies provide information about where and when snapshots can be taken and user/avatar consent is required for machinimas, i.e. films carried out in Second Life®, and ownership and copyright of all user-created content including avatars and in-world land and real estate.

Similarly to the privacy issues discussed above, all policies concerning intellectual property and copyright are in line with national legislation under whose jurisdiction the virtual world provider finds itself. For issues which are not contemplated under the specific policies, reference to national legislation of the provider is made.

The Scope of Language Education and SLA Research in Virtual Worlds

To date there is still very limited research data collected and discussed regarding language education in virtual worlds because the use of these environments for language education has only really boomed since the introduction of voice chat in 2007. Most teacher and researcher activity in virtual worlds so far has been devoted to the exploration of the potential and the creation of suitable learning scenarios, the listing of best practice guidelines and the development of an understanding of the significant features for language education, e.g. Dalgarno & Lee, 2010, Lim, 2009, Deutschmann & Panichi, 2009b, Molka-Danielsen, Deutschmann, & Panichi, 2010, the EU-funded projects AVALON, AVATAR, NIFLAR, icEurope and the devoted section of the website of ICT for Language Teaching.[5]

Research by the authors has looked at levels of learner participation and engagement in structured language learning events. Learner participation was measured in terms of "floor space" i.e. how much linguistic activity was produced by the learners during the course and

5 <http://www.ict4lt.org/en/>.

how learner participation was influenced by the linguistic behaviour of the teachers, i.e. backchannelling. This research, however, is limited in scope to discourse analysis of the teacher-learner and learner-to-learner voice chat and did not look at other activity in the environment (Deutschmann & Panichi, 2009a; Deutschmann *et. al.* 2009).

Future research may want to consider learner participation in a broader context (beyond linguistic features) and look at the other communicative dimensions afforded by the environment such as the representational, performative and artistic. In particular, we feel there is a lot of unexplored territory in terms of the pragmatics of intercultural communication and non-verbal communication.

From a more specifically linguistic perspective, the environment and the recording methods discussed above make learning events in virtual worlds readily accessible to linguistic and language acquisition research in general. One area of particular interest, given the possibilities of virtual worlds in manipulating avatar identity, is sociolinguistics. HUMlab and the department of Language Studies at Umeå University in Sweden have, for example, recently developed a project which makes use of new voice morphing tools in Second Life® to enable gender research experiments whereby males can be represented via a female avatar and vice versa and lead to reflection over how gender effects how one is treated linguistically.[6]

However, researchers also need to bear in mind that although virtual worlds are defined as "open communities", or worlds, the section of society that is represented within them may be more homogeneous than the term "open" would suggest. As a researcher, one might want to consider issues such as resident/learner profiles which would include socio-economic data thus enabling us to get a more accurate view of the typical virtual learner in the interest of broader educational issues such as access to education and the adoption of new technologies by specific educational communities. An additional distinction that needs to be made is that between investi-

6 <http://assis.pbworks.com/w/page/33613545/ASSIS-A> Second Step in Second Life.

gating learner/teacher activity in a structured, institutionally promoted learning event or string of events (i.e. a course) and language acquisition and language learning that takes place spontaneously among virtual world residents.

References

Activeworlds website (n.d.) Accessed 6 February 2011 at <http://www.activeworlds.com/>.

Association of Second Life Academic Research website (n.d.) Accessed 6 February 2011 at <http://world.secondlife.com/group/9bfca9e5-ef0a-e5e4-b27a-33ecac14863d>.

Ess & the AoIR ethics working group (2002). *Association of Internet Researchers (AOIR) Ethics Guide.* Accessed 6 February 2011 at <http:// aoir.org/documents/ethics-guide/>.

AVALON website (n.d.) Accessed 6 February 2011 at <http://ava lon. humanities.manchester.ac.uk/>.

AVATAR website (n.d.) Accessed 6 February 2011 at <http:// www.avatarproject.eu/avatar/index.php>.

Bani, M., Genovesi, F., Ciregia, E., Piscioneri, F., Rapisarda, B., Salvatori, E., & Simi, M. (2009). Learning by creating historical buildings. In J. Molka-Danielsen & M. Deutschmann (Eds.), *Learning and teaching in the virtual world of second life* (pp. 125–144). Trondheim: Tapir Akademisk Forlag.

Belz, J. A. (2003). Linguistic perspectives on the development of intercultural competence in telecollaboration. *Language Learning & Technology*, *7*(2), 68–117.

Belz, J. A. & Muller-Hartmann, A. (2003). Teachers as intercultural learners: Negotiating German-American telecollaboration along the institutional fault line. *Modern Language Journal*, *87*(1), 71–89.

Capurro, R. & Pingel, C. (2002). Ethical issues of online communication research. *Ethics and Information Technology*, *4*(3), 189–194.

Carter, B. (2010). *Presence, representation and identity in virtual reality*. Paper presented at HumLab, Umeå University, Sweden, 27 April 2010.

Carter, B. (2009). Enhancing virtual environments. In J. Molka-Danielsen & M. Deutschmann (Eds.), *Learning and teaching in the virtual world of second life* (pp. 45–60). Trondheim: Tapir Akademisk Forlag.

Dalgarno, B. & M.J.W. Lee (2010). What are the learning affordances of 3-D virtual environments? *British Journal of Educational Technology 41*(1), 10–32.

Davies, G. (Ed.-in-chief) (n.d). ICT4LT. Accessed 6 February 2011 at <http://www.ict4lt.org/en/>.

Deutschmann, M., Molka-Danielsen J., & Panichi, L. (2011). Analyzing the design of telecollaboration in second life using activity theory. In A. Cheney & R. Sanders (Eds.), *Teaching and learning in 3D immersive worlds: Pedagogical models and constructivist approaches* (pp.151–167). Hershey, PA: IGI Global.

Deutschmann, M., & Panichi, L. (2009a). Talking into empty space? – Signalling involvement in a virtual language classroom in second life. *Language Awareness, 18* (3–4), 310–328.

Deutschmann, M., & Panichi, L. (2009b). Instructional design, learner modeling, and teacher practice in Second Life. In J. Molka-Danielsen & M. Deutschmann (Eds.), *Learning and teaching in the virtual world of second life* (pp. 27–44). Trondheim: Tapir Akademisk Forlag.

Deutschmann, M., Panichi, L., & Molka-Danielsen, J. (2009). Designing oral participation in second life – A comparative study of two language proficiency courses. *ReCALL, 21*(2), 70–90.

Dooly, M. (2008). *Telecollaborative language learning: A guidebook to moderating intercultural collaboration and language learning.* Bern: Peter Lang.

Ess, C., & the AoIR ethics working committee (2002). *Ethical decision-making and Internet research: Recommendations from the AoIR ethics working committee.* Downloaded 6 February 2011 from <http://www.aoir.org/reports/ethics.pdf>.

IcEurope website (n.d.) Accessed 6 February 2011 <http://www.iceurope.uni-tuebingen.de/>.

Labov, W. (1972). *Sociolinguistic patterns.* Oxford: Blackwell.

Lim, K. (2009). The six learnings of second life: A framework for designing curricular interventions in-world. *Journal of Virtual Worlds Research, 2* (1), 4–11. Downloaded 6 February 2011 from <http://journals.tdl.org/jvwr/article/view/424/466>.

Molka-Danielsen, J., & Deutschmann, M. (2009). Examining the design of learning activities in second life through the lens of activity theory. In J. Krogstie (Ed.), *NOKOBIT Proceedings* (pp. 1–12). Trondheim: Tapir Akademisk Forlag.

Molka-Danielsen, J., Deutschmann, M. & Panichi, L. (2010). Designing authentic communication for language learning in virtual space. *Designs for Learning Journal, 2* (09), 22–33.

NIFLAR website (n.d.). Accessed 6 February 2011 at <http://cms.let.uu.nl/niflar/>.

O'Dowd, R., & Ritter, M. (2006). Understanding and working with "failed communication" in telecollaborative exchanges. *CALICO Journal, 61*(2), 623–642.

OpenSim wiki (n.d). Accessed 6 Feburary 2001 at <http://open simulator.org/wiki/Main_Page>.

Richardson, D. (n.d.). *Business Talking.* Accessed 6 Februay 2011 at <http://avalonlearning.pbworks.com/w/page/7682802/Business-Talking>.

Sadler, R. (2008). *Ethical standards for research in Virtual Worlds: A call to virtual arms.* Paper presented at the EUROCALL 2008 conference New Competencies and Social Spaces, Kodolányi János University College, Székesfehérvár, Hungary, 3–6 September 2008.

Thomas, M. (2009). Ethical issues in the study of second language acquisition: Resources for researchers. *Second Language Research, 25*(4), 493–511.

Mackey, A., & Gass, S.M. (2005). *Second language research. Methodology and design.* Mahwah, NJ: Lawrence Erlbaum.

Panichi, L., Deutschmann, M., & Molka-Danielsen, J. (2010). Virtual worlds for language learning and intercultural exchange – Is it for real? In F. Helm, & S. Guth (Eds.), *Telecollaboration 2.0. Language, literacies and intercultural learning in the 21st century* (pp. 165–195). Bern: Peter Lang.

Panichi, L., Deutschmann, M., Bryan, C., & Richardson, D. (2008). *Perceptions of learning in the CMC environment of Second Life. A Swedish-American case study.* Paper presented at the CALL CMC SIG Event conference Computer Mediated Communication and Language Learning: Research and Practice, Università di Padova, Padova, Italy, 17–19 April 2008.

Second Life website (n.d.). Accessed 6 February 2011 at <http://secondlife.com/>.

Second Life Snapshot and machinima policy (n.d.). Downloaded 6 Feburary 2011 from <http://wiki.secondlife.com/wiki/Linden_Lab_Official: Snapshot_and_machinima_policy>.

Second Life Terms of Service (n.d.). Downloaded 6 Feburary 2011 from <http://secondlife.com/corporate/tos.php>.

Second Life Intellectual Property policy (n.d.). Downloaded 6 Feburary 2011 from <http://wiki.secondlife.com/wiki/Intellectual_Property>.

Second Life Community Standards (n.d.). Downloaded 6 Feburary 2011 from <http://secondlife.com/corporate/cs.php>.

Second Life Guidelines for Using Linden Lab's Trademarks (n.d.). Downloaded 6 Feburary 2011 from <http://secondlife.com/corporate/brand/trademark>.

Wang, S., & Heffernan, N. (2010). Ethical issues in computer-assisted language learning: Perceptions of teachers and learners. *British Journal of Educational Technology, 41* (5), 796–813.

World of Warcraft website (n.d.). Accessed 6 February 2011 <http://www.worldofwarcraft.com/index.xml>.

Intercultural Competence in Computer-Mediated-Communication: An Analysis of Research Methods

MARTINA MÖLLERING & MIKE LEVY

For the past twenty years, research on computer-mediated communication (CMC) in the context of language learning has been highly topical. Whereas early small-scale studies in the field were focused on synchronous, written communication in the immediate context of the language teaching classroom, research on CMC has moved from the actual to the virtual – in many cases transnational – classroom, hence the terminology: 'email-tandem', 'network-based language teaching/learning', 'telecollaboration'.

In the early phase of research into CMC, i.e. the early to mid-nineties, the focus was on synchronous CMC in a classroom context. Set against the background of a teaching paradigm where communicative competence was at the fore, classroom activities in this phase of research into CMC typically included dialogic interaction in the form of open-ended questions for discussion. Synchronous computer-mediated communication was seen to support these activities because of its perceived similarity with spoken communication. A seminal study was Kelm's (1992) investigation of the use of synchronous computer networks in SLA, a preliminary exploration of the impact of computer-assisted classroom discourse (CACD) in second language learning environments. Beauvois (1992, 1995, 1998) likened the computer-assisted discussion between language learners in a classroom setting to "conversation in slow motion" (1992: 455) and Chun (1994) anticipated it would "facilitate the acquisition of interactive competence" (p.29). In the same vein, Kern (1995) compared the quantity and characteristics of discourse through synchronous, written classroom interaction and during an oral class discussion on the same topic. The findings attest to more active communication by learners in CMC contexts (see also Warschauer, 1996), with more turns as well as more tokens produced in each turn. Contributions by learners are said to be more complex with regards to morphosyntax as well as discourse structure and communication is much more focused on the group rather than the teacher –a trend which points to a transformation of the teacher role.

At the beginning of the new millennium, research in CMC in the context of language acquisition shifted from a focus on communicative competence to an interest in intercultural competence, or rather, as defined by Byram (1997), intercultural communicative competence. One major research interest regarding CMC in the context of foreign language education is the question of the extent to which online contact actually contributes to intercultural learning. Byram (1997) differentiates between communicative competence, which focuses on the exchange of information, and intercultural competence which stresses the ability to "decentre and take up the perspective of the reader" as well as the capacity for "establishing and maintaining relationships" (p.3). Apart from this emphasis on culture learning being an interactive process, intercultural perspectives have highlighted the interconnectedness of language learning and culture learning (e.g. Kramsch, 1993), the need for learners to be able to achieve a critical distance from their own cultures (Bredella, 1999), a reflection about self and other as a reflection of intercultural learning processes (see Krumm, 1992, 1995) and the deconstruction of stereotypes and reduction of intolerance (Bredella & Delanoy, 1999) as being central elements in the development of intercultural competence. In the final section of this chapter, we will relate our evaluation of CMC research to different underlying viewpoints of culture as they have been outlined in Levy (2007).

The shift in focus from communicative to intercultural competence has been labelled as the "Intercultural Turn" by Thorne (2010). Early research studies on"online intercultural exchange", to use the umbrella term introduced by O'Dowd (2007), report mainly on asynchronous electronic communication between language learners in different locations in a so-called virtual classroom (e.g. Fischer, 1998). This field of research has been referred to as "email-tandem learning" (c.f. Woodin, 1997; Brammerts, 1998; Little & Ushioda, 1998; Appel, 1999; Appel & Mullen, 2000; Appel & Gilabert, 2002; Kötter, 2003). Language learning in tandem can be defined as a form of open learning where learners with different languages form a partnership in order to practise and improve the language they are learning. It has been thought of as a form of autonomous learning (for caveats on autonomous learning in such settings see Little & Ushioda, 1998; Little, 2001) where the focus is on learning through authentic communication with a native speaker. Two people with different native languages work together in pairs in order to help one another improve their language skills but also to learn more about each other's culture so that there is a presumed potential for intercultural learning as part of the process.

Although there is no doubt about the fact that online exchanges offer a strong potential for intercultural learning, in the early stages, there seems to have been an assumption on the part of educators that engaging learners in e-mail exchanges with members of the target culture would automatically produce more positive attitudes and a better intercultural understanding. This stance has been criticized (e.g. O'Dowd, 2003) and a number of studies have therefore stressed the importance of embedding e-mail exchanges into structured language learning environments, thus providing a bridge between the classroom and the natural language setting (Woodin, 1997) and the need for close institutional co-operation through the planning and implementation stages (e.g. Little & Ushioda, 1998; Belz, 2001, 2002; O'Dowd & Eberbach, 2004). Focusing on a task-based approach to promoting intercultural learning in electronic learning networks, Müller-Hartmann (2000) comes to the following conclusion:

> It is important to realize that to enhance intercultural learning, the close monitoring of the process by which such learning is carried out is very important. That is to say, the virtual exchange must be thoroughly integrated into the local context of classroom instruction. [...]And it is here that the task-based approach develops its fullest potential by allowing learners to develop and ex-

> press their views, thus making real communication possible and consequently setting the stage to initiate processes of intercultural learning. p. 145)

In this chapter, the focus is on research that explores how online intercultural exchanges might contribute to intercultural learning. Many of the projects discussed are theory-driven taking their inspiration from Vygotsky, sociocultural theory or the notion of intercultural competence (see Lomicka, 2006; Byram, 1997). As well as enabling contact and interaction with native speakers, these environments for intercultural learning provide students with the opportunities to reflect on both their own culture and the culture of the language they are learning, and in the most successful projects develop into fully functioning online communities of practice (see Darhower, 2007).

Since most culture learning projects with new technologies are collaborative, the limitations and constraints of culture learning in this context are often associated not with the technology itself, but with difficulties for learners in sustaining a meaningful cross-cultural language exchange. That is why the vast majority of intercultural collaborative projects place special emphasis on the pedagogy or methodology. While this should always be the case for all the language skills, perhaps it emerges with more urgency in cross-cultural exchanges because of the recognized possibilities of failed communication across cultures (e.g. Ware, 2005, Schneider & von der Emde, 2006) and the risks learners and teachers may be exposed to (see O'Dowd & Ritter, 2006). Managing this risk requires a well-conceived pedagogy and careful selection of technologies to match purpose (see Levy, 2007).

In the following section, we will firstly provide a synopsis and discussion of a number of early key studies in the field of telecollaboration, and then add to those a summary overview of additional studies undertaken in the conventional framework of intercultural exchanges (Thorne, 2010), before we move to a very brief discussion of research under the umbrella of Telecollaboration 2.0. We will then discuss the different notions of culture underlying the approaches to researching intercultural competence in CMC in the subsequent section of this contribution.

Researching Intercultural Competence in Online Intercultural Exchanges

Research reports on intercultural competence (ICC) in online exchanges have addressed intercultural learning processes and outcomes in various ways. Furstenberg, Levet, English, & Maillet (2001) report on the CULTURA project, a web-based, cross-cultural, curricular initiative "designed to develop foreign language students' understanding of foreign cultural attitudes, concepts, beliefs, and ways of interacting and looking at the world" (p.55). Their approach is grounded in the belief that to understand another culture a learner needs more than knowledge about that culture, rather, they need to develop a curiosity toward the culture of otherness, and particularly those aspects that relate to attitudes and values (cf. Byram, 1997). Culture is here seen as elemental, as we outline in more detail in the final section of this paper, and part of the task design aims at making students aware of their own cultural orientation. With a focus on fostering mutual understanding across French and American cultures, CULTURA is said to offer a comparative approach that asks learners to observe, to compare and to analyse parallel materials from their respective cultures and to exchange viewpoints on these materials, which include films, texts and online news media.

Data on the reported stage of the project were collected in the form of:

Questionnaires:

- student evaluations of the CULTURA project, addressing usefulness and interest for cultural understanding, quality of materials and activities, web interface, nature and frequency of re-

sources used and general assessment concerning gains in understanding the target culture
- student responses to questionnaires designed to stress cultural differences with respect to topics such as family relations, power structures, work, etc.

Online discussions:
- of the responses to those questionnaires by French and American students as well as online discussions of the films and texts provided.

The mainly qualitative data analysis focuses on the positive learning outcomes achieved in the areas under investigation (Furstenberg, et al., 2001: 87ff.).

O'Dowd (2003) reports on an email exchange between Spanish and English second year university language learners, identifying key characteristics of e-mail exchanges which helped to develop learners' intercultural communicative competence and outlining elements of e-mail messages which may enable students to develop successful intercultural relationships with their partners. Following an action-research approach to researching the exchange, the data collected in his study consist of:

- participant observation
- email data
- questionnaires
- interviews
- the researcher's reflexive journal
- peer-group feedback.

Following a qualitative data analysis, he provides a descriptive account of four partnerships, identifying specific characteristics of each one which helped or hindered the intercultural learning process. As we have seen with the Furstenberg, et al. (2001) study, the view of culture as elemental comes to the fore in these findings. Helping students to identify the cultural embeddedness of their feelings and views and to express and query these in the exchange with their partners is described as one of the major supporting factors of intercultural learning. Those students who managed to achieve this by establishing a more personal relationship with their partners, asking for feedback and reflection and providing their own analyses and personal reflections, while adhering to the socio-pragmatic rules of the partner's language when writing in that language are described as particularly successful (O'Dowd, 2003: 137).

Belz (2003) adds a linguistically grounded analysis of intercultural competence to the discussion of intercultural learning in telecollaboration projects. She reports on the online contributions of two German and one American student participating in a telecollaboration project over a seven week period. The three students were chosen to identify why their correspondence did not lead to intercultural learning in terms of developing attitudes of "curiosity and openness" (Byram, 1997). Belz (ibid) provides a qualitative as well as a quantitative analysis of the data collected and comes to the conclusion that the students she researched were not able to establish and maintain functional intercultural relationships in the context of the telecollaborative project because they did not have sufficient knowledge of culture-specific patterns of interaction in their partner's language. Culture-specific patterns she identifies in this exchange are:

- the performance of critique
- the discussion of taboo topics
- the degree of directness in conversational discourse
- linguistic devices for the mitigation of opinions.

Hanna & de Nooy (2003) report on a quite different set of data. Their study examined the varying success of four anglophone students of French in participating in a web-based forum of the French newspaper Le Monde. The intercultural dimension reported on in this paper is therefore referring to a relationship between non-native speakers and native speakers, rather than to a relationship between groups of non-native speakers. Pointing out the fact that email exchanges between groups of learners "are often limited to teacher-determined topics and the cultural comfort zone of student-student interaction" and that "discussion list tasks tend not to be differentiated clearly from keypal tasks" they criticize that in conventional email exchanges there is no sense of the difference between a conversation between two people and a public discussion (Hanna & de Nooy, 2003: 73). Here, it is group membership that is a determinant of (inter)cultural positions which we will discuss in more detail in the final section of this chapter. Analysing their subjects' contributions to the forum in a qualitative manner, based on the content of their contributions, they come to the conclusion that adherence to the rules for acceptable cultural behavior in the genre "internet forum" is the measure for successful participation and that competence in the target language in the sense of correctness and fluency plays a less significant role.

The analysis of the above studies focusing on intercultural learning in online projects seems to show that insights into the conditions for the development of intercultural competence can be gained in particular from those studies that focus on instances where intercultural communication does not take place successfully. Furstenberg, et al. (2001) provide an impressive model of a comparative approach that integrates parallel materials such as questionnaires, films, texts and online news media and their evaluation of the project shows very positive results for the work with those materials as an essential component of the online exchange described. As their data collection methods and the ensuing analysis are tightly bound to the content provided in their project, a transfer into other online learning environments seems rather difficult. Hanna and de Nooy's (2003) study provides a view of intercultural competence as a one-way street: to communicate successfully, their students need to understand the rules of the genre 'internet forum' in the target culture, with native speakers setting the boundaries of what constitutes culturally acceptable verbal behavior in the genre. Failure to behave according to the norms accepted by native speakers is reported to lead to exclusion from the communicative process. In a similar vein, Belz (2003) reports on a breakdown of communication between online partners because of non-adherence to cultural norms as expressed through linguistic means. The outcomes of her linguistic data analysis vividly show the interconnectedness of language learning and intercultural learning (cf. Kramsch, 1993).

In addition to the studies outlined above in detail as some early examples of research into intercultural aspects of telecollaboration projects, the following table provides a summary overview of key studies on intercultural learning in this earlier period of telecollaboration.[1]

Table 1. Selected key studies on intercultural aspects of telecollaboration projects

Study	Telecollaborative Setting	Data Collection & Analysis	Areas of Investigation
Kramsch & Thorne, 2002	French/US students	Qualitative analysis of intra-class interaction (students' contribution to chat)	Discursive Strategies; rhetorical conventions, forms of argumentation; language differences
		Qualitative analysis (students' contribution asynchronous CMC)	Relationship (Self & Other); understanding of online relationships
O'Dowd, 2006	German students with partner classes in Ireland and the US	3 qualitative studies; data from email, web-based message boards & video-conferencing	Discursive Strategies; directness/indirectness. Relationship (Self & Other); understanding of online relationships
Thorne, 2003	French/US students	Qualitative analysis: students' contribution to synchronous and asynchronous CMC (email, instant messenger, synchronous chat)	Discursive Strategies; rhetorical conventions; forms of argumentation Relationship (Self & Other); understanding of online relationships

1 For a comprehensive overview on intercultural issues in CMC, including non-educational settings see Hanna and de Nooy, 2009; the areas of investigation listed here have been adopted from this overview.

Toyoda & Harrison, 2002	Learners & native speakers of Japanese	Series of chat conversations; 45 units with communication breakdowns analysed	Discursive Strategies; language differences; sudden topic change; flow response; intercultural communication gap
		Qualitative analysis of negotitation of meaning	Word & Sentence level: Recognition of new word; misuse of word; pronunciation error; grammatical error; inappropriate segmentation; abbreviated sentence
Ware, 2005	German/US students	Qualitative analysis of data from online transcripts, interviews, and questionnaires	Discursive Strategies; language differences; time students devote to communication
			Relationship (Self & Other); understanding of online relationships; stereotypes and preconceptions of the other

The qualitative analyses of the research data in such studies typically center on difficulties in intercultural communication between the different groups, or in some instances, even breakdown of communication. Due to the limited time frames of most exchanges, though, the data collected and the methods of analysis mostly show a point-in-time view of intercultural competence, rather than providing insights on the development of intercultural competence of individual learners.

In addition to outlining the results of analyses based on discourse data, a large number of studies also report on the impact of local factors on the successes or otherwise of telecollaboration projects. Emphasis is given to the institutional context, including factors such as academic calendars, accreditation systems and access to computers (e.g. Belz, 2001, 2002; Belz & Müller-Hartmann, 2003; Möllering, 2005; Möllering & Ritter, 2008).

In her analysis of "missed" communication in CMC, Ware (2005) points out differences in students' expectations towards a project with regard to grammatical accuracy, message length, or response time. She suggests that problems can be avoided to a certain extent if both teachers and students are aware of the situation and the expectations of their partners. Extensive contact between teachers before the exchange and introductory writing tasks which involve students telling their distant partners about how they feel about their future work together may go some way to increasing sensitivity to the needs of the other group. O'Dowd and Ritter (2006) take the analysis a step further by developing a structured inventory of factors – at three different levels: an individual, classroom and socio-institutional level – which may lead to cases of "failed" communication in online exchanges. Lamy and Goodfellow (2010) in their problematisation of telecollaboration and "learning 2.0" point out that research on telecollaboration so far reports on what they call micro-level and meso-level institutional factors; they propose an additional macro-level, that takes into account different definitions of interculturalism and its ideological affiliations with national entities and groups speaking different 'national languages' – ideologies that are being challenged in the context of Web 2.0 telecollaboration.

In July 2010, nearly 2 billion people – or 28.7% of the world population – were using the global Internet[2] and it is the emergence of Web 2.0 that has given impetus to another shift in researching online intercultural exchanges. A minimalist definition of what is commonly referred to as Web 2.0 focuses on its affordability for users to interact and collaborate with each other through the use of so-called social media, which allow them to not only access but to generate and share content in a virtual community. Examples of Web 2.0 would be technologies such as blogs, wikis, social networking sites, video sharing sites, web applications and folksonomies, with multimodal approaches to communication an overarching feature.

2 <www.internetworldstats.com>, accessed 14 February 2011.

In their discussion of 'Telecollaboration 2.0', Helm and Guth (2010) argue that in addition to what they call 'the more traditional goals of telecollaboration', namely the development of target language skills and intercultural communicative competence, the additional objective in this environment is the development of new online literacies that take into account the online social practices many people participate in. Thus, in Telecollaboration 2.0 the emphasis is on learners as "world citizens" and the aim is:

> [...] for them to learn to operate, that is to communicate, collaborate, create and negotiate, effectively in multilingual, multicultural global networks using any number of languages (be it a foreign language, a lingua franca, their own native language(s)) and communication modes (oral, visual and/or textual, synchronous or asynchronous) in more or less open or closed environments. (Helm & Guth, 2010: 71)

According to Guth and Thomas (2010) most of the research on telecollaboration to date predates the emergence of Web 2.0 technologies which leads them to speak of an "infancy of Web 2.0 tools in telecollaboration"(p.63). There is, however, emerging research on telecollaboration in Web 2.0 settings and a set of case studies, published in Guth and Helm (2010), offers practical illustrations of implementing new forms of telecollaboration, dealing with Web 2.0 applications such as Skype (Guth & Marini-Maio, 2010; Meguro & Bryant, 2010), wikis (Guth & Marini-Maio, 2010), social networking sites (Meguro & Bryant, 2010) and Second Life (Carter, 2010).

With the addition of Telecollaboration 2.0, the range of technological alternatives that language learners now have at their disposal to support the development of intercultural competence is vast. Still, however, there are fundamental considerations that apply when reflecting upon the development of understanding across cultures and languages. This involves knowledge of the self and elements in one's cultural history and background, the relationship between one's own culture and the target culture, the necessary skills to be able to become an accepted equal in a target group, and the obstacles one needs to learn how to surmount in becoming a confident, active participant. The second half of this chapter addresses such issues and makes recommendations for the design of research studies in the field.

Intercultural Competence: Underlying Notions of Culture

In considering the discussion so far, it is clear that the approaches, methodologies and data collection techniques in research on ICC have been diverse. Similarly the theoretical perspectives have been many. This diversity can be traced back to the multifaceted and multilayered qualities of the culture concept itself. Taking an a-theoretical perspective, Levy (2007) endeavoured to examine the idea of culture from five perspectives: culture as elemental; culture as relative; culture as group membership; culture as contested; and culture as individual (variable and multiple). These perspectives are complimentary and inevitably overlap. Levy's premise was that the more we know about the culture concept itself, as an object and target for learning, the better equipped we will be in terms of pedagogy and practice. Furthermore, it is argued here that the five perspectives can help to provide insight into what might be required in terms of a research design. Drawing substantially on Levy (2007), these basic principles are now discussed whilst referring back to many of the CMC projects described earlier in this chapter as examples.

Culture as Elemental

The idea of culture as elemental emphasises our cultural embeddedness. As we grow and learn our first language, we are acculturated into a particular way of life. It follows, therefore, that when a second language learner begins a new language, the learner is no more a "blank slate" culturally than they are linguistically. In the words of Savignon and Sysoyev:

> [L]earning of foreign culture does not start from "an absolute zero". By the time learners begin the study of a L2 context and its culture, they have already formed certain concepts, stereotypes, and expectations about L2 cultural realities. These expectations are not fixed and immutable. But they will influence the way learners comprehend and interpret a L2 culture (C2). (2002: 510)

We may be largely unaware of our own cultural orientation, especially in its deeper aspects, such as those that influence belief systems and values (see Bourdieu, 1971; Hall, 1966). Numerous authors over many years have made this observation, for example describing culture as invisible or silent (Furstenberg, et al., 2001; Hall, 1966; Kramsch, 1993).

Therefore, in research investigating ICC, our deep, cultural embeddedness needs to be taken into account. This leads both to task designs and research designs that assist and record the learner's journey as they gradually become more aware of their own cultural orientation (C1) as well as the target culture (C2) associated with the language they are learning. This awareness takes time to develop and only a series of self-reflection activities and intercultural encounters will bring about the desired result. Research designs need to be formulated so as to be able to record learner reflections, both of the learners' C1 and C2. This requires the use of data collection tools that will successfully generate detailed, on-going ICC data over a period of time, and this may be achieved by such instruments as questionnaires, surveys, e-mail transcripts or chat logs, and learner diaries (see O'Dowd, 2003; Furstenberg, et al., 2001; Belz, 2003; Thorne, 2003). Generally in-class activities will precede between-class activities. Therefore, research designs may also include recording of in-class discussions, offline and online. Learner reflections on the C1 may prove to be as important as their responses to the C2 in tracking change over time, stage by stage, with the gradual development of ICC. The goal, of course, is to help the learner objectify their prior cultural experiences while recording their responses as they move into new cultural contexts.

It is worth noting at this point that pedagogical task designs and the corresponding research designs are by necessity closely linked. Research designs need to be formulated with the nature of the associated tasks firmly in mind. In many instances, the research design is motivated by, and oriented to, the task design. This is evident in many of the CMC projects described in this chapter, the majority of which place a heavy emphasis on the organisation of the task and the sequencing of its subcomponents. Not surprisingly then, the research methods, procedures and data collection tools will often be shaped by the nature of the task that they bear upon, as becomes obvious when comparing for example the task design and data collection in a study such as Furstenberg, et al. (2001) to those in Hanna and de Nooy (2003), both outlined above.

Issues for the researcher that may arise as a result of cultural embeddedness include the following:

- Difficulties following individual students over a sufficiently extended period of time such that the changes occur and are recorded
- Recording the learner experiences with sufficient depth so as to capture the subtle changes in orientation to the C1 and the C2 that are occurring
- The very substantial amount of data generated for the researcher to process.

Such issues may be addressed by involving the learner-as-researcher, or ethnographer, a learner role that has been frequently advocated from a pedagogical perspective by a number of writers on ICC (e.g., Bateman, 2002; O'Dowd, 2006; Roberts, et al., 2001; Savignon & Sysoyev, 2002). Regular, personal methods of recording change such as learner diaries are also most valuable, especially if learners are prepared with some of the systematic skills of the researcher first.

Culture as Relative

In addition to its elemental qualities culture is, fundamentally, a relative concept, not an absolute one. Arguably, one culture can only be understood in terms of another (Moorjani & Field, 1988). For the purposes of learning and teaching, the culture learner is almost inevitably drawn towards an approach which contrasts what "they" do with what "we" do, across a range of criteria. However, Guest (2002: 154) identifies a number of problems associated with a contrastive approach in learning and teaching the C2, and a paraphrased list of the problems follows:

- Oversimplification of the richness and variety within cultures leading to 'caricature' rather than a deeper understanding
- Reducing cultural understanding to discrete declarative propositions about a culture
- Binary logic failing to reflect complex realities
- Reducing a culture to monolithic, static categories
- Encouraging stereotypes, 'used to exacerbate adversity, and not to encourage mutual respect'
- Detailing differences can lead to withdrawal of interest in another culture
- Increasingly cultural boundaries are becoming blurred and intermingled.

Instead of taking a contrastive analytical approach, Guest (2002: 157) argues that "small-scale interactive models" would ultimately be both more accurate and productive. In essence, Guest is recommending a move away from the learner as detached observer towards the learner as active participant in culture learning, and from a view of culture which is static and distant, to a view which is more dynamic and directly engaged. In this sense, the culture-as-relative perspective provides a contrast in approach to the culture-as-elemental perspective.

In terms of research designs, the culture-as-relative perspective emphasises again the importance of longitudinal, qualitative studies and the value of capturing the experience of the individual learner.

Also, researching the learner as active participant in culture and learning has become more feasible and practical with new technologies because the interaction logs can be recorded and saved for future analysis. These logs may also be used for teacher-directed learner reflection (see Toyoda & Harrison, 2002). Data which tracks changes over time, including the learner's attitudes to both the C1 and the C2, and through such into cultural exchanges as e-mail tandem or chat will be particularly useful (see Appel & Gilabert, 2002; O'Dowd, 2006).

Undoubtedly, issues will emerge around the temptation to formulate broad generalisations prematurely, as learners inevitably engage in a developing awareness of difference. Such events would likely be an important focus for the researcher when analysing transcripts. However, appropriate task design with in-class and out-of-class debriefing sessions will help mitigate such problems, and again these events may be recorded for research purposes.

Culture as Group Membership

Human beings live out their lives as members of groups. Early in life, the groups to which we belong are chosen for us, later in life we make more choices for ourselves. In our early years, our family, community, school and home country, with the corresponding beliefs, values and traditions, help create our primary cultural orientation. Then as we grow, work, travel, or learn another language further layers or levels are added to the cultural mix that form an individual's cultural identity. For Lindsay, Robins and Terrell:

> Culture is everything you believe and everything you do that enables you to identify with people who are like you and that distinguishes you from people who differ from you. Culture is about groupness. A culture is a group of people identified by the shared history, values, and patterns of behaviour. (1999: 26–27)

A group perspective on culture draws attention to the idea of membership and community and leads to questions such as how people identify with groups, how others identify people with groups and how different groups relate and interact with one another. Hanna and de Nooy's (2003) study, widely cited, illustrates very well some of the problems encountered when two learners of French attempt to participate in our discussion forum. Lack of intercultural competence in this context leads to rejection, not due to a lack of linguistic or socio-linguistic skills but due to perceived intentions regarding group membership.

The group perspective on culture also brings to centre stage the participants and groups that are created or accessed in any research study on ICC. Groups may range from in-class or between-class groups of language learners in an institutional language learning settings, to international groupings of learners, as in e-mail tandem for example, where two groups with a reciprocal L1 and L2 interact, and on to more authentic groups in settings that are not designed for language learners, such as the public Internet discussion forum described by Hanna and de Nooy (2003) in which language learners played a part. Here we can observe a transition from a protected institutional learning environment to an open real-world setting. Another important factor in group formation is whether the language background of learners (L1) is homogeneous or not within the groups; the group composition in terms of such factors as language background need to be aligned with the goals the researcher seeks to address (e.g., see Fernández-Garcia & Martínez-Arbelaiz, 2002: 288). The role of the language teacher as a potential participant in such groupings is also another consideration that has to be taken into account.

With culture as group membership as the focus, research designs may be directed towards:

- Insider/outsider perspectives
- Group creation, maintenance & regulation, offline & online
- Group moderation, gatekeepers etc.
- Norms & expectations; variation & conformity

- Pedagogical contexts versus authentic contexts
- NNS requirements & rehearsal with a view to NS group "membership".

Some of the research issues that may arise concern the availability of data on participants in authentic group settings which may be difficult to obtain, and potentially it may also involve ethical and/or privacy issues around collecting data in these contexts. But again the importance of recording the individual learner experience as they engage in these different intercultural exchanges remains central.

Culture as Contested

Culture is contested at many levels, both from without and within. Thus, cultures may be contested at the level of the nation state or beyond, for example when a "clash of cultures" is proclaimed in the media; or they may be contested at the level of the individual, when "culture shock" is experienced. When an individual learns another language, or moves to live in another country, culture may be contested within the individual, as differing belief systems, ideas and values meet head to head, and are compared and contrasted both consciously, and subconsciously, through feelings of disquiet and uncertainty.

It should not be particularly surprising therefore that in settings where language learners are linked with individuals from another culture that misunderstandings and communication breakdowns sometimes occur. These points of contestation are frequently of significance to the researcher of ICC because they provide prime examples of cultural differences and culture learning in action. As noted earlier, a number of online ICC projects seek to identify these conditions, that is where intercultural communication does not take place successfully (e.g., O'Dowd, 2003; Hanna & de Nooy, 2003). Importantly, such critical events around points of contestation are usually isolated and identified according to constructs determined by the researcher's theoretical orientation. Such is the case in two studies focusing on synchronous chat discussions among learners of Spanish, the first by Fernández-Garcia and Martínez-Arbelaiz (2002) and the second by Darhower (2002) which are now described to exemplify differences.

Fernández-Garcia and Martínez-Arbelaiz conducted a study using a theoretical framework from Varonis and Gass (1985), and they focused particularly on the need for discourse moves that allowed interlocutors to negotiate meaning to ensure the message was understood. The interactional modifications that resulted were held to make the input more comprehensible and thereby to facilitate language learning. In terms of points of contestation, they looked especially at misunderstandings, moments of communication "breakdown" and "repair" sequences, as defined by the theory. In contrast, Darhower (2002) also examined the interactional features of synchronous CMC chat for Spanish learners. However, he described his work as a sociocultural case study, and explored the social interactive features of online chat. He used Vygotsky's theoretical framework and discourse analysis techniques to describe and explain the most salient features of the interactions that occurred. Darhower also emphasised the notion of intersubjectivity, the building of a shared communicative perspective or context which participants gain through collaborative discourse. Darhower's study focussed upon the maintenance and "loss" of intersubjectivity. Thus, both projects focused on key points of contestation but in different ways according to their respective theoretical frameworks. Also consistent with a sociocultural case study, Darhower (2002) shows an interest in off-task discussion reflecting the broader theoretical base and a concern with the importance of learners building a shared communicative perspective in an intercultural setting (see Levy & Stockwell, 2006, for further discussion).

The two contrasting theoretical approaches illustrate well the choices that confront contemporary researchers investigating ICC. No one theoretical account is pre-eminent. In these examples, two approaches are taken that analyse very similar kinds of data in very similar settings using similar methods, but that are motivated by two different theories that generate very different results. Briefly, the results generated by the theoretical approach taken by Fernández-Garcia and Martínez-Arbelaiz (2002) steered the work toward a narrower micro-focus on specific and discrete negotiation routines, and analysis that highlighted the acquisition of lower level discourse functions. In contrast, Darhower's (2002) theoretical approach effectively guided the study toward a macro-view and an understanding of learning as participation, a perspective where learning is viewed not as acquisition, but as a process of becoming part of a greater whole. The second investigation allowed for a broader interpretation of the results such that the author was in a position to include a commentary on identity exploration and role play, off-task discussion, and the use of humour and sarcasm. Importantly, however, both studies still used the same chat transcripts as their data source, but they were analysed and interpreted differently according to the overarching theoretical models.

Culture as Individual (Variable and Multiple)

The fifth and final perspective presents culture as an individual variable, noting that while there are commonalities, individual understandings of the same culture will differ from one person to the next. In the context of language and culture learning, this means that the learner's and the teacher's understanding of their own culture (C1) will inevitably be an individual interpretation, modified by such individual factors as world knowledge, language and cultural background, experience living abroad, political awareness etc. Thus, when an individual is in a position to represent their own culture, either as a language teacher or learner, their interpretation will be subjective and personal.

The critical importance of the individual perspective is evident in many of the past studies on culture learning, particularly when individual student quotations are used to show a personal response or reaction to something that has been said or suggested in the midst of an intercultural exchange. A good example, again from O'Dowd (2003), is when in spite of the set task, one of the exchange students presents an outspoken position on regional nationalism to an online partner in an introductory email. But there are numerous other examples where authors teaching or researching culture feel the need to report on individual reactions and responses. Darhower (2002) provides another good example, where one student wants to go off-task when the teacher leaves the class, while their partner wants to remain task-focussed. The set of eight case studies reported in Tellecollaboration 2.0 provide further illuminating examples (see Guth & Helm, 2010).

The online environment adds further layers of complexity to the culture concept. Regular participation in online cultures simultaneously dilutes and expands our individual cultural orientation and mix. Our cultural profile is not static, and grows and develops through intercultural experiences. In more general terms, any cultural understanding that arises from an exchange or interaction will be subject to the perspective and frame of reference of the individual observer or participant. What one learner will come to understand or learn when observing or engaging in a intercultural exchange, another may not.

In terms of research methods and techniques, this individual perspective on culture speaks of the importance of listening to the learner's voice via such approaches as the individual case study that facilitates the recording in detail of the learner's personal growth and experience. A case study is designed in terms of its unit of analysis. An obvious focus for attention is the individual student, although case studies may also focus upon the describing the collaborative experience of a pair of participants, or yet again the focus may be a larger entity such as a discussion forum, or another online venue for language learners. Issues that may arise when an individual perspective is taken reflect some of the drawbacks with case study research such as determining the boundaries of the "case", and making generalisations.

In concluding this section on underlying notions of culture from the five perspectives, it is worth recapping the general point, that meaningful research around culture learning can be complex and challenging. Facets of the culture concept as described here would lead the researcher to carefully consider long-term, semester long qualitative research studies. As a result of its elemental qualities, research designs are recommended that are sensitive enough to capture subtle changes in a student's orientation to the first and second culture as a study moves forward. This takes time as well as data collection instruments that generate detailed information. Further, as with all in-depth, long term qualitative studies, it will take a researcher of particular skill and training to marshal and interpret the data in ways that generate results which are meaningful and helpful to others. The idea of the learner-as-researcher may be productive.

Culture is also relative. While it is natural to employ contrastive or comparative approaches to generate study data, without due care such an approach can quickly reduce another's understanding of a culture to monolithic, static categories. Culture learning is not simply an assembly of facts, nor intercultural competence a set of surface level techniques and formulas to manage intercultural interactions. It is something deeper. As such, research designs need to be sufficiently refined to capture some of the subtleties of cultural understanding as they evolve and develop in the mind of the individual. Again this suggests longer, in-depth qualitative approaches. With regard to culture as group membership, the key study by Hanna and de Nooy (2003) is instructive. Pedagogical tasks designs and research designs need, at some stage, to engage the students directly in real-world groups, such as the online forum described in this study. This involves a level of risk. Entry into such authentic groups, not designed for pedagogical purposes—where students are usually insulated from potential problems and difficulties—is sometimes not straightforward, as in the example described in this study. Again students need to be suitably prepared for the learning task, or in preparation for a research study. The idea of the insider/outsider perspective may be helpful.

Culture is also contested. For example, while great care may be taken in constructing email partnerships, past studies show that some partnerships may fail, and individual students may vary significantly in what they take away from the experience (O'Dowd, 2003). Meticulous preparation is critical both for teaching and for research purposes. Stages in task design need to be very carefully sequenced, as in CULTURA, for example (see Levet & Waryn, 2006). From a research perspective, different kinds of data may be collected at different points in the process of task completion. Finally, culture is individual (variable and multiple).

Clearly many of the points made earlier apply here, too. Researchers need to carefully document and report the background of individual students. Many past studies do not do this to a sufficient degree. When an individual student behaves in a particular way, or appears to overreact in an interaction, where possible the relevant background should be reported (see O'Dowd 2003; Guth & Helm, 2010). Past experiences, such as living overseas, particular political and social leanings and orientations make a difference to research outcomes and how far one can generalize from particular results.

Conclusion

In reviewing the research studies described in this chapter, it is noteworthy that at base much of the work completed involves the analysis of transcript data (textual, aural, visual, or in combination). There are two key points to be made here. First, this data may be difficult to collect over a period of time, especially with mobile learning with partners at a distance, but also with Web 2.0 technologies such as wikis and blogs where information is dynamic with multiple inputs and contributors. Second, when such data is reviewed, researchers are faced with a number of options when looking for critical events in the data that pertain to the development of intercultural competence. Just how intercultural competence is operationalised motivates the search by determining the critical events that are taken to influence ICC.

In providing a field of view, each theory prescribes a focal point and identifies factors that are believed to impact upon it. In this way the theory drives and shapes the data collection, interpretation and analysis. In other words, the theoretical account effectively identifies which elements are to be brought into the foreground and which are to remain in the background, or are to be disregarded altogether (e.g., Darhower, 2002; Fernández-Garcia & Martínez-Arbelaiz, 2002). The theoretical orientation (e.g., socioculturalism vs. discourse structure) and the corresponding research constructs (e.g., intersubjectivity vs. negotiation of meaning) lead to different points of focus as well as alternative processes of analysis and interpretation, even when the data itself is of a similar type (e.g., chat transcripts). The complexity and variety of the culture concept means that many theories of culture and language may be applied giving rise to very different interpretations of the same data. Sometimes combining methods may be effective, as in multimethod studies that combine two or more approaches to research in a single study. For example, a study may combine qualitative case studies, quasi-experimentation, and quantitative descriptive data collection and analysis. Such studies are heavily labour and resource intensive but they do have the potential to provide a much richer picture of the phenomenon in focus. Given the complexity of the culture concept, and the absence of an overriding theory, it would seem that a combination of frameworks, methods and interpretations would be beneficial in ICC research because at this point in our understanding of intercultural competence such an approach would lead to a deeper and more nuanced understanding of the developments taking place.

References

Appel, C. (1999). *Tandem language learning by e-mail: Some basic principles and a case study. (CLCS Occasional Papers – 54).* Dublin: Trinity College, Centre for Language and Communication Studies.

Appel, C., & Gilabert, R. (2002). Motivation and task performance in a task-based web-based tandem project. *ReCALL, 14*(1), 16–31.

Appel, C., & Mullen, T. (2000). Pedagogical considerations for a web-based tandem language learning environment. *Computers and Education, 34*(3–4), 291–308.

Bateman, B. E. (2002). Promoting openness toward culture learning: Ethnographic interviews for students of Spanish. *The Modern Language Journal, 86*(3), 318–331.

Beauvois, M. H. (1992). Computer assisted classroom discussion in the foreign language classroom: Conversation in slow motion. *Foreign Language Annals, 25*(5), 455–464.

Beauvois, M. H. (1995). E-Talk: Attitudes and motivation in computer-assisted classroom discussions. *Computers and the Humanities, 28*(3), 177–290.

Beauvois, M. H. (1998). Conversations in slow motion: Computer-mediated communication in the foreign language classroom. *Canadian Modern Language Review, 54*(2), 198–217.

Belz, J. (2001). Institutional and individual dimensions of transatlantic group work in network-based language teaching. *ReCALL 13*(2), 129–147.

Belz, J. A. (2002). Social dimensions of telecollaborative foreign language study. *Language Learning & Technology, 6*(1), 60–81.

Belz, J. A. (2003). Linguistic perspectives on the development of intercultural competence in telecollaboration. *Language Learning & Technology, 7*(2), 68–117.

Belz, J. A. & A. Müller-Hartmann (2003). Teachers as intercultural learners: Negotiating German-American telecollaboration along the institutional fault line. *Modern Language Journal 87*(1), 71–89.

Brammerts, H. (1998). Autonomous language learning in tandem via the internet. *a&e (Anglistik und Englischunterricht), 62*, 273–284.

Bredella, L. (1999). Zielsetzungen interkulturellen Fremdsprachenunterrichts.[Objectives of intercultural language teaching] In L. Bredella & W. Delanoy (Eds.), *Interkultureller Fremdsprachenunterricht* [Intercultural language teaching](pp. 85–120). Tübingen: Gunter Narr Verlag.

Bredella, L., & Delanoy, W. (Eds.) (1999). *Interkultureller Fremdsprachenunterricht* [Intercultural language teaching]. Tübingen: Gunter Narr Verlag.

Bourdieu, P (1971). Systems of education and systems of thought. In M.F.D. Young (Ed.), *Knowledge and control: New directions for the sociology of education (pp. 189–207).* London: Collier-MacMillan.

Byram, M. (1997). *Teaching and assessing intercultural communicative competence.* Clevedon, UK: Multilingual Matters.

Carter, B. (2010). Virtual harlem: Building a community. In S. Guth and F. Helm (Eds.), *Telecollaboration 2.0. Language, literacies and intercultural learning in the 21st Century* (pp. 365–374). Bern: Peter Lang.

Chun, D. M. (1994). Using computer networking to facilitate the acquisition of interactive competence. *System, 22*(1), 17–31.

Darhower, M. (2002). Interactional features of synchronous CMC in the intermediate L2 class: A sociocultural case study. *CALICO Journal, 19*(2), 249–277.

Darhower, M. (2007). A tale of two communities: Group dynamics and community building in a Spanish-English telecollaboration. *CALICO Journal, 24*(3), 561–590.

Fernández-Garcia, M., & Martínez-Arbelaiz, A. (2002). Negotiation of meaning in non-native speaker non-native speaker synchronous discussions. *CALICO Journal, 19*(2), 279–294.

Fischer, G. (1998). *E-mail in foreign language teaching: Toward the creation of virtual classrooms.* Tübingen: Stauffenberg.

Furstenberg, G., Levet, S., English, K., & Maillet, K. (2001). Giving a virtual voice to the silent language of culture: The Cultura project. *Language Learning & Technology, 5*(1), 55–102.

Guest, M. (2002). A critical 'checkbook' for culture teaching and learning. *ELT Journal, 56*(2), 154–161.

Guth, S. & Helm, F. (Eds.) (2010). *Telecollaboration 2.0. Language, literacies and intercultural learning in the 21st Century*. Bern: Peter Lang.

Guth, S. & Marini-Maio, N. (2010). Close encounters of a new kind: The use of skype and wiki in telecollaboration In S. Guth & F. Helm (Eds.), *Telecollaboration 2.0. Language, literacies and intercultural learning in the 21st Century* (pp. 413–426). Bern: Peter Lang.

Guth, S. & Thomas, M. (2010). Telecollaboration with web 2.0 tools. In S. Guth & F. Helm (Eds.), *Telecollaboration 2.0. Language, literacies and intercultural learning in the 21st Century* (pp. 39–68). Bern: Peter Lang.

Hall, E. T. (1966). *The hidden dimension*. New York: Doubleday.

Hanna, B., & de Nooy, J. (2003). A funny thing happened on the way to the forum: Electronic discussion and foreign language learning. *Language Learning & Technology, 7*(1), 71–85.

Hanna, B. E. & de Nooy, J. (2009). *Learning language and culture via public internet discussion forums*. Basingstoke, UK: Palgrave, Macmillan.

Helm, F. & S. Guth, S. (2010). The multifarious goals of telecollaboration 2.0 tools: Theoretical and practical implications. In S. Guth & F. Helm (Eds.), *Telecollaboration 2.0. Language, literacies and intercultural learning in the 21st Century* (pp. 69–106). Bern: Peter Lang Publishers.

Kelm, O. R. (1992). The use of synchronous computer networks in second language instruction: A preliminary study. *Foreign Language Annals, 25*(5), 441–454.

Kern, R. G. (1995). Restructuring classroom interaction with networked computers: Effects on quality and characteristics of language proficiency. *Modern Language Journal, 79*(4), 457–476.

Kötter, M. (2003). Negotiation of meaning and codeswitching in online tandems. *Language Learning & Technology, 7*(2), 145–172.

Kramsch, C. (1993). *Context and culture in language teaching*. Oxford: Oxford University Press.

Kramsch, C., & S. Thorne (2002). Foreign language learning as global communicative practice. In D. Block & D. Cameron (Eds), *Language learning and teaching in the age of globalization* (pp.83–100). London: Routledge.

Krumm, H.-J. (1992). Bilder im Kopf. Interkulturelles Lernen und Landeskunde[Images in one's head. Intercultural learning and area studies]. *Fremdsprache Deutsch [German as a foreign language]* *6*/1992, 16–19.

Krumm, H.-J. (1995). Interkulturelles Lernen und Interkulturelle Kommunikation [Intercultural learning and intercultural communication]. In K.-R. Bausch, H. Christ & H.-J. Krumm (Eds.), *Handbuch Fremdsprachenunterricht* [Manual of foreign language teaching] (p. 157). Tübingen: Francke.

Lamy, M.-N., & R. Goodfellow (1999). Reflective conversation in the virtual language classroom. *Language Learning & Technology, 2*(2), 43–61.

Little, D. (2001). Learner autonomy and the challenge of tandem learning via the Internet. In A. Chambers & G. Davies (Eds.), *Information and communications technologies and language learning* (pp. 29–38). Lisse: Swets and Zeltlinger.

Levet, S., & Waryn, S. (2006). Using the web to develop students in-depth understanding of foreign cultural attitudes and values. In R. Donaldson & M. Haggstrom (Eds.), *Changing language education through CALL* (pp. 95–188). Oxford: Routledge.

Levy, M. (2007). Culture, culture learning and new technologies: Towards a pedagogical framework. *Language Learning & Technology, 11*(2), 104–127.

Levy, M. & Stockwell, G. (2006). *CALL dimensions: Options and issues in computer-assisted language learning.* Mahwah, NJ: Lawrence Erlbaum.

Lindsay, R.-B., Robins, K. N., & Terrell, R. D. (1999). *Cultural literacy: A manual for school leaders.* Thousand Oaks: Corwin.

Little, D., & Ushioda, E. (1998). Designing, implementing and evaluating a project in tandem language learning via e-mail. *ReCALL, 10(*1), 95–101.

Lomicka, L. (2006). Understanding the other: Intercultural exchange and CMC. In N. Arnold & L. Ducate (Eds.), *Calling on CALL: From theory and research to new directions in language teaching.* San Marcos, TX: CALICO Publications.

Meguro, A., & Bryant, T. (2010). Finding language partners in unexpected places: Skype and social networking for USA-Japan telecollaboration. In S. Guth and F. Helm (Eds.), *Telecollaboration 2.0. Language, literacies and intercultural learning in the 21st Century* (pp. 453–463). Bern: Peter Lang.

Möllering, M. (2005). Interkulturelles Lernen in elektronischen Lernumgebungen [Intercultural learning in electronic learning networks]. In G. Blell & R. Kupetz (Eds.), *Fremdsprachenlernen zwischen Medienverwahrlosung und Medienkompetenz. Beiträge zu einer kritisch-reflektierenden Mediendidaktik* (pp. 175–185). Frankfurt: Peter Lang.

Möllering, M., & Ritter, M. (2008). Computer-mediated communication and intercultural learning. In F. Zhang & B. Barber (Eds), *Handbook of research on computer-enhanced language acquisition and learning* (pp. 361–376). Hershey, Pennsylvania: IGI-Global.

Moorjani, A., & Field, T. T. (1988). Semiotic and sociolinguistic paths to understanding culture. In A. J. Singerman (Ed.), *Toward a new integration of language and culture. Reports of the Northeast conference on the teaching of foreign languages* (pp. 25–45). Middlebury, VT: Northeast conference, 1988.

Müller-Hartmann, A. (2000). The role of tasks in promoting intercultural learning in electronic learning networks. *Language Learning & Technology, 4*(2), 129–147.

O'Dowd, R. (2003). Understanding the "other side": Intercultural learning in a Spanish-English e-mail exchange. *Language Learning & Technology 7*(2), 118–144.

O'Dowd, R. (2006). *Telecollaboration and the development of intercultural communicative competence.* Munich: Langenscheidt-Longman.

O'Dowd, R. (2007). Evaluating the outcomes of online intercultural exchange. *ELT Journal, 61* (2), 144–152.

O'Dowd, R., & Eberbach, K. (2004). Guides on the side? Tasks and challenges for teachers in telecollaborative projects. *ReCALL, 16*(1), 5–19.

O'Dowd, R., & Ritter, M. (2006). Understanding and working with 'failed communication' in telecollaborative exchanges. *CALICO Journal, 23*(2), 623–642.

Roberts, C., Byram, M., Barro, A., Jordan, S., & Street, B. (2001). *Language learners as ethnographers.* Clevedon, England: Multilingual Matters.

Savignon, S. J., & Sysoyev, P. V. (2002). Sociocultural strategies for a dialogue of cultures. *The Modern Language Journal, 86*, 508–524.

Schneider, J., & von der Emde, S. (2006). Conflicts in cyberspace: From communication breakdown to intercultural dialogue in online collaborations. In J. Belz & S. Thorne (Eds.), *Internet-mediated intercultural foreign language education* (pp. 178–206). Boston: Thomson Heinle.

Thorne, S. (2003). Artifacts and cultures-of-use in intercultural communication. *Language Learning and Technology, 7* (2), 38–67.

Thorne, S. (2010). The 'intercultural turn' and language learning in the crucible of new media. In S. Guth and F. Helm (Eds.), *Telecollaboration 2.0. Language, literacies and intercultural learning in the 21st Century* (pp. 139–164). Bern: Peter Lang.

Toyoda, E., & Harrison, R. (2002). Categorization of text chat communication between learners and native speakers of Japanese. *Language Learning & Technology, 6*(1), 82–99.

Varonis, E.. & S. Gass (1985). Non-native/non-native conversations: A model for negotiation of meaning. *Applied Linguistics,* 6(1), 71–90.

Ware, P. (2005). "Missed" communication in online communication: tensions in a German-American telecollaboration. *Language Learning & Technology, 9*(2), 64–89.

Warschauer, M. (1996). Comparing face-to-face and electronic discussion in the second language classroom. *CALICO Journal 13*(2), 7–26.

Woodin, J. (1997). Email tandem learning and the communicative curriculum. *ReCALL, 9*(1), 22–33.

Section III: Research Methods for Online Interaction and Exchange

Applying the Methodology of Learner Corpus Analysis to Telecollaborative Discourse

NINA VYATKINA

Telecollaborative pedagogy and the research methodology of learner corpus analysis are both relative newcomers on the foreign language education scene. The aim of this chapter is to show how corpus analysis methods and tools can be applied by researchers interested in examining telecollaborative discourse. I will show how the two have been successfully brought together in existing research and suggest directions for future applications. The chapter begins by describing learner corpora and the research method of contrastive interlanguage analysis. In particular, I define the terminology used in this research paradigm, describe its characteristics and purposes, and list the contexts where it has been applied. The next section shows why this methodology is uniquely suited to research on intercultural computer-mediated exchanges. In what follows, I provide concrete examples of how selected corpus research methods and tools have been applied in collecting and analyzing a telecollaborative corpus in research exploring language development in college-level learners of German. I will conclude by a discussion of results and suggestions for future research.

Language corpora and Contrastive Interlanguage Analysis (CIA)

This method has been used in both descriptive and contrastive language studies to explore variation across genres and registers – a research area made famous by Biber (1988) and Sinclair (1991). Most corpus-based studies have focused on distribution and frequency of linguistic features as used by Native Speakers (NSs) of different languages (although predominantly English). Findings from this research have attracted attention of Second Language Acquisition (SLA) and Foreign Language Teaching (FLT) researchers who expanded corpus-based research to include not only NS data but also learner data. For this purpose, learner productions are systematically collected and compiled in electronic *learner corpora*:

> Computer learner corpora are electronic collections of authentic FL/SL textual data assembled according to explicit design criteria for a particular SLA/FLT purpose. They are encoded in a standardised and homogenous way and documented as to their origin and provenance. (Granger, 2002: 7)

The research method based on comparisons between NS and learner corpora has been termed *Contrastive Interlanguage Analysis*, or *CIA* (Granger, 1998a). According to Granger, CIA studies seek to uncover "qualitative differences (misuse) and quantitative differences (over- and underuse)" of the targeted features by learners in comparison to NSs (2003: 541). Although learner corpora are relative newcomers (see Pravec, 2002; Nesselhauf, 2004, for reviews) and CIA studies span only about a decade, they have greatly enriched SLA research with findings grounded on large amounts of empirical data. Areas of inquiry have ranged from morpho-syntactic constructions to lexis to pragmatic features and discourse patterns (see collections by Granger, Hung, & Petch-Tyson, 2002; Aston, Bernardini, & Stewart, 2004; Sinclair 2004; Aijmer, 2009). CIA has proven especially productive in revealing subtle differences between learners at higher proficiency levels (high intermediate to advanced) and NSs. Considerable advances have been made by researchers working on the collection and analysis of the International Corpus of Learner English (ICLE)[1] and the Louvain International Database of Spoken English (LINDSEI)[2]. Working with a number of subcorpora encompassing the written and oral productions of English as a Second Language (ESL) learners with different first language (L1) backgrounds, these researchers have compared learner and NS use of English. For example, Granger (1998b) found that learners overuse generic adverbs and adjectives (such as *very* or *important*) but under-use their more specific and contextually restricted counterparts (such as *closely, highly* and *critical, significant*). Aijmer (2002) showed that learners used significantly more modal verbs in their writing than NSs, which contributed to an overuse of spoken patterns inappropriate in a written academic genre. Nesselhauf (2005), Gilquin, Granger, & Paquot (2007), Gilquin (2008), and Paquot (2008) explored differences in NS and learner use of phraseological expressions such as noun-verb combinations (e.g. *to have a look*) and discourse markers (e.g. *on the contrary* in writing and *sort of* in speaking). These studies again show that advanced learners' productions, without being grammatically inaccurate, differ from baseline NS writing in stylistic nuances and idiomaticity. Rather than using the terms 'overuse' and 'underuse' as disparaging labels for learner deficiencies, the above studies aim at raising awareness of learners, teachers, and researchers of second language (L2) "Nuancenkompetenz", or 'nuance competence' (Weinrich, 1993: 842). Notably, this research has resulted in a number of corpus-based pedagogical suggestions in the areas of pedagogical lexicography (Rundell & Granger, 2007) and phraseology (Granger & Meunier, 2008).

This brief overview highlights advances made in learner corpus research to date. However, much of the potential of computer-aided corpus analysis remains underexplored due to a number of limitations of existing learner corpora. First, most of them are monolin-

1 <http://cecl.fltr.ucl.ac.be/Cecl-Projects/Icle/icle.htm>.

2 <http://cecl.fltr.ucl.ac.be/Cecl-Projects/Lindsei/lindsei.htm>.

gual, i.e. researchers require an *external* NS comparison corpus in order to conduct contrastive learner corpus analyses. However, the explanatory power of such comparisons is limited because, as Vyatkina & Belz (2006) argue, "the data to which learner productions are compared were produced at a different point in time, under different circumstances, and in different contexts" (p. 320). Second, with some notable exceptions, learner corpora are highly restricted with respect to genre (most of them include only written argumentative essays) and language (predominantly L2 English). Finally, the majority of existing corpora are cross-sectional and synchronous. They comprise data collected as snapshots of performance of particular learner populations at one point in time. As Belz points out, studies based on such learner corpora "tend to describe L2 use only at a particular point in time. As a result, they are not positioned well to address questions at the heart of SLA research, namely, how does L2 competence *change* over time?" (2007: 47).

Some researchers make inferences about typical developmental stages and patterns based on corpus data collected from different groups of learners at different stages in collegiate instructional sequences (Tono, 2000) or of different age (Housen, 2002). However, as Housen (2002) notes, the aggregate view of this largely cross-sectional learner corpus research may mask variation in individual developmental paths taken by learners. Yet, despite "nearly ritualized" calls (Ortega & Byrnes, 2008: 5) for longitudinal SLA studies, dynamic accounts of variability in learner productions, more exhaustive sampling, and fine grained analyses of learner language (Ellis & Larsen-Freeman, 2006; Norris & Ortega, 2009), researchers largely shy away from the difficult and time consuming endeavor of compilation and analysis of longitudinal learner corpora. Examples of notable exceptions are longitudinal corpora of learner written German (Lüdeling, Walter, Kroymann, & Adolphs, 2005; Byrnes & Sinicrope, 2008) and learner spoken French (Myles, 2008) as well as the Lab School multimedia corpus containing textual, audio, and video data (Reder, Harris, & Setzler, 2003). In the following section, I discuss how the compilation and analysis of *telecollaborative (TC) learner corpora* address the research needs and design limitations mentioned above.

Advantages of TC Data for Learner Corpus Research

Telecollaboration is one of the forms of social networking that has been on the rise in FLT during the last decade (see Warschauer, 1996; Furstenberg, Levet, English, & Mallet, 2001; Belz & Thorne, 2006; O'Dowd, 2007; Dooly, 2008; Guth & Helm, 2010; Dooly & O'Dowd, this volume). Belz defines telecollaboration as:

> institutionalized, electronically mediated intercultural communication under the guidance of a languacultural expert (i.e., a teacher) for the purposes of foreign language learning and the development of intercultural competence. (2003a: 2)

One unique feature of TC classes is "the alternation of Internet-mediated *inter*cultural sessions with face-to-face *intra*cultural sessions" (Belz, 2006: 214, emphasis in original). During traditional classroom sessions, the teacher provides instruction in various L2 grammatical, pragmatic, and cultural topics, while during computer-mediated communication (CMC) sessions, learners practice their acquired knowledge in real-life interactions with native speakers. During subsequent instruction sessions, the teacher gives the students an opportunity to observe their own accurate and inaccurate L2 uses in excerpts from their CMC discourse as well as to discuss it *in plenum* or individually. The instructor teacher thus acts as a "facilitator" (Rogers, 1969: 105–106) who provides guidance to learners during both intercultural and intracultural sessions. Moreover, the teacher in TC courses also is in a unique position to conduct classroom-based research using corpus analysis methods. Features that make TC data especially suitable for learner corpus construction and CIA studies are addressed in the next sections.

Automatically Saved Data

Because TC language practice sessions are always computer-mediated and thus L2 productions are usually automatically saved, this presents a unique opportunity for corpus data collection. This holds true for text-based CMC genres such as email, forum, and chat as well as audio/video-based genres such as teleconferences. Provided the teacher/researcher follows ethical standards for research and an approved procedure for collecting human subject research data[3], these computer recordings of learner and NS productions can be used for construction of corpora for concurrent or future investigations. Whereas audio and video data would require subsequent transcription, text-based data obviate the need for this time-consuming part of research and can be directly transferred into an electronic database. This immediate availability of data for research greatly enhances the feasibility of the study, especially if the researcher has limited funding and is not part of a larger collaborative team.

Richness of Metadata

Smaller, custom-made corpora (Ghadessy, Henry, & Roseberry, 2001) usually contain rich participant metadata (on age, gender, language learning history) and task metadata (on topic, prompts, planning time). As Granger argues:

> the usefulness of a learner corpus is directly proportional to the care that has been exerted in controlling and encoding [learner and task] variables. (2002: 9).

3 Researchers need to plan well in advance and keep in mind that their research protocol must be approved by the Institutional Review Board (IRB) *prior* to the beginning of the data collection process, i.e., *prior* to the TC exchanges. Mackey & Gass (2005: 25–42) provide a very helpful guide for young researchers which discusses ethical issues in research involving humans, describes the process of obtaining informed consent, and gives helpful examples of necessary documents.

Additionally, such smaller specialized corpora can be organized in accordance with the teacher/researcher's own scholarly and pedagogical needs without compromising generally accepted standards for corpus collection (Seidlhofer, 2002; Flowerdew, 2005; Lee & Swales, 2006). This is especially true for TC corpora because the teacher/researcher has an insider view on the study context, which greatly enriches the ethnographic dimension (Flowerdew, 2005) and enhances the ecological validity of both the learner corpus itself and studies based on its data (Reinhardt, this volume).

Integrated NS Baseline Data

Tasks that teachers formulate for participants of TC exchanges (who are speakers of different languages) may include various configurations of languages to be used: 1) both partner classes continuously alternate the use of their respective L1 and L2 thus having an opportunity to practice their L2 but also an obligation to provide models in their L1 to their partners for whom it is an L2 (Belz, 2005a); 2) only one language is used, as L1 by one partner group playing the role of tutors and as L2 by another partner group playing the role of learners (Sauro, 2009); 3) only the L1 is used by both partner groups during intercultural (CMC) sessions, whereas L2 is practiced during intracultural (traditional, in-class) sessions (Furstenberg et al., 2001). Thus, in most TC courses, data in one and the same language are being produced by both NSs and learners of that language during the same or similar tasks. This unique feature of telecollaboration makes it a perfect locus to collect a learner corpus with an in-built NS comparison corpus. As Kasper and Rose argue, a "defensible standard" against which learner language can be measured should be "derived from successful multilingual speakers' interactions in activities relevant for a given learner population" (2002: 86). Following this line of argument, an integrated NS corpus represents a more defensible baseline for measuring learner productions than external NS corpora typically employed in CIA studies because all TC participants are multilingual speakers participating in activities that are relevant to them. The validity of the NS baseline is the highest in configuration 1 (alternating L1 and L2), as Belz and Vyatkina argue, "[t]his configuration is an advantage in contrastive interlanguage analysis because learner productions are not separated in time and space from the baseline" (2008: 45). Moreover, members of both populations in configuration 1 participate in status-equal encounters (unlike in configuration 2) and not only in similar but also in the *very same* interactions (unlike in configuration 3).

Dense developmental data

Since TC courses typically span weeks or months of CMC exchanges, corpora comprising TC data represent a subtype of diachronic, or longitudinal, corpora, which allow tracking of participant development over time. Belz and Vyatkina propose density of observation as the main feature distinguishing the subtype of *Developmental Learner Corpora* (*DLC*) from other longitudinal corpora:

> We distinguish between *longitudinal* and *developmental* analyses with regard to the density of observation of learner performance over time. While 'longitudinal' may refer to analyses in which waves of data are elicited at more distant intervals (e.g. at the beginning and end of a semester), we reserve the term 'developmental' for those analyses in which learner performance is documented at close intervals or at all points of production. (Belz & Vyatkina, 2008: 33)

All TC data are saved in computers simultaneously and automatically, which means that researchers have access to the full contingent of learners' production data for the duration of the intercultural exchanges. Such access is especially valuable for developmental studies because no intermediate stages remain unaccounted as opposed to cross-sectional designs employing only two or three data elicitation waves. In other words, a TC researcher may collect and archive every single learner and NS utterance that each participant produces over the course of the TC partnership under study. This allows analysis of development of each individual in reference not only to the NS baseline but also to previous performance of the same individual. Thus, a DLC lends itself not only to cross-sectional aggregate analyses (typical for CIA studies) but also to analyses in sequence, tracking microchanges of each focal participant over time (Belz 2003b; Belz & Kinginger, 2003; Kinginger & Belz, 2005; Vyatkina & Belz, 2006; Vyatkina, 2007).

Pragmatic and Interpersonal Linguistic Features

Another major advantage of TC corpora is the wide array of discourse types and associated linguistic features represented in the data. Notably, CMC discourse belongs to hybrid linguistic genres such as email and Internet relay chat that are "culturally conditioned on a cline of 'writtenness' and 'spokenness'" (McCarthy, 1993: 171). Kern supports this claim, positing that synchronous CMC "combines the temporal immediacy of spoken interaction [...] with the social distancing allowed for by writing", and "incorporates many features of spoken mode within a written medium" (2000: 238).

Indeed, previous research has shown that TC discourse is rich in linguistic features typical of both spoken registers (e.g. personal pronouns, see Belz & Kinginger, 2003) and written registers (e.g. pronominal adverbs, see Belz, 2005b).

Due to the oral mode quality of the CMC data captured in the written electronic medium, TC corpora lend themselves to the exploration of *interpersonal language functions*, especially in teacher-guided project-based intercultural exchanges. TC partners need to express these functions if they participate in discussions about a wide variety of contemporary topics (Belz, 2005a). Although such TC data are produced in response to classroom tasks, they nevertheless come from real-life discussions on topics collaboratively chosen by the partners themselves and thus represent authentic interactional data. On the one hand, learners are requested to complete various communicative learning tasks by interacting with NSs including getting to know each other, exchanging their opinions on assigned topics, comparing attitudes and viewpoints and the like. On the other hand, learners inevitably engage in a variety of additional communicative actions beyond classroom tasks such as personal relationship building, intercultural misunderstandings, delegation of project tasks, directions for the use of project mediating software, disagreements, and discussion of popular culture topics. TC communicative actions that have been researched (see Belz, 2007 for a review) range from language play (Belz & Reinhardt, 2004) and flirting (Belz & Kinginger, 2002) to crying (O'Dowd, 2006) to conflict (Belz, 2003b; Schneider & von der Emde, 2006). Participating in these communicative actions requires a broad array of interpersonal linguistic features (Biber, 1988). Therefore, TC corpora are uniquely conducive to exploration of development of L2 pragmatic competence as opposed to the majority of learner corpora, which are comprised of student writing in the register of monologic argumentative prose (see Pravec, 2002 for a review).

In what follows, I describe the procedure of creating one particular TC learner corpus and demonstrate what research methods have been used to perform corpus-based analyses on the material of this corpus. These specific examples are also intended to illustrate how the advantages of TC learner corpora described above play out in actual research.

Analyses of TC discourse based on *Telekorp*

The Corpus

The *Telecollaborative Learner Corpus of English and German*, or *Telekorp* (Belz, 2005a), contains all of the CMC discourse and associated metadata produced through six iterations of TC partnerships conducted between a large public US university and a German teachers' college.

In these TC courses, American undergraduate students who learned German as an L2 were paired electronically with German university students who studied English as an L2. In a series of teacher guided tasks, the partner groups communicated with each other about various intercultural topics via email and live chat using German half of the time and English the other half (see Belz, 2005a for a detailed description of the participants and the course). In terms of learner corpus classification, *Telekorp* represents a bilingual developmental learner corpus with an integrated NS comparison corpus. Because both transatlantic partner groups (Americans and Germans) used both languages alternately, *Telekorp* contains, in fact, two integrated NS-learner subcorpora: L2 German with an L1 German comparison baseline and L2 English with an L1 English comparison baseline.

The Database

The TC electronic textual exchanges were initially saved by the participants themselves in the teleconferencing client Open Text FirstClass®. On a weekly basis, a research assistant copied all production data, replaced all participant names with unique pseudonyms to protect their confidentiality, and entered them into an electronic database using FileMaker Pro® software (Fig. 1).

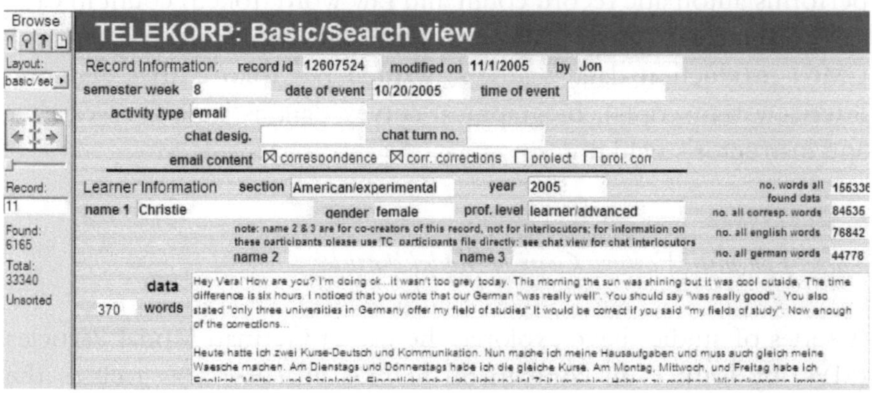

Figure 1. Example record of the *Telekorp* database

The full *Telekorp* database consists of three relational databases: 'Basic/Search View', 'Participants', and 'Full Chats'. More specifically, the production data were entered into the "data" field of the "basic" database and supplemented with a range of metadata: semester week and date of production; activity type (email, chat, survey, etc.); correspondence type (general correspondence, project discussions, error corrections, etc.); and a unique pseudonym of the author (or authors if the entry was written collaboratively). Each email constitutes one record for emails, and each turn produced by each participant constitutes one record for chats. All CMC data were further separated into the fields 'English words' and 'German words' to enable separate frequency counts for each language.

The basic view database is automatically linked to two relational databases: 'participants' and 'full chats'. The participant database is linked to the pseudonym of the first author (the person who typed the respective CMC entry) and allows for automatic display of the following learner metadata: year of participation in the TC course, section (e.g. American/ experimental), gender, and proficiency level. In sum, metadata for about 30 learner and task variables were collected at the beginning of the course via an electronic questionnaire and entered into *Telekorp*. The third relational database is linked to specific chat turn entries in the basic view and displays full chat records with sequential turns taken by all chat participants. FileMaker performs automatic record count and raw word (token) count in each field and record. Additionally, the corpus was supplemented by (non-CMC) production data (learners' written portfolio entries and oral interview transcripts), biographical survey data as well as researcher and instructor's field notes.

Target Linguistic Feature: German Modal Particles

A series of studies have explored the use of German Modal Particles (MPs) by learners in comparison to NSs in *Telekorp* as well as the effect of pedagogical interventions for teaching MPs using the same corpus. MPs function as important interpersonal markers in NS German speech but are notoriously difficult for L1 English learners because of the absence of a direct translation into English, their rampant polysemy, and strongly context-bound meaning (König & Requardt, 1991; Möllering, 2004; Weydt 2006). Based on an exploratory analysis of *Telekorp*, Vyatkina (2007) ascertained that NSs regularly used MPs in CMC exchanges conducted in German. Furthermore, she found that 97–98% of MPs in the corpus were used by the NSs and only 2–3% by the learners. This gave the researcher a rationale to develop and administer a pedagogical intervention for teaching four German MPs (*ja, denn, doch, mal*) to the American students within the framework of two consecutive TC courses using *Telekorp*-based materials. The effects of these interventions were explored in a series of studies.[4] This chapter is based on Vyatkina's (2007) unpublished study and presents (in a slightly modified format) the data coding procedure, corpus analysis tools and methods, and selected results focusing on CIA methodology. The study sought to answer the following research questions: Will the learners use more MPs after the intervention? Will the learner use be NS-like as to the frequency and distribution across the CMC media (chat and email) after the intervention?

Design

Seven American intermediate learners of German and sixteen native speakers participated in the focal TC course and exchanged emails and chats during eight weeks in fall 2005. This exchange resulted in 330 emails (33,000 German words) and 30 chat sessions consisting of

4 The effects of the first intervention were described in Belz & Vyatkina (2005) and Vyatkina & Belz (2006). The design was subsequently fine-tuned for the next iteration of the study which, after completion, presented rich material for Vyatkina's (2007) dissertation. Some effects of the second intervention were reported in Belz & Vyatkina (2008) but most material remained largely unpublished.

5,800 turns (5,300 German words). Weeks 1–4 of the exchange constituted the pre-intervention condition of the study, and weeks 5–8 the intervention/post-intervention condition.[5] The pedagogical intervention for MPs was made up of three week-long cycles each including an explicit data-driven instruction session based on the quantitative and qualitative analysis of data produced by the participants during CMC practice sessions (see Fig. 2). The instructional sessions included teacher explanations and class discussions of the MP meaning, functions, and use supported by projecting TC corpus excerpts containing MPs on the big screen, handouts, and worksheets (see Vyatkina & Johnson, 2007).

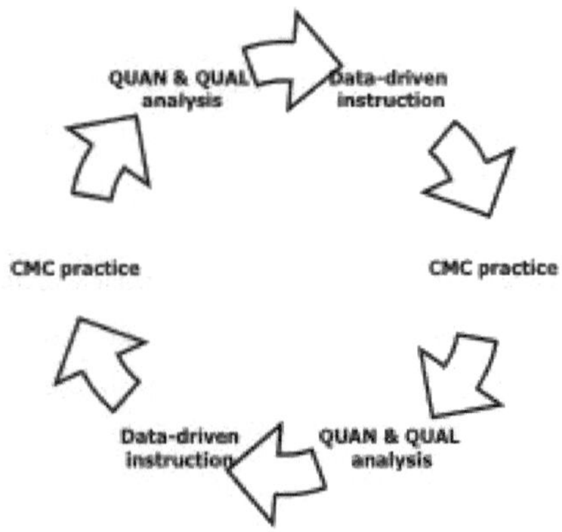

Figure 2. Cyclical pedagogical intervention

Data Coding

Textual data contained in *Telekorp* are raw, i.e. they are not coded for any linguistic categories such as parts-of-speech or syntactic struc-

5 One instructional session based on implicit enhanced condition was administered in week 4. However, it did not have any immediate production effect and is not considered here a part of the intervention (see Belz & Vyatkina, 2008 for details).

tures. Therefore, target linguistic features had to be manually tagged. McEnery, Xiao and Tono describe this "problem-oriented corpus annotation" as follows:

> First, it is not exhaustive –only the phenomenon directly relevant to a particular research question, rather than the entire contents of a corpus, is annotated. Second, the scheme for problem-oriented annotation is developed not for its broad coverage and consensus-based theory neutrality but for its relevance to the specific research question. (McEnery, Xiao and Tono, 2006: 43)

For MP coding, the *FilemakerPro* 'Find' tool was used to find each instance of the four focal words (*ja, mal, denn, doch*). Next, the word class membership of each found word was manually disambiguated to "weed out" (Poos & Simpson, 2002: 8) the homonyms with non-MP meaning. For example, the word *ja* can function in German as a modal particle and as an answering particle ('yes'), i.e. an MP homonym. As pointed out earlier, the MPs cannot be directly translated into English and require a paraphrastic description. For example, Möllering explains the meaning of the MP *ja* as follows:

> the speaker is trying to establish 'common ground' by marking a proposition as known to the hearer, thus inviting him/her to either accept the proposition as premise for the following exchange or to ask for clarification. (2004: 237)

For *Telekorp* coding purposes, the MPs were assigned the index 1 and MP homonyms the index 2, immediately following the word (e.g. *ja1; mal2*). For example:

> Das ist *ja1* cool!! 'This is [I am certain you agree] cool!!'

> Paula: ist es schweirig? 'is it difficult?'
> Simone: *ja2* 'yes'

This manual coding was the necessary initial step for automated frequency analyses performed later only on target words coded with the index 1.

Wordsmith Tools

The general learner corpus analysis technique is, according to Barlow:

> trawling through learner corpora using searching software to reveal and quantify recurrent patterns, typically lexico-grammatical patterns, that characterize the learner language associated with different learners and different settings. (2005: 336)

For MP frequency comparisons, the lexical analysis software *WordSmith Tools*®[6] (Scott, 2008) was used. It allows for retrieving examples and comparing frequencies of occurrence of focal features and their co-occurrence with other linguistic elements in specified subsets of data. Furthermore, the software automatically provides basic statistical indicators for comparing datasets such as log-likelihood index or type-token ratio. In addition to frequency, *WordSmith* provides information about, and illustrations of, the distribution of focal elements in the corpus subsets.

As *WordSmith* works with plain text files, data subsets intended for analysis were first exported from *FileMaker* into Unicode text files (to preserve special German typographic characters such as umlauts). In particular, data subsets for all learner productions before the intervention, all learner productions after the intervention, and all NS productions were extracted. For some analyses, these subsets were further subdivided into email data and chat data.

The three main tools provided by *WordSmith* are *Concord, KeyWords*, and *WordList*. The following sections describe selected comparative analyses performed with these tools on *Telekorp* MP data for the 2005 participant cohort (for the full reporting on the analyses, see Vyatkina, 2007).

6 <http://www.lexically.net/downloads/version5/html/index.html>.

Dispersion

In order to acquire an overall impression of the distribution of the target features in the corpus, the dispersion plots provided by the *WordSmith Concord* tool are useful. Dispersion plots are "maps showing where in the texts the search words were found" (Scott, 2001: 47). For this study, dispersion plots for each focal MP and each student population (learners and NSs) were retrieved from *Telekorp*. In both plots shown in Figure 3, each vertical line represents one MP use. The left and right margins represent the beginning and the end of the TC Internet exchange (spanning the total of nine weeks). The comparison of the two distribution plots for NS and learner MP use makes visible at what point the pedagogical intervention was delivered. NSs use all four focal MPs relatively evenly, with somewhat higher density of the MP *ja* and an increase in the overall density in the final third of the course. In contrast, three single lines in the left half of the learner plot represent three single MP uses in the first half of the TC exchange. The right third of the learner plot demonstrates a sharp increase (corresponding to Week 6 of the exchange, i.e., a week after the beginning of explicit instruction in Week 5) with the highest density of use for the MP *ja*. Therefore, the mere exposure to MP use in NS writing in the first half of the TC course did not trigger learner MP use, whereas the pedagogical intervention resulted in a drastic increase in MP use by the learners in approximation of the NS baseline on aggregate counts. By visually presenting the distribution of focal elements in the corpus subsets along the timeline, the plot tool is especially powerful for demonstrating the non-linear, explosive development of the target L2 feature in this study.[7]

7 The plot shows that the density of MP use by NSs also slightly increased toward the end of the correspondence (see Belz & Vyatkina, 2008 for a discussion). Although this was not the case in an earlier TC course iteration, learners' MP use also increased sharply after instruction (Belz & Vyatkina, 2005). Therefore, the MP increase in learner writing can be attributed to the instructional effect rather than to the increased exposure in the NS use.

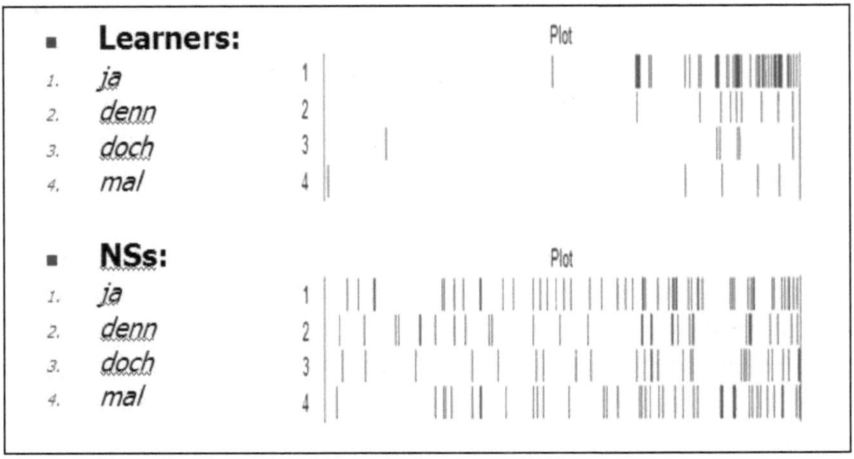

Figure 3. Dispersion plots of the MP use by learners and NSs

Wordlist

The wordlist-based analysis was performed for both CMC media types (email and chat) separately in order to investigate how common each focal MP is in comparison with other words in each respective subcorpus. For this purpose, the *WordSmith WordList* function was used. All running words from the corpus were retrieved in the form of a word list ordered by frequency. The most frequent word is ranked 1, the second frequent word 2 and so forth (Fig. 4). In addition, *WordList* provides summary statistics for each focal data subset. Table 1 presents such summary statistics for MP frequencies and the total number of German words broken down by medium (email and chat), time (pre-intervention and post-intervention), and participant group (learners and NSs).[8]

8 Email numbers declined after the first half of the course as email was mostly replaced by collaborative web-based projects in the second half.

Table 1. MP frequencies and total German words per medium, time, and participant group

medium	time	NSs		Learners	
		total words	MPs	total words	MPs
email	pre-intervention	14,685	54	10,284	3
	post-intervention	3,719	28	4,904	28
chat	pre-intervention	2,246	30	1,770	0
	post-intervention	3,421	52	3,631	43

First, the NS comparison baseline was explored. The word lists extracted from the NS chat and email subsets showed that MPs frequently appeared in NS writing, especially in synchronous CMC, i.e. chats. Among the total of 1,490 word types (or distinct words) contained in the NS chat subset, all four MPs cluster closely together and rank very high: from 47 to 57 in the frequency list. When normalized per 1000 words, the MP relative frequency ranges from 2.35 for *denn* to 3.54 for *ja*. Biber (2006) calls words that occur more than 1 time per thousand words of text highly frequent and considers them linguistic characteristics of the registers in which such words appear. Following this line of argument, MPs may be considered a linguistic characteristic of synchronous CMC discourse in German. The same holds for the NS email subcorpus, however to a lesser extent. The MP *ja* ranked 83 among 3,098 NS email word tokens and appeared on average 2 times per 1000 words and the MP *mal* ranked 132 and appeared 1.25 times per 1000 words, whereas the MPs *denn* and *doch* were still very frequent but appeared less frequently than 1 time per 1000 words. Next, word lists for the learner pre-intervention and post-intervention subcorpora were extracted. Whereas the pre-intervention chat list did not contain any MP instances, the post-intervention list contained all focal MPs. Notably, *ja* ranked 20th (Fig. 4), which places it among the most frequent words (mostly function words). In contrast, *mal, denn,* and *doch* were far below the NS baseline. A similar pattern was ascertained for emails. Therefore, the learners overused *ja* and underused three other particles in comparison with native speakers in both synchronous and asynchronous TC exchanges.

	Word	Freq.	%	Texts	%	RelC(3)
1	ICH	195	5.38	4	100.00	5.4
2	JA2	133	3.67	4	100.00	9.1
3	IST	121	3.34	4	100.00	12.4
4	DAS	81	2.24	4	100.00	14.6
5	WIR	64	1.77	4	100.00	16.4
6	UND	63	1.74	4	100.00	18.1
7	ES	57	1.57	3	75.00	19.7
8	NICHT	53	1.46	4	100.00	21.2
9	DIE	51	1.41	4	100.00	22.6
10	GUT	44	1.21	4	100.00	23.8
11	HABE	40	1.10	4	100.00	24.9
12	ABER	39	1.08	4	100.00	26.0
13	EIN	36	0.99	4	100.00	27.0
14	IN	35	0.97	4	100.00	27.9
15	SEHR	34	0.94	4	100.00	28.9
16	DU	33	0.91	4	100.00	29.8
17	EINE	33	0.91	4	100.00	30.7
18	AUCH	30	0.83	4	100.00	31.5
19	HABEN	30	0.83	4	100.00	32.4
20	JA1	30	0.83	4	100.00	33.2

Figure 4. WordList, learners, post-intervention chats

Keywords

The *KeyWords* tool allows automated comparison between two word lists. A key word is unusually frequent (or unusually infrequent) in comparison with the reference corpus (Scott, 2001). The statistic of log-likelihood is automatically calculated by this tool for marking significant and non-significant differences (Scott, 2001). Therefore, if the target feature appears among the key words while comparing two corpora, it is used in one of them with a significantly lower frequency (negative keyness) or higher frequency (positive keyness) in comparison with the other one. For this analysis, word lists for pre-intervention and post-intervention learner and NS subcorpora were extracted from *Telekorp* with email and chat data collapsed together to increase the frequency counts. Key word comparisons were conducted between the following pairs of subcorpora: 1) pre-intervention and post-intervention learner corpus; 2) pre-intervention and post-intervention NS corpus; 3) pre-intervention learner corpus and NS corpus; 4) post-intervention learner corpus and NS corpus. The MP *ja* appeared as a key word for distinguishing between the learner pre-intervention and post-intervention corpus but no other MPs were key for this comparison (Fig. 5). Therefore, although learners increased their use of all MPs after the intervention, only the increase in their use of *ja* was significant. No MPs functioned as key words between the NS pre-intervention and post-intervention corpus, which means that the NS baseline did not change over time.

N	Key word	Freq.	%	RC. Freq.	RC. %	Keyness	P
1	JA	1		50	0.58	-79.28	0.0000000000

Figure 5. MPs as key words between the pre-intervention and post-intervention learner corpus

The pre-intervention learner and NS corpus were distinguished by three MPs that appeared as key words: *ja*, *denn*, and *mal* (see Fig. 6). For the post-intervention learner-NS comparison, no MPs functioned as key words, which means that the learner MP use was not significantly different from NS use after the intervention. The frequency of the MP *doch* in both learner and NS CMC writing was too low to play a role in the differences found.

N	Key word	Freq.	%	RC. Freq.	RC. %	Keyness	P
1	MAL	1		24	0.14	-34.62	0.0000000011
2	DENN	0		22	0.13	-38.44	0.0000000000
3	JA	1		29	0.17	-42.99	0.0000000000

Figure 6. MPs as key words between the pre-intervention learner and NS corpus

Concordance

Whereas *WordList* and *KeyWord* were used to compare frequencies of occurrence of separate words in different datasets, the next series of analyses was conducted to explore characteristic co-occurrence of patterns of words, or collocations (Firth, 1968; Sinclair, 1991; McEnery, et al., 2006). The *WordSmith Concord* tool was used, which "locates all references to any given word or phrase within our corpus, showing them in standard concordance lines with the search word centered and a variable amount of context at either side" (Scott, 2001: 47, see Fig. 7–9). Having search words stacked and their left or right neighbors (collocates) alphabetized and highlighted facilitates comparison and finding regular patterns (O'Halloran & Coffin, 2004).

Collocations of German MPs have been thoroughly explored in NS oral discourse (e.g. Möllering 2004; Thurmair, 1991). These studies have shown that MPs frequently appear in collocation with the following linguistic structures: pronouns; modal verbs; other MPs; and formulaic expressions specific for each MP. Browsing the *Telekorp* concordance lines showed that the same linguistic structures were frequent neighbors of the focal MPs in both the NS and learner CMC writing. Following this preliminary finding, concordance lists for each MP and each data subset were further explored for specific contextual use.

The results of this analysis will be exemplified by collocations of *ja*, the most frequent MP in both the NS and learner discourse. It was found that, despite the similarity in the types of linguistic structures collocating with *ja*, there were also marked differences in the frequency and contextual meaning of these collocates. In terms of overall frequency, learners underused *ja* in collocations with pronouns, modal verbs, and other MPs and overused *ja* in formulaic patterns of appraisal in comparison with NSs. Moreover, a detailed contextual analysis of *ja* collocations with pronouns revealed additional fine-grained differences between the two populations.

NSs were found to use the MP *ja* in collocation with forms of the 2nd person personal and possessive pronouns *Du, ihr, dein* ('you', 'your') in 27.12% of all *ja* occurrences, and with forms of the 1st person personal and possessive pronouns *ich, mein* ('I', 'my') in 13.56% of all occurrences. In contrast, learners used *ja* in collocation with the 1st person pronouns with much higher frequency than with the 2nd

person pronouns: 33.33% of all *ja* occurrences with 'I', 'my' and 5.88% with 'you', 'your' (see Fig. 7, 8 for examples).

Concordance
Das sind aber kurze Ferien Dannhabt ihr ja1 viel länger frei als wir! Aber unser Se
deen nicht überrannt. Vielleicht findet ihr ja1 in einer ruhigeren Stunde Zeit uns ein
u bekommen. Vielleicht interessiert dich ja1 noch, was ich sonst in meiner Freizei
abe ich keines gesehen). Kannst es Dir ja1 mal1 im Internet anschauen
Knieschmerzen aufhören. Ich habe Dir ja1 gesagt, dass ich Sport studiere. Da h
durch Komma getrennte Sätze. Da Du ja1 sehr gut deutsch schreibst (und rede
eutsch schreibst (und redest?) wirst Du ja1 schon wissen, das unsere Wörter of
Schulen Naja2, vielleicht schaffst Du es ja1 dann mal1 bei mir vorbei zu kommen
... dafür ist man auf der Welt... Du lernst ja1 noch nicht so lange deutsch Weihna
2! Wie war es denn1? Davon hast du mir ja1 in deiner E-Mail geschrieben. Eine be
E-Mails antworten kannst. Du musst ja1 auch drei mal2 so viele schreiben wie

Figure 7. Collocations of *ja* with 2nd person pronouns, NSs

e Polin und keine Deutsche." Ich denke ja1 das die Kinder sind sehr gemein zu
haben ich muss gehen...aber ich mache ja1 die uebersetzung nachher! ja2 ich mu
wahrscheinlich zu teuer, und ich wuerde ja1 nicht mit meinen Eltern an Weiternac
ne haare und blau-graue augen ich liebe ja1 schon blaue Augen ich hab eigentlich
verdiene ein bisschen Geld! Ich brauche ja1 Geld um Buecher fuer die Universitae
. Bis zum naechsten mal2! -Chip Ich will ja1 dorthin reisen, aber dass meine
hr arm scheint und sie neue ist? Ich bin ja1 in der Mitte und bin ein bisschen verb
, aber ich habe Angst fuer(?) ich Schrieb ja1 zwei, oder? ach *schrieb ja2, bestim
koennten Ich weiss es nicht, wir ich sie ja1 ins Internet stellen kann *wie ich... u
h am 24. abends ja2 ich auch =) ich hab ja1 keinen! bin SINGLE =) ich auch!!! ich

Figure 8. Collocations of *ja* with 1st person pronouns, learners

MPs also collocated with the plural form of the 1st person pronoun *wir* ('we') in both NS and learner data. However, the two populations used this pronoun differently. Waugh (2006) has shown that in spoken interactions personal pronouns may play an 'inclusive' interpersonal role, placing the speaker and the hearer in one and the same social group, or an 'exclusive' role, placing the hearer outside the speaker's social group. In *Telekorp* data, German NSs used *wir* frequently and mostly inclusively, for referring to both German and American partners (Fig. 9). Americans, on the other hand, used *wir* only twice, both times exclusively, for referring to Americans as opposed to Germans.

Concordance

l2 sehr nett und witzig fand. Aber dafür haben wir ja1 die mails. Benutzt du icq oder skype auch? D
alles richig zu kooridinieren. Am Ende waren wir ja1 zu siebt. Hoffentlich haben wir euch mit unser
ich für immer lieben würden. Also dann hören wir ja1 gleich im Seminar voneinander! Ich freue mich
der da und wir können chatten. Dann können wir ja1 den Rest besprechen. Freu mich auf morgen.

Figure 9. Collocations of *ja* with the inclusive pronoun *wir*, NSs

Based on this classification, personal and possessive pronoun instances in *Telekorp* can be grouped into speaker-oriented pronouns ('I', 'my', and exclusive 'we', 'our') and hearer-oriented pronouns ('you', 'your', and inclusive 'we', 'our'). After calculating frequencies for these categories, NSs were found to use the MP *ja* in collocation with hearer-oriented pronouns in 45.76% and with speaker-oriented pronouns in 15.25% of all occurrences. Learners, in contrast, were found to use *ja* in collocation with hearer-oriented pronouns in 5.88% and with speaker-oriented pronouns in 37.25% of all occurrences (Figure 10). Therefore, NSs use the MP *ja* with the highest frequency in hearer-oriented utterances, which is in line with the interpersonal MP meaning component "reference to shared knowledge" (Möllering, 2001, p. 132). In contrast, learners use the MP *ja* most frequently when they refer to themselves (as a person or as a group of Americans as opposed to Germans).

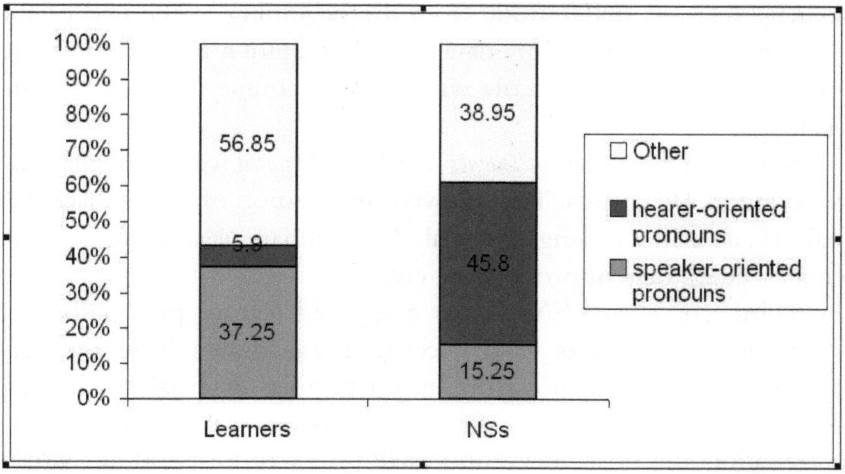

Figure 10. Proportion of collocations of *ja* with hearer-oriented and speaker-oriented pronouns, learners and NSs

Summary and Discussion

This chapter focused on applications of some corpus-based research methods and automated corpus analysis tools to TC discourse. First, the methodology of Contrastive Interlanguage Analysis, or CIA, was briefly reviewed and selected examples of CIA studies were listed. Next, advantages of combining CIA with research on telecollaboration were explained. Finally, examples from research that employed CIA for exploring a TC learner corpus were given, including the description of concrete applications of WordSmith Tools lexical analysis software. In this section, I summarize how a number of unique features of TC data facilitated a successful application of CIA methods and tools.

First, the *computer-mediated nature of the production data* allowed for automated saving of all of the TC discourse in computers. This allowed the researcher to explore the full course of L2 development of language learners under study from the beginning to the end of the TC exchange. The text-only data did not require a transcription and could be used simultaneously with the TC course for research and teaching.

Second, a *rich variety of learner and task metadata* were collected and saved in the TC corpus. This allowed the creation of data subsets for analysis according to language (only German language data), medium (email – chat), date of production, etc.

Third, an *integrated NS corpus* compared learner productions to NS baseline which was valid because it was drawn from the very same interactions and not from an unspecified external NS corpus. In particular, contrasts were computed between learner and NS pre-intervention and post-intervention MP use. Word list and key words corpus analysis tools were used to demonstrate that learners drastically underused MPs in comparison to NSs before the intervention but there was no significant difference between the populations after the intervention. Moreover, after the intervention, the learners were found to use MPs with different frequency according to the CMC medium in the same fashion as the NSs (fewer MPs in emails than in chats). Finally, the most frequent MP in both NS and learner discourse was *ja*. This finding confirms the results of previous research (Cheon-Kostrzewa & Kostrzewa, 1997; Kasper & Rose, 2002) showing that the L2 acquisition path often leads from most frequent to less frequent language features.

Fourth, because *Telekorp* archived *dense developmental data* and not only pretest/posttest data, it was possible to include a developmental component into the analysis and compare learner post-intervention productions to their own pre-intervention productions as a baseline. Moreover, the *Plot* function of the *Concord* tool facilitated a comparison of the dispersion of individual MPs between learners and NSs. It was found that the learner development was rather uneven: not monotonic over the TC course but rather explosion-like after the intervention (Figure 3). Furthermore, the individual developmental paths of each participant can be tracked over time in addition to analysis of aggregate cohort data. Such analyses are beyond the scope of this chapter, and the reader is referred to a series of studies which qualitatively and quantitatively analyze the development of individual participants from this study (Vyatkina, 2007; Belz & Vyatkina, 2008) and from another TC cohort (Belz & Vyatkina, 2005; Vyatkina & Belz, 2006).[9]

Fifth, applying CIA to TC discourse proved to be very efficient in demonstrating *L2 pragmatic development,* namely productive use of *interpersonal features,* as the result of pedagogical intervention. Fluency in using such features greatly helps learners develop advanced L2 competence with 'economical' means, as Weydt, Harden, Hentschel, and Rösler argue:

> Von einem gewissen Kenntnisstand des Deutschen an ist es viel ökonomischer, die immer wiederkehrenden Abtönungspartikeln zu lernen, als noch weiter an der Grammatik oder am übrigen Vokabular zu arbeiten. Man wird mit einem vergleichsweise geringen Aufwand an Arbeit ein erhebliches Mehr an Fähigkeit erreichen, idiomatisches Deutsch zu sprechen.[10.] (1983: 9)

This study confirmed the feasibility of explicit data-driven teaching of MPs. Despite ample exposure to the MPs in the NS discourse, only two learners used a total of 3 MPs at the pre-intervention stage. After the intervention, learners showed a dramatic increase in MP frequency and range in approximation of the NS baseline after 2–3 weeks of instruction. This result provides striking evidence in favor

9 It is worth noting that *all* participants made great strides in developing their production and/or awareness of German MPs although each of them followed his/her own developmental path. Some of them started using MPs right after the first instructional session while others waited until they became cognitively ready, and yet others did not start using MPs during the TC course but expressed a strong intention to use them in the future. These individual differences point to the limitations of aggregate quantitative studies and to the need to supplement them with qualitative case studies.

10 'From a certain level of knowledge of German onward, it is much more economical to learn the modal particles that always pop up than to work further on grammar or the rest of vocabulary. At a relatively low cost in work, one can attain a considerable enhancement in the ability to speak idiomatic German.' (Author's translation)

of explicit instruction in pragmatics, especially in comparison with untutored MP acquisition in study abroad settings that typically happens only after 20–30 months of exposure (Cheon-Kostrzewa & Kostrzewa 1997; Rost-Roth, 1999).

Sixth, the analysis of MP *collocations* showed that all patterns typical of NS data were found in the learner usage, however, some of these patterns were underused and others were overused. Although no significant aggregate frequency difference was found in the post-intervention data, there appears to be a rather large difference between NSs and learners with regard to MP contextual use. This analysis sheds light on the MP *semantic prosody* in NS and learner CMC writing, i.e. the contextual meaning "which is established through the proximity of a consistent series of collocates" (Louw, 2000: 57). In particular, it was found that NSs tended to use more "harmonic" MP/pronoun collocations and learners more "disharmonic" collocations (Aijmer, 2002: 68). In other words, collocations of MPs and hearer-oriented pronouns in NS discourse reinforced the interpersonal nature of both linguistic features, whereas the interpersonal nature of MPs conflicted with the speaker-oriented function of personal pronouns preferred by learners. This finding, again, lends support to explicit teaching of such fine-grained nuances of meaning with the help of corpus-based awareness-raising activities (see Vyatkina & Johnson, 2007 for pedagogical suggestions).

Conclusion

This chapter has demonstrated that TC discourse lends itself to explorations by corpus analysis methods and more studies in this direction are welcome and needed. Educators considering TC exchanges are encouraged to collect TC corpora and to include a research component in their planning process. First, they need to carefully follow the IRB procedures for protection of human subjects and agree these procedures with their TC partners since they may differ from institution to institution and from country to country. Next, they should decide upon and carefully follow the procedure for saving, archiving, and organizing the TC data. Although using database software is advisable for archiving both primary data and metadata, one should at least devise a transparent system of folders for saving the data as separate text files. The annotation of corpus data will depend on particular research objectives.

Both corpus-driven and corpus-based (Tognini-Bonelli, 2001) studies may be conducted on TC corpora. The former are exploratory studies that involve browsing through raw corpus data, looking for potentially interesting features and patterns, and formulating hypotheses for future testing. The latter are studies that focus on testing hypotheses which may come from previous research conducted in non-TC settings or one's own exploratory corpus-driven studies. For such studies, problem-oriented corpus annotation for target features needs to be conducted prior to analysis.

TC corpus research designs can be particularly recommended for SLA researchers interested in developmental interventional studies exploring effects of TC corpus-based pedagogical interventions (Belz & Vyatkina, 2008), studies of hybrid media and genres, as well as studies of interactional linguistic and discourse features. It is worth mentioning that although this essay reported on the use of proprietary corpus software such as *FileMaker* and *WordSmith*, open source software should be highly recommended for future studies. An example of user-friendly open source software with incorporated corpus annotation and analysis tools is *UAM Corpus Tool*[11], (O'Donnell, 2011) and a number of other tools have been developed that are freely available for research purposes. Finally, the importance of using different lenses for learner corpus analysis should be especially pointed out. Corpus research is uniquely suited for combining quantitative and qualitative methods, aggregate and microgenetic analyses,

11 <http://www.wagsoft.com/CorpusTool/>.

and such combinations are necessary for providing thorough and multifaceted accounts of learner development.

References

Aijmer, K. (2002). Modality in advanced Swedish learners' written interlanguage. In S. Granger, J. Hung & S. Petch-Tyson (Eds.), *Computer learner corpora, second language acquisition and foreign language teaching* (pp. 55–76). Amsterdam/Philadelphia: John Benjamins.

Aijmer, K. (2009). *Corpora and language teaching.* Amsterdam/Philadelphia: John Benjamins.

Aston, G., Bernardini, S., & Stewart, D. (2004). *Corpora and language learners.* Amsterdam/Philadelphia: John Benjamins.

Barlow, M. (2005). Computer-based analyses of learner language. In: R. Ellis & G. Barkhuizen (Eds.), *Analyzing learner language* (pp. 335–357). Oxford: Oxford University Press.

Belz, J. A. (2003a). From the special issue editor. *Language Learning & Technology, 7*(2), 2–5.

Belz, J. A. (2003b). Linguistic perspectives on the development of intercultural competence in telecollaboration. *Language Learning & Technology, 7*(2), 68–117.

Belz, J. A. (2005a). Telecollaborative foreign language study: A personal overview of praxis and research. In D. Hiple & I. Thompson (Eds.), *Selected papers from the 2004 NFLRC symposium on distance education, distributed learning, and language instruction.* Honolulu: National Foreign Language Resource Center, University of Hawai'i. Downloaded 1 May 2011 from <http://www.nflrc.hawaii.edu/networks/nw44/belz.htm>.

Belz, J. A. (2005b). Corpus-driven characterizations of pronominal *da*-compound use by learners and native speakers of German. *Die Unterrichtspraxis/Teaching German, 38*(1), 43–59.

Belz, J. A. (2006). At the intersection of telecollaboration, learner corpus research, and L2 pragmatics: Considerations for language program direction. In J.A. Belz & S. L. Thorne (Eds.), *Internet-mediated intercultural foreign language education* (pp. 207–246). Boston, MA: Heinle and Heinle.

Belz, J. A. (2007). The role of computer mediation in the instruction and development of L2 pragmatic competence. *Annual Review of Applied Linguistics, 27*, 45–75.

Belz, J. A., & Kinginger, C. (2002). The cross-linguistic development of address form use in telecollaborative language study: Two case studies. *Canadian Modern Language Review 59*(2), 189–214.

Belz, J. A., & Kinginger, C. (2003). Discourse options and the development of pragmatic competence by classroom learners of German: The case of address forms. *Language Learning, 53*(4), 591–647.

Belz, J. A., & Reinhardt, J. (2004). Aspects of advanced foreign language proficiency: Internet-mediated German language play. *International Journal of Applied Linguistics, 14*(3), 324–362.

Belz, J. A., & Thorne, S. L. (Eds.) (2006). *Internet-mediated intercultural foreign language education.* Boston, MA: Heinle and Heinle.

Belz, J. A., & Vyatkina, N. (2005). Learner corpus analysis and the development of L2 pragmatic competence in networked intercultural language study: The case of German modal particles. *Canadian Modern Language Review, 62*(1), 17–48.

Belz, J. A., & Vyatkina, N. (2008). The pedagogical mediation of a developmental learner corpus for classroom-based language instruction. *Language Learning and Technology, 12*(3), 33–52.

Biber, D. (1988). *Variation across speech and writing.* Cambridge: Cambridge University Press.

Biber, D. (2006). *University language: A corpus-based study of spoken and written registers.* Amsterdam: John Benjamins.

Byrnes, H., & Sinicrope, C. (2008). Advancedness and the development of relativization in L2 German: A curriculum-based longitudinal study. In L. Ortega & H. Byrnes (Eds.), *The longitudinal study of advanced L2 capacities* (pp. 109–138). New York: Routledge.

Cheon-Kostrzewa, B., & Kostrzewa, F. (1997). Der Erwerb der deutschen Modalpartikeln. Ergebnisse aus einer Longitudinalstudie (II). *Deutsch als Fremdsprache, 3*, 150–155.

Dooly, M. (2008). Telecollaborative language learning: A guidebook to moderating intercultural collaboration and language learning. Bern: Peter Lang.

Ellis, N.C., & Larsen-Freeman, D. (2006). Language emergence: Implications for applied linguistics—Introduction to the special issue. *Applied Linguistics, 27*(4), 558–589.

Firth, J. R. (1968). Linguistic analysis as a study of meaning. In F. R. Palmer (Ed.), *Selected papers of J. R. Firth 1952–59* (pp. 12–26). London: Longman.

Flowerdew, L. (2005). An integration of corpus-based and genre-based approaches to text analysis in EAP/ESP: Countering criticisms against corpus-based methodologies. *English for Specific Purposes, 24*, 321–332.

Furstenberg, G., Levet, S., English, K., & Mallet, K. (2001). Giving a virtual voice to the silent language of culture: the Cultura project. *Language Learning and Technology, 5*(1), 55–102.

Ghadessy, M., Henry, A., & Roseberry, R. (Eds.) (2001). *Small corpus studies and ELT: Theory and practice.* Amsterdam/Philadelphia: John Benjamins.

Gilquin, G. (2008). Hesitation markers among EFL learners: Pragmatic deficiency or difference? In J. Romero-Trillo (Ed.), *Pragmatics and corpus linguistics: A mutualistic entente* (pp. 119–149). Berlin/New York: Mouton de Gruyter.

Gilquin, G., Granger, S., & Paquot, M. (2007). Learner corpora: The missing link in EAP pedagogy. *Journal of English for Academic Purposes, 6*(4), 319–335.

Granger, S. (Ed.) (1998a). *Learner English on computer.* London: Longman.

Granger S. (1998b). Prefabricated patterns in advanced EFL writing: Collocations and formulae. In A. Cowie (Ed.), *Phraseology: theory, analysis and applications* (pp. 145–160). Oxford: Oxford University Press.

Granger, S. (2002). A bird's-eye view of learner corpus research. In S. Granger, J. Hung & S. Petch-Tyson (Eds.), *Computer learner corpora, second language acquisition and foreign language teaching* (pp. 3–33). Amsterdam: John Benjamins.

Granger, S. (2003). The international corpus of learner english: A new resource for foreign language learning and teaching and second language acquisition research. *TESOL Quarterly, 37*(3), 538–546.

Granger, S., Hung, J. & Petch-Tyson, S. (Eds.) (2002). *Computer learner corpora, second language acquisition and foreign language teaching*. Amsterdam: John Benjamins.

Granger, S., & Meunier, F. (Eds.) (2008). *Phraseology in foreign language learning and teaching*. Amsterdam: John Benjamins.

Guth, S., & Helm, F. (Eds.) (2010). *Telecollaboration 2.0. Language, literacies and intercultural learning in the 21st century*.. Bern: Peter Lang.

Housen, A. (2002). A corpus-based study of the L2-acquisition of the English verb system. In S. Granger, J. Hung & S. Petch-Tyson (Eds.), *Computer learner corpora, second language acquisition and foreign language teaching* (pp. 77–116). Amsterdam: John Benjamins.

Kasper, G., & Rose, K. (2002). *Pragmatic development in a second language*. Malden, MA: Blackwell.

Kern, R. (2000). *Literacy and language teaching*. Oxford: Oxford University Press.

Kinginger, C., & Belz, J. A. (2005). Socio-cultural perspectives on pragmatic development in foreign language learning: Microgenetic case studies from telecollaboration and residence abroad. *Intercultural Pragmatics, 2*(4), 369–421.

König, E., & Requardt, S. (1991). A relevance-theoretic approach to the analysis of modal particles in German. *Multilingua, 10*(1/2), 63–77.

Lee, D., & Swales, J. (2006). A corpus-based EAP course for NNS doctoral students: Moving from available specialized corpora to self-compiled corpora. *English for Specific Purposes, 25*(1), 56–75.

Louw, B. (2000). Contextual prosodic theory: Bringing semantic prosodies to life. In C. Heffer, H. Sauntson & G. Fox (Eds.),

Words in context: A tribute to John Sinclair on his retirement (pp. 48–94). Birmingham, UK: University of Birmingham.
Lüdeling, A., Walter, M., Kroymann, E., & Adolphs, P. (2005). Multi-level error annotation in learner corpora. *Proceedings from Corpus Linguistics 2005*, Birmingham. Downloaded 1 May 2011 from <http://www.corpus.bham.ac.uk/pclc/#corpora/>.
Mackey, A., & Gass, S. (2005). *Second language research. Methodology and design.* Mahwah, NJ: Lawrence Erlbaum Associates.
McCarthy, M. (1993). Spoken discourse markers in written text. In: J. Sinclair, M. Hoey & G. Fox (Eds.), *Techniques of description: Spoken and written discourse* (pp. 170–182). New York: Routledge.
McEnery, T., Xiao, R., & Tono, Y. (2006). *Corpus-based language studies: An advanced resource book.* London: Routledge.
Möllering, M. (2001). Teaching German modal particles: A corpus-based approach. *Language Learning & Technology*, *5*(3), 130–151.
Möllering, M. (2004). *The acquisition of German modal particles.* Bern: Peter Lang.
Myles, F. (2008). Investigating learner language development with electronic longitudinal corpora: Theoretical and methodological issues. In L. Ortega & H. Byrnes (Eds.), *The longitudinal study of advanced L2 capacities* (pp. 58–72). New York: Routledge.
Nesselhauf, N. (2004). Learner corpora and their potential for language teaching. In J. Sinclair (Ed.), *How to use corpora in language teaching* (pp. 125–152). Amsterdam: John Benjamins.
Nesselhauf, N. (2005). *Collocations in a Learner Corpus.* Amsterdam: John Benjamins.
Norris, J., & Ortega, L. (2009). Towards an organic approach to investigating CAF in instructed SLA: The case of complexity. *Applied Linguistics, 30*(4), 555–578.
O'Donnell, M. (2011). UAM Corpus Tool [Computer software]. University of Madrid, Spain. Downloaded 12 November 2011 from <http://www.wagsoft.com/CorpusTool/index.html>.
O'Dowd, R. (2006). The use of videoconferencing and email as mediators of intercultural student ethnography. In J. A. Belz & S. L.

Thorne (Eds.), *Internet-mediated intercultural foreign language education* (pp. 86–120). Boston: Heinle and Heinle.

O'Dowd, R. (Ed.) (2007). *Online intercultural exchange: An introduction for foreign language teachers.* Clevedon, UK: Multilingual Matters.

O'Halloran, K., & Coffin, C. (2004). Checking overinterpretation and underinterpretation: Help from corpora in critical linguistics. In C. Coffin, A. Hewings & K. O'Halloran (Eds.), *Applying English grammar: Functional and corpus approaches* (pp. 275–297). London: Arnold.

Ortega, L., & Byrnes, H. (Eds.). (2008). *The longitudinal study of advanced L2 capacities.* New York: Routledge.

Paquot, M. (2008). Exemplification in learner writing: a cross-linguistic perspective. In S. Granger & F. Meunier (Eds.), *Phraseology in foreign language learning and teaching* (pp. 101–119). Amsterdam: John Benjamins.

Poos, D., & Simpson, R. (2002). Cross-disciplinary comparisons of hedging: Some findings from the Michigan Corpus of Academic Spoken English. In R. Reppen, S.M. Fitzmaurice, & D. Biber (Eds.), *Using corpora to explore linguistic variation* (pp. 3–23). Amsterdam/Philadelphia: John Benjamins.

Pravec, N. (2002). Survey of learner corpora. *ICAME Journal, 26*, 81–114.

Reder, S., Harris, K., & Setzler, K. (2003). A multimedia adult learner corpus. *TESOL Quarterly, 37*(3), 546–557.

Rogers, C. R. (1969). *Freedom to Learn.* Columbus, OH: Charles E. Merrill.

Rost-Roth, M. (1999). Der Erwerb der Modalpartikeln. Eine Fallstudie zum Partikelerwerb einer italienischen Deutschlernerin im Vergleich mit anderen Lernervarietaten. In N. Dittmar & A. Giacalone Ramat (Eds.), *Grammatik und Diskurs/Grammatica e discorso. Studi sull'acquisizione dell'italiano e del tedescho/Studien zum Erwerb des Deutschen und des Italienischen* (pp. 165–209). Tübingen, Germany: Stauffenburg.

Rundell, M., & Granger, S. (2007). From corpora to confidence. *English Teaching Professional, 50*, 15–18.

Sauro, S. (2009). Computer-mediated corrective feedback and the development of L2 grammar. *Language Learning and Technology, 13*(1), 96–120.

Schneider, J., & von der Emde, S. (2006). Dialogue, conflict, and intercultural learning in online collaborations between language learners and native speakers. In J. A. Belz & S. L. Thorne (Eds.), *Internet-mediated intercultural foreign language education* (pp. 178–206). Boston: Heinle and Heinle.

Scott, M. (2001). Comparing corpora and identifying key words, collocations, frequency distributions through the WordSmith Tools suite of computer programs. In M. Ghadessy, A. Henry & R. Roseberry (Eds.), *Small corpus studies and ELT: Theory and practice* (pp. 47–67). Amsterdam/Philadelphia: John Benjamins.

Scott, M. (2008). WordSmith Tools (Version 5) [Computer software]. Liverpool, UK: Lexical Analysis Software.

Seidlhofer, B. (2002). Pedagogy and local learner corpora. In S. Granger, J. Hung & S. Petch-Tyson (Eds.), *Computer learner corpora, second language acquisition and foreign language teaching* (pp. 213–234). Amsterdam: John Benjamins.

Sinclair, J. (1991). *Corpus, concordance, collocation.* Oxford: Oxford University Press.

Sinclair, J. (Ed.) (2004). *How to use corpora in language teaching.* Amsterdam: John Benjamins.

Thurmair, M. (1991). "Kombinieren Sie doch nur ruhig auch mal Modalpartikeln!": Combinatorial regularities for modal particles and their use as an instrument of analysis. *Multilingua, 10*(1/2), 19–42.

Tognini-Bonelli, E. (2001). *Corpus linguistics at work.* Amsterdam: John Benjamins.

Tono, Y. (2000). A computer learner corpus based analysis of the acquisition order of English grammatical morphemes. In L. Burnard & T. McEnery (Eds.), *Rethinking language pedagogy from a corpus perspective* (pp. 123–132). Frankfurt am Main: Peter Lang.

Vyatkina, N. (2007). Development of second language pragmatic competence: the data-driven teaching of German modal particles based on a learner corpus. The Pennsylvania State University, Unpublished doctoral dissertation.

Vyatkina, N., & Belz, J. A. (2006). A learner corpus-driven intervention for the development of L2 pragmatic competence. In K. Bardovi-Harlig, J. C. Félix-Brasdefer, & A. Omar (Eds.), *Pragmatics and language learning (Vol. 11)* (pp. 315–357). Honolulu: National Foreign Language Resource Center, University of Hawai'i.

Vyatkina, N., & Johnson, K. E. (2007). *Teaching German modal particles: A corpus based approach.* University Park, PA: CALPER Publications.

Warschauer, M. (Ed.) (1996). *Telecollaboration in foreign language learning.* Honolulu: Second Language Teaching and Curriculum Center, University of Hawai'i.

Waugh, L. (2006, September). Indices of identity and markers of ideological stance by proficient L2 speakers in their L1: Evidence from French conversational interaction. Lecture given at the Pennsylvania State University.

Weinrich, H. (1993). *Textgrammatik der deutschen Sprache.* Mannheim, Leipzig, Wien, Zürich: Dudenverlag.

Weydt, H. (2006). What are particles good for? In K. Fischer (Ed.), *Approaches to discourse particles. Studies in pragmatics 1* (pp. 205–217). Amsterdam: Elsevier.

Weydt, H., Harden, T., Hentschel, H., & Rösler, D. (1983). *Kleine deutsche Partikellehre.* Stuttgart: Ernst Klett.

Using Eye-Tracking to Investigate Gaze Behaviour in Synchronous Computer-Mediated Communication for Language Learning

BREFFNI O'ROURKE

This chapter focuses on the application of eye-tracking –i.e., the recording of a subject's point of gaze during visual tasks– to research in synchronous, text-based computer-mediated communication (hereafter just SCMC) for language learning. It differs from the other chapters in two ways that need to be addressed at the outset. First, eye-tracking requires apparatus and software with which many investigators in CMC are not closely familiar, and to which they do not typically have routine access. Second, little work has so far been done using eye-tracking, either in CMC studies generally or in SCMC for language learning specifically[1]. As a chapter on a method that is so far embryonic, perhaps it requires more self-justification than others.

A trivial justification is that researchers are well advised to consider what can in principle be done, not just what is relatively easily done, and in doing so to look at prospective as well as established research methods. But obviously, methods ought to be chosen on the basis of their potential to address particular research questions. So we need to consider what eye-tracking might be able to tell us about SCMC. When I turn to that later, I will argue that this technology can offer insights into micro-aspects of individual SCMC behaviour that have consequences for the sequential unfolding of discourse, and for learners' attention to language form. In short, eye-tracking can bring us much closer to the first-person experience of

1 The only two examples that I am aware of, O'Rourke (2008) and Smith (2010), are discussed below.

SCMC in ways that are interesting in themselves, but also tightly connected to other phenomena, individual and dialogic, that researchers already are interested in. I hope to convince the reader that these micro-level aspects of SCMC, which have been relatively overlooked in the literature so far, deserve much closer attention than they usually get.

Individual Processes in SCMC

It is easy to see why SCMC has usually been approached with the tools and assumptions of fields concerned chiefly with spoken communication, like discourse analysis of various kinds (e.g., Cherny, 1999; Darhower, 2002; Herring, 2004; Paulus & Phipps, 2008; Weininger & Shield, 2004), conversation analysis (Garcia & Jacobs, 1998, 1999; Hutchby, 2001; Negretti, 1999), pragmatics (Burke & Kraut, 2008; Lange, 2008; Morand & Ocker, 2003; Park, 2008a, 2008b; Sykes, 2005), and interactionist SLA (Fuente, 2003; O'Rourke, 2005; Ortega, 1997; Smith, 2003; Sotillo, 2010). Clearly, the discourse of SCMC shares a range of important characteristics with spoken discourse, characteristics frequently discussed in the literature (e.g., Chun, 1994; O'Rourke, 2005; Smith, 2003; Werry, 1996) and not requiring elaboration here. But much is obscured or lost when SCMC is viewed solely through a lens not designed to detect its distinctive properties. Discourse analysis and conversation analysis, in particular, emphasise social ordering: the shared, public, co-constructed aspects of linguistic interaction. But it is a fact whose consequences are rarely fully drawn in the second language literature that the practical mechanics of co-construction work very differently in SCMC than in speech. These differences are attributable ultimately to the temporal relationship between linguistic production and perception and to the differing nature of 'communicative space' in the two modes. In face-to-face communication, utterances are perceived, by both speaker and hearer, as they are produced, and production and perception are by their nature public; that is, they are simultaneously observable to both speaker and addressee. Hence, both time and communicative space are continuous and shared. As a result, the raw facts of communication –the words spoken, their source, the ordering of turns or the existence of overlaps: what I will call the discourse text – are all *mutually manifest* (Sperber & Wilson, 1995): they are facts immediately accessible to all parties, and the further fact that they *are* equally accessible is itself accessible to all parties.[2] Hence, these raw facts constitute a subset of the parties' *mutual cognitive environment* (ibid.), the set of assumptions that are mutually manifest to them. Let us call this subset a *mutual textual environment.* To put it simply, parties to spoken face-to-face interaction are 'on the same page' (I use the metaphor advisedly!), and know they are.

In SCMC, though, a message's production and perception are, for the addressee, temporally split, occupying two distinct stretches of time. I compose my message now, but you will read it only later, and maybe considerably later – indeed, perhaps not at all. This can be termed *local asynchronicity*, to distinguish it from the global synchronicity that follows from the fact that the communicating parties are online simultaneously. Furthermore, because message composition is invisible to addressees, each party to the dialogue inhabits a private as well as a public communicative space (and usually, of course, a separate physical space as well). The facts of production and perception are thus not immediately mutually manifest. There is a mutual textual environment in a certain sense: the record of the text as it appears in the output window is identical for all parties. However, this is a system-generated artifact that will generally not correspond to the actual turn-by-turn experience of any participant, and need not in any case

2 By contrast, it is improbable that for any dialogue there exists a reliable consensus regarding implicatures, presuppositions, illocutions, perlocutions, tone, or other inferred or interpretational aspects of talk. There may not even be consensus at any given moment regarding encoded, semantic meaning. These phenomena are part of discourse, but not of what I am calling discourse text.

be referred to by participants at all beyond reading the most recent two or three partner send-units (Garcia & Jacobs, 1998, 1999).[3]

These facts will be illustrated in more detail below. For the time being, the main points are that in SCMC, the record that appears in the output window presents only one perspective on a dialogue that has multiple perspectives, none of them definitive, and that the assumption of a single, monolithic, mutual textual environment must be abandoned in favour of the recognition of multiple textual environments. And this in turn means that individual, private experience is a discrete communicative phase for SCMC interlocutors in a sense that it is not for face-to-face ones: not only do interlocutors occupy separate physical spaces, they also experience the sequentiality of the discourse text in different ways, they read their partners' send-units in private, and they compose and often edit their own send-units in private. In SCMC, the first-person experience of the discourse text is not a shared one.

This does not mean that SCMC discourse does not show social ordering or joint construction. It means that in SCMC, the production of an orderly discourse involves distinctive mechanisms that have quite clear-cut, recurring phases of private activity, receptive and productive. A research programme that omits this individual, first-person perspective cannot aspire to a full understanding of SCMC. Yet the great majority of research to date has failed to give due weight to the private phases of SCMC interaction. I will argue in the next section that this follows from over-reliance on output logs as a data source, and that eye-tracking in particular offers much richer insights into first-person experience.

3 The units sent with each press of the Enter key are sometimes less than complete turns, and sometimes more than single utterances. I use the term *send-unit* when it seems important to distinguish such units from these other kinds of unit.

Capturing the First-Person Perspective: Beyond Output Logs

This first-person perspective may be interesting in itself, and necessary for a full picture of SCMC, but what relevance does it have for the use of SCMC in language learning specifically? I think there are two kinds of answer to this. Let us take a rough and ready distinction between broadly interactionist and broadly sociocultural approaches to language learning. As a first approximation, we can say that in the interactionist model, communicatively-focused interaction shapes language in a way that makes it optimal for learning, which is conceived of as an individual cognitive process. The main role of interaction is as a generator of input to a learning device (Long, 1985; Mackey, 1999; Pica, 1994; Scarcella & Higa, 1981; Varonis & Gass, 1985). Sociocultural perspectives, meanwhile, hold that learning is best understood as a social achievement that actually takes place *in* dialogue (Firth & Wagner, 1997; Lantolf, 2000; Lantolf & Appel, 1994; Lantolf & Poehner, 2008; Lantolf & Thorne, 2006). Interactionist approaches clearly have a stake in processes that belong in the private phases of SCMC – in particular, the cognitive processes of monitoring (Krashen, 1985; Levelt, 1989), attention, and noticing (Schmidt, 1995). (See also Reinhardt, this volume.) The relevance of the first-person perspective seems clear here. But for both interactionist *and* sociocultural approaches there is a further reason for focusing on the individual aspect, namely, that the details of the discourse text are often not explicable without consideration of how the text came into being, which means looking at the individual processes of text production.

But output logs alone, the data source on which many studies have relied to date (e.g., Fernández-García & Martínez Arbelaiz, 2003; Negretti, 1999; O'Rourke, 2005; Ortega, 1997; Tudini, 2003), can provide little basis for inferences about private actions. Output logs, often called transcripts, are textual records of chat sessions. They correspond to the dialogue as it appears in the output window of chat participants; in some systems they are saved automatically, in others users must explicitly save using a menu command, and in still others users can save only by manually copying the text and pasting into a file. Since logs show every utterance generated by the participants, in the order in which they are registered by the system's server, they give the impression of completeness. However, in an earlier publication (O'Rourke, 2008), I suggested that among the information missing from output logs are individual paralinguistic and non-linguistic behaviours, such as gestures and vocalisations (as investigated by Smith & Gorsuch, 2004), drafting processes prior to sending, and information on attentional focus. In addition, the property of interactional tempo – the overall speed of the exchange and the time between send-units – is not reliably deducible from output logs. I also suggested (O'Rourke, 2008) that there are other data sources that can serve to fill in these gaps, among them retrospective user report, keystroke logs with or without timestamps, video screen-capture, conventional video recording of the user in his or her physical environment, and eye-tracking.

On the basis of a brief SCMC extract, the article (ibid.) goes on to show how such additional data can provide information entirely missing from output logs and can also strengthen certain conclusions only tentatively inferrable from logs. For example, raw output logs clearly allow us to identify discourse activities like the resolution of communicative problems (negotiation for meaning). In addition, logs may license inferences about (i) timing, notably when turn ordering suggests that adjacent messages were composed in overlap, and (ii) attention to form: apparent uptake by a learner of native-speaker recasts may suggest noticing. If we go beyond simple logs to data sources that furnish precise information on timing (screen-captured video or precisely time-stamped output logs), we can reconstruct with greater confidence the tempo of the exchange (an aspect of interaction that plays an important part in shaping the subjective experience of an SCMC dialogue) and establish, with greater certainty than that permitted by simple logs alone, which pairs of send units were composed in overlap. These details of timing and simultaneity underlie the characteristic disrupted adjacency of output logs. Timing information allows us to see differences in composition speed between individuals, which are also likely to contribute to the subjective experience (as when a slow typist is conversing with a much faster one, for example).

With screen-captured video or keystroke logs, we can in addition see drafting processes (Smith, 2008; Smith & Gorsuch, 2004; Smith & Sauro, 2009), including the correction of typographical errors. More interestingly, we can identify cases where messages are abandoned completely, often in deference to new topics initiated in 'interrupting' messages from a partner, and cases where the user alters earlier parts of the draft (rather than the latest text at the draft's 'right edge'), suggesting deliberate monitoring during the drafting phase. The analyst can also see where the user paused during drafting, which in particular cases, given the evidence of further edits to the draft, might be reasonably be taken as an indicator of cognitive processes like lexical search or sentence framing. Pauses might also be caused by, or occasion, scanning of the output window, in search of new send-units from the partner or of previous occurrences of words or structures. With video, then, we can get much closer to the details of the learners' interaction with their own text and, sometimes at least, with the previous text as recorded in the output window.

Table 1 summarises the advantages and limitations of the data sources discussed so far.

Table 1. SCMC data sources

Data source	***Kind of evidence***	***Advantages***	***Limitations***
Standard output logs	Utterance form and content; Discourse activities	Easy to collect	Turn sequence a system artifact corresponding to no user´s experience; Intended turn adjacency sometimes uncertain; No evidence of exchange tempo
Timestamped output logs	As above, with additional timing infor-	Help to reconstruct turn sequences and give	Timestamps sometimes too imprecise

	mation	indication of exchange tempo	for accurate sequence reconstruction
Retrospective user report	Impressions and recollections of affect, individual decision processes, reading processes, attention and noticing	Phenomenologically rich	Limited reliability
Keystroke logs	All individual keystrokes (by one or more parties), including use of edit-keys	Reveal drafting processes	Separate software required; Data less easily read than output logs
Screen-captured video	Video showing all activity as it appeared on recorded subject's screen: subject's drafting, other participants' output	Reveals drafting processes and timing	Separate software required; Data analysis requires repeated playback of small segments and use of a transcription scheme
Video-recording of subject(s) in physical environment	User attention, concentration, affect, boredom, distraction, drafting and revision processes, exchange tempo, etc.	Captures many aspects of first-person experience of SCMC, including ones highly relevant to language learning	Set-up relatively complex and intrusive; Collection of large amounts of data impractical; Transcription and analysis of data in fine detail presents challenges

The final type of data considered by O'Rourke (2008) was gaze data, provided by eye-tracking equipment. Following a brief introduction to the principles of eye-tracking, this illustration will be expanded below using the example of three styles of eye-tracker analysis.

Eye-Tracking Basics

An eye-tracker is a device that determines the precise movements of a subject's point of gaze with respect to visual stimuli: objects, physical scenes, still or moving images, or texts. Gaze movements are calculated from eye movements, which are in turn estimated by one of a number of methods, depending on the particular tracker. The device used in work reported here incorporates hidden near-infrared diodes which set up reflections on the pupils. The reflections are detected and tracked by a camera, and point of gaze is continuously calculated and recorded by software. Earlier eye-tracking technology was strictly laboratory-bound, and was intrusive for subjects, requiring the head to be fixed in one position using bite-bars or head frames. Many newer eye-trackers are portable and allow the subject free or minimally constrained movement. Lightweight devices may be worn on the head or incorporated in purpose-made spectacles, or housed in a specially designed computer monitor, with no physical contact with the subject at all.

One application of eye-tracking is in real-time interactivity: for example, an eye-tracker may function as a computer input device, allowing the user to activate a function by simply looking at the appropriate interface element. Our interest here, though, is in research applications. In the broadest terms, eye trackers allow investigators to explore the interface between the sense of sight and the visible environment: investigators record, for later analysis, the gaze of subjects during the performance of tasks such as operating a flight simulator, scanning a picture, navigating a website, or reading a text. This allows researchers to make inferences, with more certainty than they otherwise could, about the dynamics of subjects' focal attention. The research interest will typically lie in the inferences that can be drawn beyond the basics of what is looked at and when. In cognitive domains, for example, deploying point of gaze as a variable in carefully designed experiments makes possible very precise inferences about the nature of mental processes beyond simple apperception. This is notably the case for reading, where eye tracking has made possible great advances in our understanding of how text is mentally processed (Rayner, 2009). Eye-trackers have also been used in psycholinguistics more generally for investigation of real-time processing in L1 (Knoeferle & Crocker, 2009; Tanenhaus, Spivey-Knowlton, Eberhard, & Sedivy, 1995) and L2 (Cieślicka, O'Rourke, & Singleton, 2008).

The essential nature of eye movements in reading are well established (Rayner, 2009). In contrast to *pursuit*, where the eyes smoothly follow a moving object, reading consists of a succession of alternating *saccades*, or jumps, and *fixations*, where the gaze comes to rest, or nearly so. Saccades take about 30 milliseconds (ms) and span 7 to 9 letter spaces; fixations encompass one or two characters (there may be smaller movements within this radius) and last 225–250 ms on average, in a range of 50–600 ms.

Procedures and data formats

The eye-tracker used to gather the data discussed below was a Tobii 1750 <www.tobii.se>. It incorporates concealed near-infrared lights and a camera in the frame of an otherwise ordinary LCD computer monitor. The tracker allows considerable freedom of head movement. The eye-tracking process is unobtrusive: after a brief calibration procedure, the investigator starts the recording with a mouse-click.

ClearView[4], the software application that is used to set up and manage studies (e.g., organising subject and stimulus data, initiating and saving recordings), in addition provides access to various data visualisation and analysis tools. In the case of an SCMC study, where the stimulus is an interactive program interface rather than a static

4 Now superseded by Tobii Studio.

image, data of three kinds are recorded: (1) a screen-captured video recording; (2) time-stamped *event data*, i.e., key-presses and mouse-clicks; and (3) *gaze data*, which are sampled by this particular eye-tracker at 50 Hz (50 samples a second, or one every 20 milliseconds). The key elements of each data point are the timestamp in milliseconds (20, 40, 60, 80 …) and the screen *x* and *y* coordinates (in pixels) of the subject's gaze at the moment in question. Gaze data are 'raw', in the sense that there is no distinction between saccades and fixations: each data point simply represents the coordinates of the gaze at a given moment, provided the tracker has been able to determine it. Data will be absent when the subject blinks or looks away from the screen.

For present purposes, we can focus on two ways in which the data can be more usefully represented for the SCMC researcher. First, recalling that the eyes are not always absolutely still even during fixations, raw gaze data can be converted into *fixation data* by grouping together, as fixation events, sequences of gaze-points spanning a user-defined duration (say, 40 ms) that are clustered within a certain user-defined radius (say, 20 pixels). For example, what would appear in the *gaze* data file as five successive gaze samples located within 20 pixels of one another, time-stamped at 1000, 1020, 1040, 1060, 1080, would be registered in the *fixation* data file as a single fixation, with timestamp 1000 and duration 100 ms. So the resulting fixation data file is essentially a time-stamped list of the screen coordinates and durations of each successive fixation. Fixation data can be exported for further processing in spreadsheet or statistical applications.

Second, ClearView can present the data in the more intuitive *gaze replay* format. In this representation, the software plays back the screen video while superimposing on it a moving dot representing the point of gaze. This animated gaze point is generated from the numerical gaze data in real time as the video plays. This representation in turn can be exported into a standard video format (AVI), and played, manipulated and annotated in any suitable qualitative data analysis program. This kind of data representation permits analysis by direct observation.

Three Illustrations

In this section, I will try to illustrate some of the ways that eye-tracking can bring us closer to the detailed mechanics of SCMC. Three different kinds of analysis will be presented. The first will be a brief summary of the illustrative gaze analysis presented in (O'Rourke, 2008), and looks at reading patterns in NS-NNS interaction. The second extends this preliminary investigation by exploring two full-length SCMC sessions. And the third, finally, illustrates the issue of private textual environments. The focus is on method rather than outcomes, and each example highlights a slightly different approach to the analysis of eye-tracker data.

All data presented are from a collection of output logs and eye-tracker data from one-off SCMC tandem sessions (O'Rourke, 2007) set up for the purpose of the study. The participants were undergraduate university students, all native speakers of English, learning French, German or Spanish either as a degree subject or as an elective module. Each session was about 45 minutes long and involved interacting in a MOO[5] with a native speaker of the target language (TL). Participants were instructed simply to chat to their partner; no specific task was given, though possible topics of talk were displayed on-screen for reference. They were told to start in English and switch to the TL half way through, or vice versa. The native speakers of English sat in front of a Tobii 1750 eye tracker connected to an ordinary PC. Participants were informed that eye-tracking was taking place and had formally consented to the recording of the data and its use for research purposes.

5 A kind of text-based virtual environment. For present purposes only the chat-like communication function is relevant.

Analysis 1: Interpretation of a Brief Extract Using "Gaze Replay"

In illustrating the limitations of output logs, I set out above some of the additional information available using additional data sources, as discussed by O'Rourke (2008), on the basis of a short tandem SCMC extract. Here I will highlight some additional facts that can be derived by observing the gaze-replay data of the extract.

In one sense, this kind of analysis is straightforward: it amounts to reconstructing the story of what happened, from one participant's point of view, in the exchange in question, and in some cases this is very clear from close observation of gaze replay. The analyst is likely to be interested in specific instances of attention to linguistic items, particularly if he/she is working within the interactionist paradigm. But there are two related challenges. The first is ambiguity in the data. It is not always clear whether an apparent brief fixation, particularly on a line of only one or two words, indicates reading at the level of awareness that we would regard as significant. Presumably, we are interested in at least (i) deliberate re-reading of one's own output, before or after sending, since this amounts to a form of monitoring, potentially for linguistic form; and (ii) reading of currently relevant or previous output from one's partner at a level of awareness that might permit noticing to occur (Schmidt, 1995). Difficulties of interpretation therefore arise in the case of fleeting fixations that do not form part of the left-to-right fixation-saccade-fixation pattern characteristic of canonical reading. This problem typically arises in the case of subjects who are non-touch typists, looking at the keyboard for long stretches and perhaps looking up occasionally at the draft in progress. Do isolated, brief fixations potentially permit noticing to take place? Should we consider them to be strategic, or are they more or less reflexive?

This challenge leads to the second. Observational, interpretational analysis must aspire to replicability and minimise subjectivity. Hence, operational definitions need to be found to which the researcher holds him- or herself accountable. An operational definition for the act of *reading own draft before sending*, for example, might encompass the minimum qualifying number of fixations; whether or not these must occur left-to-right (bearing in mind that *regression* of gaze to earlier parts of a text are common in reading); whether the sequence of fixations must encompass the whole of the draft from start to end, and so on. There seems to be no other way of validating such definitions than assuring oneself that they largely match one's subjective impressions of what constitute clear cases of reading, neither significantly over- nor under-identifying them. There will thus always be some arbitrary element to this procedure, but the important thing from the point of view of replicability is that the researcher adheres to the definitions established.

This method of analysis yields evidence that may corroborate or undermine inferences which could be drawn from other sources. In the extract discussed by O'Rourke (2008), the subject, Ciara, a student on an elective German module, is in conversation with Steffi, her native speaker (NS) partner, in German. There are three cases where other sources suggest uptake of implicit recasts or attention to model lexical tokens in the partner's output:

- Editing data from keystroke logs or screen video would show that Ciara changes *Ich geht mehr gut* to the more nearly target-like *Es geht mehr gut* (the target form is *Es geht mir gut* "I am well"). Since the NS partner has produced, in the immediately previous turn, the variant *Mir geht es gut*, this raises the possibility that Ciara was influenced by that turn to make the *ich* to *es* correction. The gaze replay allows us to confirm this: before making the edit, Ciara re-reads the model NS utterance in the output window, then fixes on the word *Ich* in her own draft, and finally makes the change.
- There is an apparent implicit correction by Steffi of Ciara's spelling *Sociologie* (Steffi: *Studierst du also Soziologie?* "Are you studying sociology?"). When Ciara uses the word a second time, she spells it correctly with <z> instead of <c>, which might suggest to an analyst using only the log that she has taken up Steffi's correction. Again, the gaze replay confirms this: before beginning her draft (the relevant part of which reads *und wir mussen fuer ein Jarh*

Soziologie machen), she fixes briefly on Steffi's model in the output window, briefly on her own misspelling before that, begins her draft, and refers back to Steffi's model three times while typing the word *Soziologie*.

- Edit data show a correction of an incipient misspelling *Gessell-schaft*, previously modelled by Steffi, to the correct *Gesellschaft*. Here too, the gaze data confirm that she consults Steffi's model three times while typing the word and correcting her erroneous beginning, *Gesse[…]*.

But in addition, gaze data can show up learner actions where they are not detectable from any other data source. In this extract, the gaze replay shows that Ciara compares her *studiere* ("study" 1st person singular) to Steffi's *studierst* (2nd person singular); and that after typing *Philosophie* she looks back at Steffi's token of *Soziologie*, before adding *(?)*, inviting confirmation from Steffi. This suggests that she was considering *Soziologie* as a partial orthographic model for *Philosophie*.

Gaze replay thus permits close analysis of short extracts which can yield detailed insight into individual linguistic-cognitive strategies in L2 SCMC. But it can be used also to go beyond specific incidents and establish the subject's habitual reading behaviours; this is what we turn to next.

Analysis 2: Patterns of Monitoring in Two Complete Sessions

O'Rourke (2008) suggested that there are three particular phases in individual SCMC use that count as opportunities for attention to linguistic form: reading while drafting (*simultaneous monitoring*); after drafting but before sending (*pre-send monitoring*); and after sending (*post-send monitoring*). In this extract, Ciara watches the keyboard while typing, glancing up every few seconds. She interrupts her typing to read partner interruptions, to focus on noticed errors in her draft, and occasionally to scan back for particular model items in previous text. She reads a completed draft prior to sending only once; but she reads her own message immediately after sending on four occasions out of the five in the extract.

The interest of such reading and re-reading patterns lies in the potential to empirically scrutinise conjectures that SCMC inherently fosters focus on form in ways not available in oral communication (Beauvois, 1997; Kitade, 2000; Lai & Zhao, 2006; Ortega, 1997; Pellettieri, 2000; Salaberry, 2000; Tudini, 2003; Warschauer, 1998). Intensive case studies can raise and sharpen methodological and empirical questions, but authoritative answers must come from larger-scale investigations. No claim to such authority can come from the following results, which come from gaze-replay analysis of only two full sessions, but they do give indications of what we might expect to find in a full-fledged study as well, including a hint of the range of individual variation. The subjects are Ciara, again, and Erik, who like Ciara is taking German as an optional module. The native-speaker partner is the same in both cases.

In the case of simultaneous monitoring (i.e., reading one's own draft while typing), the following patterns are evident. First, both subjects watch the keyboard primarily as they type (visible as the disappearance of the gaze point towards the bottom of the screen). Episodes of switching gaze back to the screen occur at periodic intervals during longer drafts; when typographical errors occur; always when revising (deleting and/or inserting); and at what seem to be natural pauses, typically at clause or sentence boundaries. Brief glances at any such point may be prolonged if the subject notices a partner "interruption", and this can sometimes be seen to lead to a reassessment of the relevance of the current draft (i.e., discourse-level monitoring). These patterns are closely similar for both subjects.

Since the patterns are so uniform, quantification would not add importantly to the analysis in this case. However, it is possible to process the numerical *fixation data* in order to produce, quasi-automatically, static visual representations of monitoring (see below), using the following procedure.

First, event data (keypresses and mouse-clicks) and fixation data are merged and sorted by timestamp, to yield a single chronological list in which fixations are interspersed with keypresses. In this merged list, drafting phases are readily identified as those stretches of events and fixations occurring between an initial keypress and the pressing of the *Enter* key, which publishes the draft. Within drafting phases, gaze transitions from screen back to keyboard can be established with a considerable degree of accuracy on the basis of what one can term the *fixation interval*, the time that elapses between the end of one fixation and the start of another (itself easily calculated from fixation timestamps and durations).

A fixation interval can logically correspond to one of three different phenomena: (1) a saccade; (2) a cluster of 'fixations' of less than the criterial values (40 ms and 20 pixels were the values used in the present study); (3) a blink; or (4) a gaze transition from the screen to elsewhere. Now, Rayner (2009) gives 30 ms as a 2-degree saccade duration typical of reading; Sirevaag and Stern (1998), citing earlier work, consider blinks of less than 300 ms to be "normal", and ones of 300–500 ms to be "long duration". We can therefore be confident that a fixation interval of greater than 500 ms corresponds neither to a saccade, nor a blink, nor to a long series of very short, scattered sub-fixations. Such a long gap between fixations is thus highly likely to be due to a gaze transition away from the screen. If a half-second-long gap occurs within a drafting phase, and especially if it is followed by keystrokes rather than by further fixations, we can infer with confidence that this is a gaze transition to the keyboard. The moment of gaze transition from keyboard to screen then corresponds straightforwardly to the next fixation recorded in the data. In this way, each keypress can be labelled as being associated with either screen or keyboard gaze with the help of spreadsheet formulae, and the merged keypress and fixation data can be manipulated in a text editor to produce visualisations such as those in figures 1–4. In these visualisations, non-indented lines represent phases of keyboard-directed gaze while typing, while the indented lines represent fixations and keypresses while the subject is looking at the screen.

Key:

#	Backspace (delete backward)
_	Trailing space
*	One fixation
________	New send-unit

```
Ja
            *
, Gesse
            ******
#
            *****#*
ellscha
            *************
ft
            ****
- danke
            *
!
```
(Ja, Gesellschaft- danke!)

Figure 1. Simultaneous monitoring – Ciara (L2 phase) corrects *Gesellschaft*

```
not really its kind of hard
          **
co
          *#*
#
          ***
because i never
          **
studie
          *d*
 chemistry
          **
before and it seems to be based alot on that!
          **
_____________________________________
yea
          *##
es
          *********
but
          ***####
so the course will probably get alot hat
          ****#
rder!
          **
but in 2nd year we get to speicialise
          **
 so i can drop chemistry if i want
          *,**
 what about you
          *
what course w#
          *ar*e
 you studying?
          ****
```

(*not really its kind of hard because i never studied chemistry before and it seems to be based alot on that! / yes so the course will probably get alot harder!but in 2nd year we get to speicialise so i can drop chemistry if i want, what about you what course are you studying?*)

Figure 2. Simultaneous monitoring – Erik (L1 phase)

```
         g*
rr im so angry, i thought i had a 9 am this morning but
the teacher
         *_
never showed up!
___________________________________
yeah, tired too, but luckily it's almost xmas!
___________________________________
i know, i practically ran down dawson street.
         ***
```

(grr im so angry, i thought i had a 9 am this morning but the teacher never showed up! / yeah, tired too, but luckily it's almost xmas! / i know, i practically ran down dawson street.)

Figure 3. Simultaneous monitoring – Caitlin (L1 phase)

```
on m'a dit que c parce_
         *
u
         *e
 l y a bcp_
         **
d
         *
e
         *
ntreprises francaises qi#ui
         *
 sont install
         *
e_
         *
ici, car c
         * *
moi##
         *##*#
lest#
         *
 impots sont moins chere
         *
 qu'en_
         *
france
```

(on m'a dit que c parce ue l y a bcp d'entreprises francaises qui sont installe ici, car les impots sont moins chere qu'en france)

Figure 4. Simultaneous monitoring – Caitlin (L2 phase)

In figure one, we see that Ciara, though her gaze is on the keyboard while typing, looks up repeatedly while correcting the word *Gesellschaft.* As noted above, we can tell from the gaze replay data that she is checking the spelling model provided (implicitly) by her partner. In figure 2, we can see that a large number of Eric's screen-gaze periods are associated with edits, in this case, backspaces. Figures 3 and 4 illustrate the simultaneous monitoring patterns of Caitlin (who is taking French as a degree subject and is a regular user of MSN Chat in French), and a striking difference between her L1 and L2 habits is evident: In English (figure 3), she tends to type complete drafts – up to 67 keypresses in the sample given – without looking at the screen at all, whereas in French (figure 4) she looks up much more often: her longest keyboard-gaze period is only 27 characters, and there are several stretches much shorter than that. This suggests that the L1 / L2 distinction might be an influential factor in simultaneous monitoring behaviours: at least some users might be more careful monitors of their own output in L2 than in L1, though one possibility that would need investigation is that this is more an index of confidence levels in L2 typing than a strategic concern with formal L2 accuracy more generally.

Overall, the picture that emerges of simultaneous monitoring is that it is driven chiefly by low-level editing considerations, in particular, the need to delete accurately. The periodic glances we see are too brief to be plausibly focused on morphosyntax or expression, so that learners are likely to note only spelling errors at best. However, since learners sometimes notice interruptions during these occasional glances, they may be led to consider the topical relevance of the draft they are currently working on, as evidenced by the fact that they on occasion completely delete a draft and start a new one relevant to the interruption.

We turn next to pre-send monitoring, operationally defined as at least two fixations on the input field following the completion of a candidate draft (i.e., a draft that is potentially sendable). Table 1 shows the relevant quantities in Ciara and Erik's sessions. This is not a consistent behaviour for either of these subjects, and there is no significant difference between L1 and L2. However, like simultaneous monitoring, pre-send monitoring sometimes appears to be focused on the relevance of the current draft in light of a newly-arrived interlocutor turn.

Table 2. Number (%) of instances of re-reading draft before sending (pre-send monitoring)

	Ciara	Erik
L2	8 (31%)	4 (24%)
L1	6 (27%)	6 (40%)

Post-send monitoring is more prevalent overall, and in Erik's case, nearly categorical (table 2).

Table 3. Number (%) of instances of re-reading after sending (post-send monitoring)

	Ciara	Erik
L2	14 (54%)	15 (88%)
L1	11 (50%)	15 (100%)

Since Erik's pattern is so consistent, the question arises whether there is a pattern discernible behind Ciara's approximately 50/50 split. A sample of instances where Ciara does not re-read her own turn after sending suggests that partner interruptions may be a factor; this hypothesis is borne out by a complete survey (table 3).

Table 4. Interaction between Ciara's post-monitoring behaviour and partner interruptions

	Subject re-reads	**Subject doesn't re-read**
Interruption	11 (38%)	18 (62%)
No interruption	14 (74%)	5 (26%)

In the absence of an interruption, Ciara re-reads on three out of every four occasions, whereas the tendency is reversed where there is an interruption. So it seems that after sending, Ciara will attend to a new partner turn, if there is one, rather than re-reading her own; but otherwise she will generally re-read her own turn. Ciara's drafts are interrupted by partner send-units on 26 occasions, Erik's on only ten, so it is possible that this tendency is not an idiosyncrasy of Ciara's, but that she is simply quantitatively more affected by it. If this is the case, then we can conjecture that post-send monitoring is a default tendency, and that the medium itself pushes users towards engaging in it.

Finally in this analysis, we turn to a reading behaviour that does not count as monitoring in the usual sense: the reading of "old" text in the output window, which I will call *look-back*. This is an action whose boundaries are not as clear-cut as the foregoing monitoring behaviours, but in the case of Ciara and Erik's sessions, it is possible to distinguish between two types of look-back. First, there is target-focused *scanning* behaviour, where the subject evidently looks for an instance of a form which he or she recalls. There are three clear-cut instances of this, all in Ciara's L2 phase. First, while drafting, she locates *Oesterreich* and *Oberoesterreich* ("Austria" and "Upper Austria") in her partner's output, fixes on them several times, then types *Oesterreich* in her draft. Second, also while drafting, she locates two tokens of *Einwohner* in her partner's output, then corrects the capitalisation of her own token, *einwohner*. And finally, during a wait period (awaiting a partner turn), she scans back and fixes for several seconds on her own erroneous item *Frienden*, which should be *Freunde*. There is no subsequent self-correction, but her gaze behaviour suggests that she may have noticed that the word "doesn't look right", at least.

Second, during wait-periods, there are several instances of re-reading recent, but sometimes also considerably older turns, in an apparently unsystematic but quite sustained fashion (table 4), which we might call *browsing*. In a gaze replay, browsing typically involves the reading of several older turns, some in sequence and some not.

Table 5. Occurrences of browsing

	Ciara	**Erik**
L2	3	2
L1	7	8

Since browsing is more common in L1 than L2, it cannot be explained primarily as a strategic exploitation of the medium for L2 processing or learning. An alternative conjecture is that this kind of re-reading functions to refresh memory of past, especially recent discourse text, and possibly to organise or re-organise the subject's representation of it. The next analysis illustrates why such re-organisation might be necessary.

Analysis 3: Reconstructing One User's Experience of the Discourse Text

Towards the start of the chapter, I pointed out that each party to an SCMC dialogue has a different experience of the sequentiality of the discourse text. The gaze-replay function allows us to reconstruct the sequence experienced by a subject, an exercise that allows us to explore more closely the ways in which SCMC discourse can unfold. Consider the following log extract, from Caitlin's L1 phase (certain minor typing errors corrected):

1.	Caitlin:	so how is everything?
2.	Isabelle:	well I'm a bit tired... more than a bit, but on the whole it's fine
3.	Isabelle:	what about you ?
4.	Caitlin:	grr im so angry, i thought i had a 9 am this morning but the teacher never showed up!
5.	Caitlin:	yeah, tired too, but luckily it's almost xmas!
6.	Isabelle:	that's tough... especally when you had a hard time to get up...
7.	Caitlin:	i know, i practically ran down dawson street.
8.	Isabelle:	I am looking forward to the holidays, really
9.	Caitlin:	will you be going home?
10.	Isabelle:	so you live near the campus ?
11.	Isabelle:	yes I am going back to France for one week
12.	Caitlin:	yes, i leave at trinity hall in rathmines
13.	Caitlin:	just a week? will you be travelling the other time or studying?
14.	Isabelle:	your'e lucky then. I have hour and a half of transport every day
15.	Caitlin:	opps i live at...
16.	Caitlin:	really? how far away do you live?
17.	Isabelle:	near Blandchardstown
18.	Caitlin:	so for a 9 am you have to leave your house at 7h30, that's when i get up
19.	Isabelle:	exactly !
20.	Caitlin:	oh yeah, i used to swim out there on sundays. at the NAC
21.	Caitlin:	there was always traffic even on a sunday afternoon.
22.	Isabelle:	yes, it's a very big building this NAC
23.	Caitlin:	have you ever been there?

By examining the replay of her gaze during this stretch of dialogue, we can reconstruct Caitlin's sequential experience of it. "Experience" is meant to encompass both the composition of her own turns and the initial reading (ignoring re-reads) of her partner's, both of which are visible from the gaze replay. Hence, if a turn from Isabelle appears before one from Caitlin in the output log, but the replay shows that Caitlin composed her turn before reading Isabelle's, then Caitlin's sequential experience was in fact Caitlin-Isabelle. Caitlin's sequential experience of the discourse text in this extract was as follows:

1. Caitlin:	so how is everything?
4. Caitlin:	grr im so angry, i thought i had a 9 am this morning but the teacher never showed up!
3. Isabelle:	what about you ?
2. Isabelle:	well I'm a bit tired... more than a bit, but on the whole it's fine
5. Caitlin:	yeah, tired too, but luckily it's almost xmas!
6. Isabelle:	that's tough... especally when you had a hard time to get up...
7. Caitlin:	i know, i practically ran down dawson street.
8. Isabelle:	I am looking forward to the holidays, really
9. Caitlin:	will you be going home?
10. Isabelle:	so you live near the campus ?
12. Caitlin:	yes, i leave at trinity hall in rathmines
11. Isabelle:	yes I am going back to France for one week
13. Caitlin:	just a week? will you be travelling the other time or studying?
15. Caitlin:	opps i live at...
14. Isabelle:	your'e lucky then. I have !hour and a half of transport every day
16. Caitlin:	really? how far away do you live?
18. Caitlin:	so for a 9 am you have to leave your house at 7h30, that's when i get up
17. Isabelle:	near Blandchardstown
20. Caitlin:	oh yeah, i used to swim out there on sundays. at the NAC
19. Isabelle:	exactly !
21. Caitlin:	there was always traffic even on a sunday afternoon.
22. Isabelle:	yes, it's a very big building this NAC
23. Caitlin:	have you ever been there?

The obvious point is simply that the order in which Caitlin reads the turns (including her own) is substantially different from the order found in the output log. The screen video shows that some turns were drafted simultaneously, obviously a very common occurrence in SCMC, thus the order perceived by Isabelle must be different again. So in addition to the output log, there are as many versions of the order of turns as there are parties to the dialogue, a fact that the gaze data bring home to us emphatically.

More specifically, this insight into Caitlin's sequence disambiguates certain relations between turns. For instance, from the log alone we might conclude that Caitlin's (4) *grr im so angry [...]* is a response to Isabelle's (3) *what about you ?* However, in reality Caitlin began drafting unit 4 before she saw the unit (Isabelle's 3) to which it seems to relate. It was actually a new conversational initiative, in the absence of any immediate response from Isabelle.[6] In other words, rather than the action sequence the log suggests at first glance:

1.	Caitlin:	so how is everything? [*Initiative: wellbeing inquiry*]
2.	Isabelle:	well I'm a bit tired […] [*Answer*]
3.	Isabelle:	what about you? [*Reciprocation of wellbeing inquiry*]
4.	Caitlin:	grr im so angry […] [*Answer*]

the conversation actually unfolded as parallel topic strands:

1. Caitlin: so how is everything? [*Initiative: wellbeing inquiry*]	
[*17 seconds pass*] ➔➔➔	4. Caitlin: grr im so angry […] [*New initiative*]
2. Isabelle: well I'm a bit tired […] [*Response*]	
3. Isabelle: what about you? [*Reciprocation of wellbeing inquiry*]	

Similarly, consider 14–20, repeated below in the log order (self-repair in 15 omitted):

14. Isabelle:	you're lucky then. I have hour and a half of transport every day

6 As it happens, Caitlin's response token "yeah" and the elliptical formulation "tired too" in 5 indicate that it is a response to the turn represented in units 2 and 3. But it could have been otherwise: in only slightly different circumstances it might have been impossible for either Isabelle or a reader of the log to know that the apparent coherence was only coincidental.

16. Caitlin:	really? how far away do you live?
17. Isabelle:	near Blandchardstown
18. Caitlin:	so for a 9 am you have to leave your house at 7h30, that's when i get up
19. Isabelle:	exactly !
20. Caitlin:	oh yeah, i used to swim out there on sundays. at the NAC

Up to turn 19, this too seems a perfectly coherent exchange, but the log sequence is misleading, because the superficial dialogic order is not the one that was actually intended. Similarly to the previous example, there is a long pause, after turn 16, that leads Caitlin to offer a further turn rather than wait silently for Isabelle's response. The resulting structure, inferrable from the screen video and gaze replay, looks like this:

14. Isabelle: you're lucky then. I have hour and a half of transport every day [*Assertion*]

16. Caitlin: really? how far away do you live? [*Surprise display, supplementary question*]	
[*22 seconds pass*] →	18. Caitlin: so for a 9 am you have to leave your house at 7h30, that's when i get up [*inference, projecting confirmation*]
17. Isabelle: near Blandchardstown [*answer*]	
20. Caitlin: oh yeah, i used to swim out there on sundays. at the NAC [*recognition display*]	
	19. Isabelle: exactly ! [*confirmation of inference*]

There is a great deal more that could be said of this extract and what screen video and gaze replay data tell us about it. The first point that I hope has emerged clearly is that there are multiple sequences in SCMC –the one recorded in the output window / log and the ones experienced by the participants. The further point is that in making sense of the discourse text, both the participants and the analyst must derive an abstract text, recorded nowhere, such as those represented in the examples above. This abstract text is not unilinear but consists, at certain points, of multiple topic strands running in parallel: it is vital to note that it is not possible to create a single, coherent linear text from the above extract simply by re-arranging the turns. SCMC discourse text is not just an ordinary conversation jumbled up; it is a form of conversation that is multilinear even with just two participants, and its coherence must be actively inferred and tracked by the participants, and by the analyst.

Experimental Paradigms

The above analyses are based on quasi-naturalistic data elicitation sessions, but of course eye-tracking lends itself just as well to experimental methods. At the time of writing, the only full-fledged eye-tracking / L2 SCMC study that has been published is one by Smith (2010), who uses such a paradigm. Space considerations preclude giving more than a brief synopsis.

The focus of Smith's investigation is noticing of recasts by learners of English. The learner's task is a narrative re-telling, and recasts were provided by the researcher in the role of chat partner. Noticing was operationalised as a fixation of 500 ms or more on the target item. In addition to the (necessarily tentative) findings on recasts – which in many respects corroborate previous research– Smith highlights the issues that arise for the eye-tracking method itself as used in this kind of research. He notes that "it seems to provide a good indication of noticing (at least at some level)" (p. 92); and he suggests that

> [t]he most useful types of output generated by the ClearView software in this study is found in the video files [...] The text output file alone [...] is limited in its usefulness for examining interactional chat data without the screen capture file. [...] in chat interaction one needs not only a measure of duration but also an indication of multiple fixations on a given point of text such as a morphological ending, lexical item, etc. (Smith, 2010: 93–94).

He is certainly right that the textual/numerical fixation and event data cannot tell us which linguistic items the subject is looking at, and cross-referencing to the gaze replay is therefore essential. In principle, though, it ought to be possible to create tools, based on optical character recognition (OCR) algorithms, which could produce a database of the screen coordinates of each word on the chat interface at each moment of the recorded session. The word focused on by the subject at any given fixation could then be automatically identified from the gaze coordinates. And as we have seen (simultaneous monitoring, Analysis 2 above), the fixation data alone allow us to see global reading patterns without reference to gaze replay.

Smith's final point is particularly relevant for further eye-tracking work in cognitive SLA:

> the cut off length of 500 ms for considering a fixation as evidence of noticing may be too short or too long. With little guidance in this area one way to better establish this cut off may be to carefully correlate such a measure of noticing with other sources such as think-aloud protocols or stimulated recall. It is precisely this need to correlate the eye-gaze measure of noticing with other, more established measures that is a first step in legitimizing this approach as a tool in future inquiry into noticing and SCMC. (Smith, 2010: 94)

Conclusion

The disparate, tentative findings set out above hint at a view of SCMC in which it is not the visual, inscriptional, or permanent nature of the medium which has the greatest influence on the participants, but rather the unique nature of its communicative space. Oral communication is a simultaneous, shared experience based on a mutual textual environment. SCMC partitions this into multiple private communicative phases that are only partially aligned in time, and this leads to a discourse text that requires of the participants more attentional resources than does the tracking of face-to-face talk. And as we saw when looking at reading patterns, the tracking of topical relevance in particular is a driving concern behind many monitoring and reading patterns.

The more general points that I have tried to make are that the SCMC experience in general, and that of L2 learners in particular, cannot be understood without getting to grips with the nature of private experience, and that eye-tracking constitutes an ideal tool for tackling it. As the tools become more accessible and easier to use, it may be that we will learn as much about the finer detail of SCMC in L2 as we have begun to learn about the broader canvas. Certainly it seems clear, at the very least, that researchers must go beyond output logs for many investigations relevant to language learning. For many purposes, screen video will suffice, and happily that is a technology that is readily available and easy to use. Eye tracking offers screen video and more, but there are obstacles to its use by second language researchers. Most obviously, eye-trackers are still very expensive, and likely to remain so. There are various ways around this: it may be possible to rent an eye tracker for a brief period for a relatively affordable outlay; making common cause with colleagues in psycholinguistics may make for a more persuasive funding application, promising a greater return on investment in the form of a wider research agenda; and of course, given the many applications of eye tracking, it is quite possible that one or more eye trackers may already be available in psychology, computer science, engineering, health sciences or other departments.

A further obstacle is the learning curve involved in using an eye tracker. Actually setting up and running a data-gathering session is not difficult with the Tobii 1750 and ClearView, but understanding and selecting the most appropriate operating parameters is more challenging. Also taxing is the unwieldy nature of the data, compared to output logs: the researcher has to consider how best to organise the numerical data for analysis (e.g., which software tools to use, how to customise them, how to filter data, etc.), and how to present results of the analysis of the visual (gaze replay) data. Behind these problems of analysis and presentation are more fundamental issues of validity and reliability in this new kind of data, since there are as yet no standard operational definitions for such questions as what ought to count as reading in SCMC, or how long a fixation needs to be to license an inference of noticing.

None of these problems are insurmountable; it is surely worthwhile to confront them. Eye-tracking promises a depth of detail in analysis of SCMC discourse that is unattainable through any other means, and indeed insights of a different *kind* than we can otherwise aspire to. This is a method with the potential to deepen our understanding both of the individual and the social aspects of SCMC discourse, and to explore the nature of their interplay. Along the way, it is possible that we can hope to gain insights into the nature of L2 learning processes more generally, whether from a sociocultural or an individual-cognitive perspective.

References

Beauvois, M. H. (1997). High-tech, high-touch: from discussion to composition in the networked classroom. *Computer Assisted Language Learning, 10*(1), 57–69.

Burke, M., & Kraut, R. (2008). *Mind your Ps and Qs: the impact of politeness and rudeness in online communities.* Paper presented at the Proceedings of the 2008 ACM conference on Computer supported cooperative work.

Cherny, L. (1999). *Conversation and community : discourse in a social MUD.* Stanford, Calif. Cambridge: CSLI; Cambridge University Press.

Chun, D. (1994). Using computer networking to facilitate the acquisition of interactive competence. *System, 22*(1), 17–31.

Cieślicka, A., O'Rourke, B., & Singleton, D. (2008). The processing of multi-word units: Evidence from readers' eye movements. In K. Myczko, B. Skowronek & W. Zabrocki (Eds.), *Perspektywy glottodydaktyki i językoznawstwa. Tom jubileuszowy z okazji 70. urodzin Profesora Waldemara Pfeiffera* [*Perspectives on foreign language teaching and linguistics. Festschrift on the occasion of the 70th birthday of Professor Waldemar Pfeiffer*] (pp. 39–55). Poznań: Wydawnictwo Naukowe UAM.

Darhower, M. (2002). Interactional features of synchronous computer-mediated communication in the intermediate L2 class: a sociocultural case study. *CALICO Journal, 19*(2), 249–277.

Fernández-García, M., & Martínez Arbelaiz, A. (2003). Learners' interactions: a comparison of oral and computer-assisted written conversations. *ReCALL, 15*(1), 113–136.

Firth, A., & Wagner, J. (1997). On discourse, communication, and (some) fundamental concepts in SLA research. *Modern Language Journal, 81*(3), 285–300.

Fuente, M. J. (2003). Is SLA interactionist theory relevant to CALL? A study on the effects of computer-mediated interaction in L2 vocabulary acquisition. *Computer Assisted Language Learning, 16*(1), 47–81.

Garcia, A. C., & Jacobs, J. B. (1998). The Interactional Organization of Computer Mediated Communication in the College Classroom. *Qualitative Sociology, 21*(3), 299–317.

Garcia, A. C., & Jacobs, J. B. (1999). The Eyes of the Beholder: Understanding the Turn-Taking System in Quasi-Synchronous Computer-Mediated Communication. *Research on Language & Social Interaction, 32*(4), 337–367.

Herring, S. (2004). Computer-mediated discourse analysis: An approach to researching online behavior. In S. A. Barab, R. Kling & J. H. Gray (Eds.), *Designing for virtual communities in the service of learning* (pp. 338–376). Cambridge: Cambridge University Press.

Hutchby, I. (2001). Conversation and technology: From the telephone to the Internet. Cambridge: Polity.

Kitade, K. (2000). L2 learners' discourse and SLA theories in CMC: Collaborative interaction in internet chat. *Computer Assisted Language Learning, 13*(2), 143–166.

Knoeferle, P., & Crocker, M. (2009). Constituent order and semantic parallelism in online comprehension: Eye-tracking evidence from German. *Quarterly Journal of Experimental Psychology, 62*(12), 2338–2371.

Krashen, S. D. (1985). *The input hypothesis: Issues and implications.* London: Longman.

Lai, C., & Zhao, Y. (2006). Noticing and text-based chat. *Language Learning & Technology, 10*(3), 102–120.

Lange, P. G. (2008). An implicature for um: signaling relative expertise. *Discourse Studies, 10*(2), 191–204.

Lantolf, J. P. (Ed.) (2000). *Sociocultural theory and second language learning.* Oxford: Oxford University Press.

Lantolf, J. P., & Appel, G. (Eds.) (1994). *Vygotskian approaches to second language research.* Norwood, NJ: Ablex.

Lantolf, J. P., & Poehner, M. E. (Eds.) (2008). *Sociocultural theory and the teaching of second languages.* London: Equinox.

Lantolf, J. P., & Thorne, S. L. (2006). *Sociocultural theory and the genesis of second language development.* Oxford: Oxford University Press.

Levelt, W. J. M. (1989). *Speaking: From intention to articulation.* Amsterdam: John Benjamins.

Long, M. H. (1985). Input and second language acquisition theory. In S. M. Gass & C. G. Madden (Eds.), *Input in second language acquisition* (pp. 377–393). Cambridge, MA: Newbury House.

Morand, D. A., & Ocker, R. J. (2003). *Politeness theory and computer-mediated communication: A sociolinguistic approach to analyzing relational messages.* Paper presented at the 36th Annual Hawaii International Conference on System Sciences (HICSS'03) – Track1. doi: 10.1109/HICSS.2003.1173660.

Mackey, A. (1999). Input, interaction and second language development: An empirical study of question formation in ESL. *Studies in Second Language Acquisition, 21*, 557–587.

Negretti, R. (1999). Web-based activities and SLA: A conversation-analysis research approach. *Language Learning and Technology, 3*(1), 75–87.

O'Rourke, B. (2005). Form-focused interaction in online tandem learning. *CALICO Journal, 22*(3), 433–466.

O'Rourke, B. (2007). Models of Telecollaboration (1): E-Tandem. In R. O'Dowd (Ed.), *Online Intercultural Exchange* (pp. 41–61). Clevedon: Multilingual Matters.

O'Rourke, B. (2008). The other C in CMC: What alternative data sources can tell us about synchronous computer mediated communication and language learning. *Computer Assisted Language Learning, 28*(3), 227–251.

Ortega, L. (1997). Processes and outcomes in networked classroom interaction: defining the research agenda for L2 computer-assisted classroom discussion. *Language Learning & Technology, 1*(1), 82–93.

Park, J.-r. (2008a). Linguistic politeness and face-work in computer-mediated communication, Part 1: A theoretical framework. *Journal of the American Society for Information Science and Technology, 59*(13), 2051–2059.

Park, J.-r. (2008b). Linguistic politeness and face-work in computer mediated communication, Part 2: An application of the theoretical framework. *Journal of the American Society for Information Science and Technology, 59*(14), 2199–2209.

Paulus, T. M., & Phipps, G. (2008). Approaches to case analyses in synchronous and asynchronous environments. *Journal of Computer-Mediated Communication, 13*(2), 459–484.

Pellettieri, J. (2000). Negotiation in cyberspace: The role of *chatting* in the development of grammatical competence. In M. Warschauer & R. Kern (Eds.), *Network-based language teaching: Concepts and practice* (pp. 59–86). Cambridge: Cambridge University Press.

Pica, T. (1994). Research on negotiation: What does it reveal about second-language learning conditions, processes, and outcomes? *Language Learning, 44*(3), 493–527.

Rayner, K. (2009). Eye movements and attention in reading, scene perception, and visual search. *The Quarterly Journal of Experimental Psychology, 62*(8), 1457–1506.

Salaberry, M. R. (2000). L2 morphosyntactic development in text-based computer-mediated communication. *Computer Assisted Language Learning, 13*(1), 5–27.

Scarcella, R. C., & Higa, C. (1981). Input, negotiation and age differences in second language acquisition. *Language Learning, 31*(2), 409–437.

Schmidt, R. (1995). Consciousness and foreign language learning: a tutorial on the role of attention and awareness in learning. In R. Schmidt (Ed.), *Attention and awareness in foreign language learning* (pp. 1–63). Honolulu, Hawai'i: University of Hawai'i, Second Language Teaching and Curriculum Center.

Sirevaag, E. J., & Stern, J. A. (1998). Ocular measures of fatigue and cognitive factors. In R. Backs & W. Boucsein (Eds.), *Engineering psychophysiology: Issues and applications* (pp. 269–288). New Jersey: Erlbaum.

Smith, B. (2003). Computer-mediated negotiated interaction: an expanded model. *Modern Language Journal, 87*(1), 38–57.

Smith, B. (2008). Methodological hurdles in capturing CMC data: the case of the missing self-repair. *Language Learning & Technology, 12*(1), 85–103.

Smith, B. (2010). Employing eye-tracking technology in researching the effectiveness of recasts in CMC. In F. M. Hult (Ed.), *Directions and Prospects for Educational Linguistics* (pp. 79–97). London: Springer.

Smith, B., & Gorsuch, G. J. (2004). Synchronous computer mediated communication captured by usability lab technologies: new interpretations. *System, 32*(4), 553–575.

Smith, B., & Sauro, S. (2009). Interruptions in chat. *Computer Assisted Language Learning, 22*(3), 229–247.

Sotillo, S. (2010). Quality and type of corrective feedback, noticing, and learner uptake in synchronous computer-mediated text-based and voice chats. In M. Pütz & L. Sicola (Eds.), *Cognitive processing in second language acquisition: Inside the learner's mind* (pp. 351–370). Amsterdam: John Benjamins.

Sperber, D., & Wilson, D. (1995). *Relevance: Communication and cognition.* Oxford: Blackwell.

Sykes, J. (2005). Synchronous CMC and pragmatic development: effects of oral and written chat. *CALICO Journal, 22*(3), 399–431.

Tanenhaus, M., Spivey-Knowlton, M., Eberhard, K., & Sedivy, J. (1995). Integration of visual and linguistic information in spoken language comprehension. *Science, 268*(5217), 1632–1634.

Tudini, V. (2003). Using native speakers in chat. *Language Learning & Technology, 7*(3), 141–159.

Varonis, E. M., & Gass, S. M. (1985). Non-native/non-native conversations: a model for negotiation of meaning. *Applied Linguistics, 6*(1), 71–90.

Warschauer, M. (1998). Interaction, negotiation, and computer-mediated learning. In V. Darleguy, A. Ding & M. Svensson (Eds.), *Educational Technology in language learning: Theoretical reflection and practial applications* (pp. 125–136). Lyon: National Institute of Applied Sciences, Centre of Language Resources.

Weininger, M. J., & Shield, L. (2004). Promoting oral production in a written channel: an investigation of learner language in MOO. *Computer Assisted Language Learning, 16*(4), 329–349.

Werry, C. C. (1996). Linguistic and interactional features of Internet Relay Chat. In S. C. Herring (Ed.), *Computer-Mediated Communication: Linguistic, social, and cross-cultural perspectives* (pp. 47–64). Amsterdam: John Benjamins.

Notes on Contributors

FRANÇOISE BLIN is a Senior Lecturer in French at Dublin City University (Ireland). She has been working in CALL since the late eighties and holds a PhD in Educational Technology from the Open University (UK). Her more recent work focuses on the applications of Cultural Historical Activity Theory to CALL research, design, and practice. She is the current President of EUROCALL and co-editor of *ReCALL* (with June Thompson). She is also a member of the editorial boards of the *Alsic, CALICO*, and *CALL* journals.

MELINDA DOOLY is a teacher educator at the Science Education Faculty of the Universitat Autònoma de Barcelona (Spain). She teaches English as a Foreign Language Methodology (TEFL) and research methods courses, focusing on telecollaboration in education. Her research addresses teacher preparation and the use of CALL and CMC. She has published widely in the areas of teacher education and the use of technology. Dr. Dooly's current research interest is in project-based telecollaborative language learning and very young learners.

MATS DEUTSCHMANN, PhD, is Associate Professor in Language Didactics at the Department of Language Studies, Umeå University, Sweden. He has over ten years' experience in the field of online language learning and over the past five years he has worked extensively in virtual worlds. His research includes didactic design for collaborative language learning in online contexts, the language pragmatics of online education, the use of innovative technology for raising engagement and active participation, and most recently, the use of virtual worlds in research on language and identity. He has been involved in a number of international projects involving the use of virtual worlds in language learning, for example "AVALON", "Euroversity" and "A Second Step in Second Life" (ASSIS). He has published extensively in the field and is co-editor of the book *Learning and Teaching in the Virtual World of Second Life*, (2009) eds. Molka-Danielsen, J. & Deutschmann, M.,Tapir Academic Press, Trondheim.

MIRJAM HAUCK is a Senior Lecturer and Associate Head of the Department of Languages (Faculty of Education and Language Studies) at the Open University in the UK. She has written numerous articles and book chapters on the use of technologies for the learning and teaching of languages and cultures covering aspects such as task design, tutor role and training, the affordances of the new media, and e-literacy skills. Her current research and publications explore the impact of mediation and the relevance of multimodal communicative competence on the development of intercultural communicative competence in online environments.

MIKE LEVY, PhD, is professor of second language studies and Director of the Brisbane Universities Language Alliance (BULA) at the University of Queensland, Brisbane, Australia. His research includes studies on the distinctive role of technology in mediating language learning, teacher education and learner training. He is also examining the nature of multitasking and the coordination of talk and action in pair work at the computer. He teaches postgraduate courses in CALL and qualitative research methods. His publications include WorldCALL (Routledge, 2011), CALL Dimensions with Glenn Stockwell (Erlbaum, 2006) and Teacher Education in CALL with Philip Hubbard (Benjamins, 2006). He is Chair of the Steering Committee for WorldCALL (<www.worldcall.org>).

MARTINA MÖLLERING is Head of the Department of International Studies at Macquarie University. She is Professor of European Languages and also lectures on computer-mediated communication in the Masters and Professional Doctorate programs in Applied Linguistics. Her current research areas are corpus-based approaches to language teaching and computer-mediated communication in second language acquisition, of which she is author of several articles, chapters and books. One of her latest research interests is the linguistic analysis of Turkish-German identity construction as represented in literature and film.

ANDREAS MÜLLER-HARTMANN is Professor of Teaching English as a Foreign Language (TEFL) and Director of the Institute for Foreign Languages at the University of Education, Heidelberg, Germany. He holds a Ph.D. in American Studies from the University of Osnabrück, Germany. His research interests include task-supported language learning (TSLL), the development of intercultural communicative competence, the use of technology in the EFL classroom and teacher education. He has co-written books on TEFL in the secondary classroom (2004) and task-supported language learning (2011) (with Marita Schocker-v. Ditfurth), and TEFL in the primary classroom (2009) (with Michael Legutke and Marita Schocker-v. Ditfurth). He has co-edited books on qualitative research in foreign language learning and teaching (2001) and task-based language learning with technology (2008). He teaches TEFL, TSLL, CALL and American Cultural Studies.). At present, he is co-directing state-funded classroom research on the implementation of task-supported language learning in EFL in the German school system.

ROBERT O'DOWD teaches EFL and Applied Linguistics and is secretary for International Training at the University of León, Spain. He has a PhD on the use of networked technologies in the foreign language classroom and has published widely on the theme of online intercultural exchange. He is currently coordinating the INTENT project – a European Commission Lifelong Learning Project on telecollaboration in university education (<www.intent-project.eu>). His homepage is: <http://www3.unileon.es/personal/wwdfmrod/>.

BREFFNI O'ROURKE is Assistant Professor in Applied Linguistics and Manager of Language Learning Technologies and Resources in the School of Linguistic, Speech, and Communication Sciences, Trinity College Dublin. His research and teaching interests include technology and language, especially technology and language learning; comparative perspectives on cognitive and sociocultural approaches to second language learning; learner autonomy; the nature of written language, and discourse analysis.

LUISA PANICHI, BA (Monash, AUS), Dottore Magistrale in Foreign Languages and Literatures (Pisa, IT) holds a full time teaching position at the Language Centre of the University of Pisa and has over 20 years' experience in modern language education at tertiary level. She has published in the field of Learner Autonomy, Language Awareness, Tandem Learning and CMC and CALL and is the co-author of a text book on Business English. She has been active in teaching and researching in virtual world education since 2007 and was local project leader for the EU funded AVALON project for language learning in virtual worlds. Luisa currently holds a full-time PhD position in the Department of Modern Languages at the University of Hull, UK, where she is researching learner participation in virtual world language education. She is currently also co-coordinator of the recently funded EU network EUROVERSITY and is frequently invited to speak at seminars on virtual world education across Europe.

JONATHON REINHARDT (Ph.D, Penn State University) is Assistant Professor of English Language/Linguistics at the University of Arizona, USA, where he also co-directs the *Games To Teach Project* at the Center for Educational Resources in Culture, Language, and Literacy. His research interests include the application of social-informed frameworks to technology-mediated L2 learning and teaching, especially in digital game and social network-mediated contexts, as well as corpus-informed L2 pedagogy and teacher development. He has published most recently in *CALICO* Journal, *Int'l Journal of Corpus Linguistics*, and *English for Specific Purposes.*

BRENNA RIVAS is a post-doctoral researcher at Southern Methodist University on a grant that examines the impact of different community service programs on the school readiness of young English learners. Her research examines technology-mediated intervention strategies for helping English language learners develop vocabulary and early reading skills.

NINA VYATKINA is Assistant Professor of German Applied Linguistics, Coordinator of the German Language Proficiency Sequence, and Co-Director of the Center for German Business Language at the University of Kansas. She is the 2009 recipient of the ACTFL-MLJ Paul Pimsleur Award for Research in Foreign Language Education. Her research interests include language learner development in instructed settings, computer-mediated communication, learner corpus analysis, and interlanguage pragmatics. Her articles have appeared in *Canadian Modern Language Review, Foreign Language Annals, Language Learning and Technology, L2 Journal,* and *Modern Language Journal.*

PAGE WARE is an associate professor at Southern Methodist University. Her research focuses on the use of interactive technology to promote second language writing and intercultural understanding. She directs a professional development grant, funded by the Office of English Language Acquisition, that provides secondary teachers with strategies to support language learners in the classroom.

TELECOLLABORATION IN EDUCATION

Edited by
Melinda Dooly & Robert O'Dowd

The series' focus is on the pedagogical processes and outcomes of engaging learners in different geographical locations in virtual contact and collaboration together. This contact can take place through the application of online communication tools such as e-mail, synchronous chat and threaded discussion as well as the tools of Web 2.0: like wikis, blogs, and online publishing. The series is also particularly interested in innovative teaching practices involving telecollaboration that integrate the use of newly emerging forms of Internet tools such as social networking or 3D virtual worlds.

A major aim is to reflect the diversity of research and practice in this area of knowledge, providing a space for transversal dialogue among teachers and teacher trainers, administrators, researchers, and educators working in different subject areas as well as various areas of education.

Telecollaboration in Education deals with the application of such activity in different subject areas (e.g. Foreign Languages, History, Science) and in different educational contexts, including but not limited to primary, secondary, university and adult education. Publications within the series include scholarly monographs and collected papers editions as well as cutting-edge projects that exemplify good practice in the application of distanced collaborative efforts. Training manuals for educators in the organisation and application of telecollaboration are also a possible type of publication within the series. Language of publication is English.

Vol. 1 Sarah Guth & Francesca Helm (eds)
Telecollaboration 2.0. Language, Literacies and Intercultural Learning in the 21st Century.
2010. ISBN 978-3-03943-0440-5

Vol. 2 Randall Sadler
Virtual Worlds for Language Learning. From Theory to Practice.
2012. ISBN 978-3-0343-0573-0

Vol. 3 Melinda Dooly & Robert O'Dowd (eds)
Researching Online Foreign Language Interaction and Exchange.
2012. ISBN 978-3-0343-1155-7